LET THE WHOLE
WORLD SING

LET THE WHOLE WORLD SING

The Story behind the *Music of Lausanne II*

Corean Bakke

CORNERSTONE PRESS CHICAGO
CHICAGO, ILLINOIS

Published by Cornerstone Press Chicago, the publishing arm of Jesus People USA Covenant Church. Jesus People USA is a community of Christians serving the poor, the homeless, and the elderly in the Uptown neighborhood of Chicago. On a national and international level, Jesus People is known for Cornerstone *magazine, the bands on the* Grrr recordS *label (REZ, Cauzin' efekt, CRASHDOG, and the Crossing), and for Cornerstone Festival. If you would like more information about Jesus People USA and its outreaches, write JPUSA care of Cornerstone Press Chicago, 939 W. Wilson Ave., Chicago, IL 60640.*

Authors, publishers, and friends have graciously given their permission for the use of material used in these stories behind the music of Lausanne II: Steven Ayguku; David Anderson; *Asian Church Today* (Volume 6, No. 4, October-December 1989, page 8); Appianda Arthur; Baptist World Alliance; Cliff Barrows; William Brown; Gary Clark; Robyn Claydon; *The Christian Century* © 1989 Christian Century Foundation. Reprinted by permission from the August 16-23, 1989 issue; Froilan Cruz; Edward Dayton; Ted Engstrom; Samuel Escobar; Leighton Ford; Gary Granada; Rey Halili; Bill Hogue; Martha Kelsey; Dale Kauffman; Treena Kerr; Sundo Kim; Bagong Kussudiardja; Paul Landry; Melba Maggay; Ken Medema; Bill Myers; National Council of Churches; Seth Newman; Rich Piscopo; Romulo Pizaña; Philemon Quaye; Margaret Shishak; Vigo Søgaard; Charles Swindoll; Joni Eareckson Tada; Anita Teh; Ralph Torres; Soliny Vedrine; Wilmer Villacorta; Peter Waggoner; *World Christian.*

Two people, quoted in this book, are not included on the list of permission given. Attempts to locate them were unsuccessful. With these two exceptions, all requests for permission to use material were granted. Exceptions are Virgilio Enriquez, associate director for operation at the Congress, who is somewhere in the Philippines, and Rev. M.S. Anwari in Jakarta, Indonesia.

Scripture quotations marked (NIV) taken from the HOLY BIBLE, NEW INTERNATIONAL VERSION. Copyright © 1973, 1978, 1984 by International Bible Society.

Scripture quotations marked (NKJV) from the New King James Version Bible, copyright ©, 1979, 1980, 1982. Thomas Nelson, Inc., Publishers. Used by permission.

Scripture quotations marked (NRSV) from the New Revised Standard Version Bible, copyright © 1989, by the Division of Christian Education of the National Council of the Churches of Christ in the United States of America. Used by permission.

Cover design by Kevin Frank.
Printed in the United States of America.
97 96 95 94   4 3 2 1

Library of Congress Cataloging-in-Publication Data

Bakke, Corean, 1938-
    Let the whole world sing : the story behind the music of Lausanne II / Corean Bakke.
      p.   cm.
    Includes index.
    ISBN 0-940895-18-8
    1. Church music--Congresses.   2. Hymns--History and criticism--Congresses
  3. Hymns.   4. Ethnicity--Religious aspects--Christianity--Congresses.   5. Christianity and culture--Congresses.   6. International Congress on World Evangelization (2nd : 1989 : Manila, Philippines) I. Title.
ML3001.B16   1994
264'.2--dc20
                                                    94-24994
                                                     CIP
                                                     MN

For Ed Dayton

795

CONTENTS

Part Two: The Music of Lausanne II

ACKNOWLEDGEMENTS

I never expected to write a book about my involvement with the music and worship of Lausanne II Intermational Congress for World Evangelization. The copious notes I accumulated, writing down every phone conversation, and the collection of faxes, letters, and memos sent and received, were intended to help me complete the doctor of ministry requirements at Chicago Theological Seminary.

At the end of the Congress in Manila I told Ed Dayton, the program director, a few of these stories. He encouraged me to talk them into a tape recorder and then get them onto paper. But by the time I came to the end of the loose ends connected with the Congress, seminary classes had begun and I had returned to finish my work there.

A year later, knowing the stories were still unwritten, my husband revived the subject. He had also heard some of them and was convinced they ought to be preserved. Would I please get to work and do that? Every now and then, he checked. Had I begun yet? No one else, he reminded me, could write those stories. He worried that I might delay until they were too dim to retrieve.

By June of 1991 I had completed a first draft. In January of 1992 I revised that draft, casting it into a missiological framework. My friends did not understand that word. Missiological?

For the next year I looked for a publisher as the manuscript gathered dust in my attic office. But it was like a square peg in a round hole. I got nowhere.

A telephone call revived the search for a publisher: an inquiry relating to a new event requiring international worship, and questions about the worship at Lausanne II. Many calls later, a conversation with Michael Anderson, graphic artist at Cornerstone Press Chicago, resulted in an appointment with Jane Hertenstein. She was very encouraging. I felt energized once again and began another revision, omitting the obscure words and shaping it into a simple story.

I wanted the book to include photographs, and began the search to locate the professional quality proofs of the Congress. Åke Lundberg assisted with that search, describing what I needed to find. The Billy Graham Center Archives in Wheaton , Illinois, located the red three-ring binders with all the proofs and made them available to me. Åke, who had managed and put together the photo staff for the Congress, made all the prints I requested. The photos in this book were taken either by Åke Lundberg or one of the following Congress photographers: Phil DeJong, Gary Fong, Ron Londen, or Greg Schneider.

Tony Payne supported my desire to reprint the hymnal, but only in a revised and more professional format. He reformatted the music for this second edition. Pat Peterson at Cornerstone agreed to input the nonroman script, retaining the ethnic integrity of the hymnal as Tony and I had envisioned it from the beginning.

Those who read the manuscript and offered me their suggestions include Jack Kenyon, Dietrich Gruen, Bryant Myers, Ed Dayton, Tom Houston, Donald Hustad, Bill O'Brien, Robin Erickson, Tony Payne, and my husband, Ray Bakke.

The staff at International Urban Associates generously assisted. Steve Ujvarosy kept my computer and me in a working relationship. Lisa Tomkins, Roger Johnson, and Azmera Alemayehu-Love supplied phone and fax numbers from their data base.

Many others involved in the Congress recovered details needed to make the story complete and accurate. I appreciate their willingness to interrupt their own demanding agendas and give me assistance.

Donald Hustad, longtime friend and mentor, wrote the foreword. Paul McKaughan, coordinator of the Congress, wrote an afterword.

To all these friends, I extend my gratefulness.

COREAN BAKKE

FOREWORD

One of the things I've learned in teaching is that our best students often "stand on our shoulders," learning truths and achieving goals that for various reasons are out of our reach. This awareness brings feelings that are not always comfortable, but it happens nevertheless.

I remember Corean Bakke as a quiet, sensitive, artistic young woman in the Moody Chorale at Moody Bible Institute in the mid-1950s. It was often apparent that much was going on in her brain and heart that didn't spill out in our conversation. Not surprisingly, she fell in love with one of the most gregarious, loquacious tenors in the choir, and they have gone on to become leaders, he as a specialist in Christian outreach in urban areas, and she in a multitude of artistic ventures—as a piano recitalist, as a storyteller and preacher, as a worship planner, and as an expert in the preservation of ethnic musics. It is the last activity which resulted in the writing of this book, based on her experiences as program associate for worship for Lausanne II in Manila in 1989.

I was a participant in Lausanne I in Switzerland in June 1974 and, more importantly, served as chairman of the music committee for the earlier World Congress on Evangelism in Berlin in 1966, which was a forerunner of the two Lausannes. At that time, Western missionary leaders were just beginning to acknowledge their historical shortsightedness in espousing a cultural as well as a spiritual conversion among nationals in other parts of the world. However, our preoccupation in Berlin was the need to accommodate to the new, popular, Western church music styles which were invading Britain and Europe in the wake of Geoffrey Beaumont's Twentieth Century Folk Mass and the sounds of the Beatles. So rhythmic folk-rock forms accompanied mostly by guitars and theater drums got most of the attention.

There were incidents of ethnic expression at the Berlin Congress, some of which were accidental. Hymns, including some excellent theme hymns developed in a contest sponsored by Christianity Today, were sung in four languages— Spanish, French, German, and English. Rachel Saint, missionary from Ecuador, was there with two converts from the Auca Indian tribe. A few years earlier, some of their jungle brothers had killed Rachel's brother Phil and three other Latin American missionaries because they were considered a threat to their culture's security. In an informal gathering, the two Indians sang a new Christian praise hymn in their language set to one of their almost monotone folk melodies. The song's original words told the story of the Andes Mountains being scooped out of the plain by the beak of an enormous woodpecker. I remember that one bystander said, "Isn't it wonderful to be at this Congress, to hear the very best Christian music [perhaps that of George Beverly Shea] along with the most primitive [that of the Indians]." In an article written after that experience, I asked whether the Indian tribe in Ecuador would agree with that evaluation, or whether American Gospel music might be less meaningful to them than the woodpecker song. The Congress had at least one expression of religious dance as well, when the native American singer Sonny Claus mimed the Lord's Prayer in sign language.

There is little point in condemning our forebears for their sins committed in ignorance, whether in promoting the medieval Crusades, in justifying human slavery, in destroying God's gifts in nature, or in compromising human culture. We can only rejoice when the light finally dawns and a better understanding of Christian responsibility emerges.

This book tells the story of how Corean Bakke tackled the cultural issues head-on, achieving a notable breakthrough at Lausanne II. With her deep-seated conviction that all the cultures present at Manila should be faithfully represented in their own speech/music/movement languages, she worked tirelessly to bring Christian artists together from around the world. Each of those persons—singers, instrumentalists, actors, mimers, dancers, and puppeteers—becomes the center of an engaging story of careful planning, of a succession of seemingly insurmountable problems, and of final denouement.

One thing is evident: Corean Bakke either kept a daily chronicle of every conversation and happening during those months of planning, or she has an incredible memory. This is not light reading, partly because readers will find themselves sharing her emotional ups and downs in her narrative of successes and failures. Probably not many will rush to apply for a similar responsibility, unless they match Corean in conviction, determination, persistence, and patience! Through these pages she will convince you that it would never have happened apart from God's will and not a few miracles.

Some will ask: What is the point of reporting such a project, except to help someone else prepare for the occasional international gathering of Christian believers? The story may explain the significance of today's use of Asian, Latin American, and African hymns in mainline USA churches—partly to accommodate the growing diversity of our congregations, and partly to remind us that ours is a truly "catholic" (universal) church. And, as our globe rapidly becomes a village, it may encourage us to resist the tendency to homogenize cultures. I have always expected that the new song in the eternal kingdom of God would be sung by a choir that was literally multicultural and multilingual.

> You are worthy to take the scroll and to open its seals,
>   for you were slaughtered and by your blood you ransomed
>   for God saints from every tribe and language and people and nation;
>   you have made them to be a kingdom and priests serving our God,
>   and they will reign on earth.
>
>   Revelation 5:9, 10 (NRSV)
>
>   DONALD P. HUSTAD

INTRODUCTION

This story has many characters. It begins with an introducion of them and their identities at a Congress called Lausanne II in Manila.

Steven Agyaku: traditional African drummer from Ghana. He played in the small ensemble.

Ray Bakke: Lausanne associate for large cities, and my husband. Because of his contacts with people and organizations around the world, he was a valuable in-house consultant during the planning stages of my work for Lausanne II.

Froilan (Froji) Cruz: Filipino mimer from Indonesia. He assisted in communicating across language barriers and performed as soloist and as supporting cast in the Balinese productions.

Nyoman Darsane: artist from Bali. He did drama, music, and puppets in Balinese style.

Ed Dayton: program director for the Congress from the United States. As an efficiency expert, he was asked to take this job because the time for planning was so short.

Allan Eubank: founder and director of the Thai Folk Drama Troupe in Chiang Mai, Thailand. He brought that troupe to the Congress.

Pedro Eustache: flutist from Venezuela. He played in the small ensemble.

Gary Granada: Filipino soloist. He participated in the urban plenary session.

Dale Kauffman: founder and director of King's Kids international from Hawaii. He recruited a group of kids for the Congress and coordinated special youth participation on opening night.

Graham and Treena Kerr: Congress cohosts from the United States. Graham is known to many television audiences as the "Galloping Gourmet." Treena worked with him as producer.

Kerygma Canta: musicians from Asociacion Misionera Evangelica a las Naciones (AMEN Mission International).

Korean Choir: singers from Kwang Lim Methodist Church in Seoul.

Nagieb Labeb: soloist from Egypt. He sang in the traditional Middle Eastern style and accompanied himself on the *'aoud*.

Ken Medema: musician from the United States. He performed multiple tasks at the Congress: song leader, accompanist, director of the small ensemble, and soloist.

Renthungo (Ren) Merry: classical guitarist from Nagaland, India. He played in the small ensemble.

Tony Payne: assistant dean at the Wheaton Conservatory of Music in the United States. He compiled the hymnal using Graphic Notes Music Publisher Software and arranged the opening choir processional.

Romulo Pizana: founder and director of His Sounds, a Filipino choir in Manila. He prepared a large choir for the Congress, using His Sounds as the nucleus.

Russian Choir: participants from the Union of Soviet Socialist Republics.

Byron Spradlin: founder and executive director of Artists in Christian Testimony based in the United States. He directed stage activities.

Deyanira Toruño: soloist from Nicaragua. She sang in the small ensemble.

Beverly Vander Molen: assistant to Ken Medema. She also directed stage activities.

Part One

Part One

Lausanne II in Manila
An Overview

In order to tell you my story—about making an international hymnal and assembling an international worship team—I must tell you about the event which brought us all together.

During July of 1989, an international Congress on world evangelization convened in Manila. It was called Lausanne II because it followed a similar event in Lausanne, Switzerland, fifteen years earlier.

Four thousand three hundred people came from 170 countries. Some have called it the most representative gathering in the history of the Church. They came to see where, since Peter's dynamic sermon on the Day of Pentecost nearly two thousand years ago, the Church stood in terms of sharing the gospel with all of humanity.

Over the course of ten days, they attended 425 workshops identified with 45 tracks, sat through 33 plenary sessions, listened to 54 speakers, watched 19 videos, and heard in nine official languages by tuning their radio-headset dials to the spot marked with nail polish—all of which focused on the whole Church taking the whole gospel to the whole world.

They lived in hotels in the city of Manila and traveled to and from the Philippine International Convention Center by shuttle buses. They shared two thousand umbrellas as they dashed through monsoon winds and rain. They alternated between melting in the heat outdoors and freezing in the air-conditioning indoors. They ate box lunches, wore hospital-style identification bracelets for security checks, and carried briefcases decorated with the Lausanne Committee for World Evangelization logo, a fish superimposed on a globe.

The idea of having the Congress had begun six years earlier. It was to be in Lausanne, same as before. But costs became prohibitive. Singapore was the second choice, both affordable and efficient. Staff personnel moved to Singapore and settled in for the huge task of getting the physical resources organized. But news of construction delays and projected censorship difficulties uprooted plans and people. The committee named Manila as the third and final site.

The changes increased work and costs, ruining carefully planned timetables and budgets, but the ceiling fell in one month prior to the Congress. Filipino immigration officials refused to allow the Congress computers, with all advance preparation data, to enter the country. Congress representatives refused to pay bribes to release those computers. What had been a difficult job before, organizing 4,300 people's lives for ten days in a foreign country, became a nightmare.

The travel agency, buried under the task of making travel arrangements for all the participants, added to the nightmare. People were not getting their tickets on time. Cost piled upon cost; frustration piled upon frustration.

Many people who came were inexperienced travelers. They missed their flights, lost their passports and their money, refused to follow housing accommodation assignments. Some of these difficulties were to be expected because the committee wanted to reflect the global composition of the Church. It deliberately strategized to mix a significant percentage of younger leaders, women, and Third-World peoples in with the mostly male, mostly older, and mostly Western participants who had attended Lausanne I.

This is the context for my story.

When the Congress finished, all the plenary talks and track reports and video scripts were edited into a single volume of 463 pages, forming a historical record of what was said at the Congress. Almost at the beginning of that book, there is a little chapter titled "The Music of Lausanne II." It occupies a scant two pages.

My story is a mere drop in the bucket.

AN INTERNATIONAL TASK

The Challenge of
International Worship

Lausanne II in Manila was not my first experience with the Lausanne Committee for World Evangelization (LCWE). In the fall of 1984 I accompanied my husband to Stuttgart, Germany, where we attended the international committee meeting of LCWE. The committee members came from all over the world.

As was my habit, I took special notice of the worship music, led by Clive Calver and Graham Kendrick, two folk-style musicians from Great Britain. They led us in songs from a words-only book published in Great Britain.

Most of the songs were unfamiliar to me, so I mostly listened and observed. I noticed many other people also did not participate. They seemed to come from specific geographical regions: from South America, from the Middle East, from parts of Asia and Africa. The people familiar with the songbook were from places actively connected to Great Britain. The rest of us were out of the British loop.

We could have learned the unfamiliar songs had we been given some help, such as musical notation or melodic support. But words-only books are just that: poetry and prose.

I retreated to reflection. Was this worship style appropriate for an international gathering? Did these songs, all of them British, suit these folk from every continent? Could any one country's worship songs and any one style of music speak for all the diversity in that hall? The answers seemed so obvious.

Then why was this happening?

It was the easiest, most efficient way to plan worship. One phone call to a song leader with a portfolio of songs and the organizer could move on to care for other details. I discovered from that experience that the worship music at any event is determined by the song leader. In retrospect, that simple fact is obvious. Why had I never thought of it before? Because the music of before had always included me, never excluded me.

I struggled with the singleness of worship style at Stuttgart, a style which omitted many of those who came. Was there an alternative? If not, could an alternative model be developed? What would it look like?

Talk of a larger international gathering was in the air at Stuttgart. I began work on an alternative model, determined to find a way to avoid allowing international worship to be dominated by a single style from a single country and culture. Continually I asked myself the question, How could an international event incorporate the music of all peoples in the world?

The following summer my husband again traveled as the Lausanne associate for large cities. I went along, carrying my question with me. In Toyko, as we checked into our hotel room, I noticed a sign on the neighboring door:

Asian Music Symposium
for
Music in the Life of Man
A World History
Tokyo National University of Fine Arts & Music
HEAD OFFICE

I told Ray he could walk around that night without me. I intended to get acquainted with our neighbor. With notebook and pen in hand, I knocked on the door. Gen'ichi Tsuge, a Japanese ethnomusicologist, answered. He was working on a twelve-volume set of books on world music for UNESCO. I asked how he divided up the world for this project. He gave me the following:

Asia–Oceano
West Africa and North Africa–the Arabic World
Africa South of the Sahara
North America
Latin America
Western Europe
Eastern Europe

This sevenfold division brought some clarity to my confusion and a new way to ask my question: What single musical style might appropriately represent each region? I knew by firsthand experience the power of Western technology to transport Western values to all parts of the world and the tendency for peoples everywhere to adapt Western pop music to their own cultures. It seemed that the authentic voice of each region ought to go deeper than the twentieth-century expression.

My experience at Stuttgart with all British songs sensitized me to the origins of worship music. I went behind title and tune to seek out the poet, the composer or arranger, and the publisher. And I began collecting hymns and hymnals from around the world.

In the fall of 1986, on a visit to Madison, Wisconsin, I saw a copy of the small hymnal prepared for Amsterdam '86, an international conference for evangelists. The cover held so much promise. A graphic artist had taken the name of the hymnal, *Songs of Praise*, and designed a cover repeating this title in multiple languages.

I opened to the first page and found a foreword by Cliff Barrows:

> Music transcends the natural boundary of language, culture and race. God has given mankind this universal gift in order that we might praise him more perfectly. It is a glorious privilege here in Amsterdam '86 to blend our hearts and voices in praise to our wonderful Lord. What better preparation for that day when a countless multitude from all nations, kindreds, peoples and tongues stand before the throne and sing praises to the Lamb.

These introductory words complemented a wonderful cover design. But hopes fell when I opened to the contents. All songs were in English. Except for two, all forty-six songs originated in America or the United Kingdom.

I pondered the implications. The music which transcends language, culture, and race is often assumed to be Western music. I had great difficulty accepting the idea that when all nations, kindreds, peoples, and tongues stand before the throne and sing praises to the Lamb they will be singing in English. The cover design and foreword had led me to think otherwise.

Why were the songs not compatible with the message the cover and foreword seemed to suggest? Perhaps because no one had yet collected or felt the need for songs from other languages, cultures, and races, even though evangelists from 140 countries were coming to worship in Amsterdam. Perhaps efficiency had again decided the matter. Perhaps a phone call to Word, Inc., had set the process in motion and the hymnals had arrived as requested.

The problem of a single musical style dominating a worship event for persons from multiple styles and cultures was one I had experienced at age eight. When my parents moved from Montana to the Ozarks of southern Missouri, I suddenly found myself in a church music environment totally unlike the one I had left behind. The new songs were written in shaped notes, a different shape for each degree of the scale. Four-part chords had a strange, distorted appearance. That was just the tip of the iceberg as I struggled with a new way of singing in worship.

That early experience motivated my escape into the world of classical music, where the sights and sounds of music fit my earliest notions of what was appropriate and best. Not until after teaching music for many years, completing graduate studies in music, and performing as a piano recitalist, did my "conversion of the ears" occur. Joyce Scott, missionary in Kenya, helped me to move beyond familiar musical styles and become curious and respectful about others.

I discovered the world of ethnomusicology, a world seldom encountered in my formal musical studies. My newfound interest grew by leaps and bounds as I traveled in Asia and Africa with my husband. Each worship service became a rich opportunity for recording new songs and photographing new musical instruments.

My own niche as pianist expanded as I became interested in finding compositions which reflected the distinctive sounds from different parts of the world. I began learning this nontraditional music and putting together piano recitals to reflect diversity of sound—recitals where I explained the new and unfamiliar.

Not surprisingly, when I encountered the hymnal used in Amsterdam, my personal musical journey connected with the necessity of finding suitable hymnals for international events.

I kept looking. I found the *International Conference Hymnal* prepared by World Evangelical Fellowship. It includes four languages for most songs: English, French, German, and Spanish. The tune is presented with one verse only of one language only. The remainder of the verses and languages follow. This format, with the music positioned as islands among the a, b, c, and d parts of the text, is formidable. I would not describe it as "user friendly." An international event for artists in Bali in February of 1989, with World Evangelical Fellowship connections, supplied these hymnals. But during the time I was there they were not used. We sang without hymnals.

The World Council of Churches has always tried to be inclusive. Their hymnal, *Jesus Christ—Life of the World*, prepared for the Sixth Assembly in Vancouver, Canada, was easier to use even though it included four languages on many songs. In addition, this hymnal had many songs from non-English languages, but I had no way of knowing whether the hymns it included were well known and used.

Whenever opportunities came about, I talked about the problem of international worship hymnal resources and how they seemed to come up short by primarily using English-origin hymns translated into Spanish, German, and French; by concentrating on contemporary hymnody and omitting the traditional music of the Church (with the exception of some Eastern Orthodox music); by assuming no need for Eastern European, Asian, or African languages or hymns.

Would I be stuck between the inappropriateness of a single musical style for international worship and the impossibility of finding a hymnal with adequate resources?

My question, reshaped by Gen'ichi Tsuge, Japanese ethnomusicologist, continued pressing for answers: How could international worship reflect music of the world's seven geographical divisions?

Appointment to the Challenge

In September of 1987 I was invited to attend the first ad hoc meeting in preparation for Lausanne II. I presented a proposal for international worship. It began by stating the problem, "The Domination of Worship in International Settings by Westerners," and continued:

International gatherings of Christians are becoming more frequent. When such gatherings include corporate worship, questions are raised regarding the selection of appropriate worship vehicles for the occasion. When the group includes persons from many worship traditions as well as from many different cultures, languages, and theological concerns, the problem becomes very complex.

It concluded by suggesting the preparation of a worship book:

The success or failure of a worship book could guide others in similar efforts. Particular international gatherings merit a special book.

My question about international worship, raised in Stuttgart in the fall of 1984, impacted by the Japanese ethnomusicologist in 1985 and the Amsterdam hymnal for evangelists in 1986, ceased being a theoretical question in the fall of 1987. I began actively promoting an alternative model.

I also entered Chicago Theological Seminary that fall in the doctor of ministry program. As part of that program, I had to develop and implement a unique ministry project, one which I would afterwards describe, critique, and defend as a viable ministry model. If I were given the opportunity to design and implement international worship for Lausanne II, that could be my project. The timing was perfect.

Ed Dayton, appointed program director for Lausanne II in January, 1988, knew of my concern for worship. In March he sent me a letter:

> I need some more thoughts on the general area of worship. Based upon what you know, and what others might know, if you are going to develop a worship team to think through the worship portion of the '89 Congress, who would you suggest, and how would you go about it? . . . What are your thoughts about compiling a hymn book as part of the Congress notebook? What are the constraints? What's the timing? How do you see this fitting into the worship?

In May I wrote Ed a five-page letter including this response to his questions:

> The plan which has evolved in my head since Stuttgart is an attempt to include all parts of the globe in worship leadership. . . . I would look for musicians from each place to lead worship. I would like to see these musicians leading the entire conference in the worship and musical styles of their cultures. The instruments of those parts of the world . . . could enable the worship at the Congress to reflect the whole church. It would be true that many would have to learn how to participate in these culturally diverse styles, but that is what international gatherings are all about.

In that same letter, I discussed a hymnal:

> The hymnal should include hymns from all parts of the globe, including the old hymns of the church, known by all and sung in translations. The new hymns should be introduced and taught to the conference. The hymnal needs to have music as well as words so that the musicians have a resource book to take home with them, and so that the learning of new songs at the conference isn't by rote. The nature of the conference, its

themes and purpose will also determine the kind of hymns and songs needed.... The selections for this hymnal would be difficult. Guidelines could be drawn-up by a team. Selections would then need to be tested on several congregations before completing the selection.... A hymnal at the Congress has the potential to be a very significant book.

I suggested thirteen people to approach in developing a worship team. Ed then asked me to send copies of that five-page letter to all thirteen of them, inviting responses to the ideas presented. He also distributed copies to people he was working with as program director.

Ed recognized my enthusiasm but cautioned me about volunteering for too much responsibility:

I think you need to make a decision as to whether you believe you can handle all the work that might be involved in producing the hymnal, as well as managing the worship program. I am very open to having you do both, but want to be sure that you are still alive by the time of the Congress!

In July I wrote back:

Your offer to allow me to coordinate both the worship and the hymnal is what I want to do. One of the responders pointed out that is probably the better way and I agree with her. I know it will be a gigantic task, but that will be my task for this coming year. As I explained to your secretary, I'm clearing my desk, emptying the drawers, and making room for this new undertaking. It is so very perfect for the degree program I'm in. I couldn't ask for a better project nor for better timing.

In that same letter, under "priority items necessary for my job to begin," I put as the first one, "I need an official appointment stating my position and responsibilities, to whom I am accountable, and with whom I will be working."

By September, ten responses to my five-page letter had arrived. I prepared a report for Ed in which I shared those responses, and I worked some more on a philosophy of worship and music:

I see Lausanne II as an event which bridges between large international gatherings largely designed and controlled by Westerners, and future international gatherings which reflect the geographical shift of the church, from Europe and North America to Asia and/or Africa.

I think of worship in the context of Manila as being a corporate offering of ourselves, using the Romans 12 text as the basis for this kind of worship. The involvement by the people is what constitutes this kind of worship.

Bringing indigenous hymnody into juxtaposition with traditional hymnody is a way to present the offering of all parts of the global church. Bringing indigenous instruments alongside Western instruments is also that kind of offering, strongly stated visually as well as audibly.

The problem of whose indigenous hymns and instruments will be used has to be solved in a less than satisfactory way. Not all can be used, but the attempt to include representative examples and make them integral to the Congress would go a long ways toward bridging.

Perhaps the difficulty of doing this explains why it is not more often done. Going the route of hiring specialists is much easier. They come with their specialty all pre-packaged, ready to go, and the entire event is locked into a particular expression of worship. It is my hope that we can avoid that but it will require more work, more expense, and a willingness to be simple rather than showy.

Another consideration here is the desire to say to various cultures that their resources are as appropriate in worship as the Western, more sophisticated resources. By using their simple instruments, we would bless them and lift them up as yet another part of the corporate sacrifice to our God. By not using them, we imply that their instruments and songs are less desirable, appropriate only if nothing else is available.

Lausanne II is an opportunity to take responsibility for these attitudes of superiority and a chance to work to change them. . . . By sharing time and space with emerging worship expressions we attempt to correct superior attitudes. We also give permission to others to take the risk and depart from Western cultural models. A basic worship team, composed along these concepts, would include a singer, guitarist, flutist, and drummer. The singer would need to have a strong, articulate singing voice in order to lead. The flutist would augment the singer by doubling on the tune. The guitarist would provide a simple accompaniment. The drummer would maintain the beat. These instruments are commonly used in nearly all parts of the world. With adequate amplification, the assembly could be led in this way. This style of simple singing could be useful for the worship times connected with the morning Bible studies, and for brief moments of worship worked into the breaks during the day. Because the team would be small, it would also be flexible.

Evening times of celebration would be more expansive. . . .

The most colorful response came from Peter Wagner, professor of church growth at Fuller Theological Seminary:

Dear Ed:

In response to your memo on worship planning for the Congress, I would suggest asking Corean Bakke to be worship coordinator.

I do this somewhat reluctantly simply because I don't have a better idea. So let me tack on some comments for what they're worth. ·

1. Stuttgart. My impression was the opposite of Corean's. I have been to every LCWE meeting ever held and Stuttgart had by far the highest tone of spirituality, due principally to the worship....

2. Classic worship experts like Corean . . . have a need for conducting a music appreciation or ethnomusicology course when they lead a group. This more frequently meets a need of the director than the worshippers. Out there in grassroots, growing churches, the deepest worship occurs with use of the familiar as over against the exotic.

3. I have attended WCC meetings in which Corean's scheme was followed. It's like watching a special on crocodiles or penguins on Channel 28. Interesting, at times fascinating, but with a personal impact of zero. Performance is high. Meaningful participation is very low.

4. This all has to do, of course, with the theology of worship. If worship is ministry to God resulting in an intimacy with the Father, such a spiritual experience is next to impossible in an environment containing scores of cultures such as we will have in the plenary sessions. Worship is so culturally sensitive that we may as well agree to have worship leaders from different regions give demonstrations or performances and not expect much to happen in the audience. I think Corean can coordinate that kind of use of worship time well. It's the best we can do.

Ed wrote on August 2, 1988:

You were approved as program associate for worship.

I interpreted my appointment as program associate for worship as empowerment for cultural diversity. It was the chance to develop a practical answer to my four-year-old question about the possibilities for international worship.

Partners for the Challenge

I looked for someone who shared my vision for international worship, someone I could talk with because I had more questions than answers.

In December of 1986 I attended the Urbana Missionary Conference and met Byron Spradlin. I went to his enormously popular workshop on art and mission, happy to get a seat. Afterwards, I introduced myself and asked whether he had any free time. We made an appointment to have breakfast together.

Byron founded and directs Artists in Christian Testimony, a mission organization which integrates ministry and the arts. We discovered we both valued creativity and were passionately dedicated to protecting and helping the more fragile forms of creativity. We affirmed the necessity of including indigenous artists from around the world in international programming and lamented the dominance of Western forms. We began a correspondence, sharing our thoughts and involvements.

The following September we met again, this time in Chicago at my home. I told him my wish to model a music leadership style at Lausanne II using instruments available to all people no matter what their geographical location or their economic situation might be. All people had access to, or could make for themselves, drums, flutes, and stringed instruments. But how could these simple instruments be used effectively in leading worship for four thousand people?

Seated at my dining-room table, Byron suggested a plan for enabling basic musical instruments and indigenous musicians to reach their full potential leading the worship at Lausanne II. He knew only one musician who could support and participate in this kind of music leadership venture. Ken Medema could enable this international style of leadership to succeed. He could hold the fragile parts together and make them effective in front of four thousand people.

I had heard Ken only once, the previous July in Washington, D.C., at Leadership '88. He was a most unusual kind of performer. He sat at a grand piano which had a DX7 synthesizer and drum machine on top, and played and sang and interacted with the audience. During a concert, he slipped off the piano bench so that an African-American pianist could accompany a small group of singers. I marveled as he wove all the pieces together into a wonderfully cohesive whole. He did all of this without benefit of sight.

For two days, I mulled over Byron's suggestion and decided it was a good one. Using the phone number he gave me, I called Beverly Vander Molen, Ken's assistant, and introduced myself as the newly appointed program associate for worship. I shared with her my vision for putting together an international worship team.

She and Ken had already discussed the possibility of going to Lausanne II, and Ken had made up his mind. He would be available to go if women as well as men were involved, if other cultures and styles and races were involved, and not just North American whites. As Beverly and I talked, she saw that many of the things which troubled Ken and herself were the very things I was hoping to avoid at Lausanne II. Immediately, a working rapport developed.

At this point I was not sure what I wanted Ken to do. Byron had suggested Ken be the one to mold the exotic and unexpected instruments together into an ensemble. Beverly suggested Ken be the song leader as well. She told me he was very versatile and could lead every kind of song, from unaccompanied Genevan Psalter melodies to African folk hymns to traditional Gospel songs.

I hesitated because I had never heard Ken lead congregational singing. I knew him only as a solo performer. Beverly was asking me to take a giant leap of faith.

Could she provide me with a cassette tape of Ken leading worship? No, for they rarely taped his public performances. But she would send me a concert video and some of his cassette albums.

When the ad hoc committee met that fall, I presented Ken's name as vocalist, keyboard accompanist, and leader for the small ensemble. I felt apprehensive about suggesting him as song leader at this relatively early stage, in addition to all of the above.

The ad hoc group responded by spending considerable time discussing the matter of song leader. The kind of person they wanted seemed to be a non-Western person who did everything in the Western way: someone who had charisma and appropriate stage presence for an international event of four thousand people, who could take charge and make decisions, who would wear well for ten days, who spoke English fluently. No one knew such a person.

The positive and supportive part of that discussion came from Ted Ward. He knew Ken from when he had taught at Michigan State University, where Ken was his teaching assistant. Ted told the committee that he was thrilled to see Ken's name presented, that he knew of no one better qualified than Ken to participate musically at Lausanne II.

There was an important precedent for having Ken as both accompanist and song leader. In 1873, when Dwight Moody went to Scotland to conduct evangelistic meetings, he took Ira Sankey along as his sole musician. Sankey sat at a small, portable, foot-operated harmonium and played as he led singing and sang solos. His effectiveness is obvious when the stories are read.

The model of a standing song leader, with assisting musicians at the keyboard and console, developed later and became the norm for many worship situations, including small church congregations and stadium-sized congregations. The idea of returning to the old style of song leadership for the Congress gradually gained acceptance in the absence of any winning recommendation for the stand-up model which most of the committee desired.

In January I met with Beverly and Ken for the first time, at the Chicago

O'Hare Hilton. After our morning get-acquainted discussion, we took a lunch break. They had already set up an appointment for lunch with another person who wanted to meet them. When Harold Best, dean of the Conservatory of Music at Wheaton College, joined us, the discussion moved away from Lausanne II musical matters to the broader areas of music composition, music education, and musical relevancy in the late twentieth century. Surprised and unsure how to view this unexpected turn of events, I got out my notebook. As they talked I discovered they were articulating much of what I was going after intuitively. I wrote all through lunch.

One of Harold Best's comments perfectly described my role as program director of worship. He spoke of the "Abrahamic Model," a model whereby we "go, not knowing where we are going." He also spoke of the need to "give power back to the indigenous people." He ardently supported indigenous renewal.

Ken affirmed all that Harold said but anchored the theory in reality when he said, "We will not always get it right, but we will know when we did not get it right."

At the day's end, Ken, Beverly, and I had two major tasks: the selection of musicians for the small ensemble and the selection of hymns and songs for use during worship times at Lausanne II.

The ad hoc committee instructed me to form the small ensemble as a microcosm of Lausanne. Therefore, no one else besides Ken could be a white North American. That same committee also requested the addition of a female vocalist.

The musicians, minus the female vocalist whose plane arrived late, met each other one day before the Congress began. This was a very risky thing, putting together a musical ensemble that had never played together. We took great care in arranging placement of the instruments and the musicians. Everyone needed to be close to Ken to hear and see instructions. At the first rehearsal, I watched as Ken began the task of molding musicians from the four corners of the earth into a cohesive group. He knew exactly what he wanted to do. Overnight, four individuals became a versatile musical unit.

Ken did many other things at Lausanne II besides rehearsing and directing the small ensemble. He memorized the hymnal. He led and accompanied the participants in their singing. He played a concert. He played the opening night processional and accompanied the Filipino choir.

When the Soviet delegation became an impromptu choir and sang in their own language, he again provided the accompaniment. He sang and played musical responses to the platform announcements given by Graham and Treena Kerr. He felt the emotion within the hall over the testimony of a pastor from China and asked to be led to the piano where he sang and played a tribute on our behalf.

In the planning stages, the program committee considered the possibility of prerecorded music for postludes. We did not want to presume on Ken unreasonably. But he protested the idea of prerecorded music and made himself available, improvising on music from the just-finished plenary session. Postludes became times when music lovers in the auditorium came forward with their pocket-sized tape recorders and stood near the front to record everything to the last note. Ken became aware of this faithful audience. When he finished, he could hear the sounds of many recorders rewinding.

He sat through every plenary session in the ten days of the Congress, listening to everything said from the platform and responding in his inimitable way filled with exuberance and sensitivity, passion and creativity.

None of Ken's own songs were put in the Congress hymnal. He led songs written by others, and for those songs he wrote this foreword:

> This book of hymns and choruses, drawn from many lands and cultures, is offered to Lausanne II and to Christians around the world with the hope that the urgency of our call, the unity of our family, and the extent of our sacrifice will be reflected in its pages. Because we are commanded, because our hearts burn within us, because we must find a way to speak our deepest and truest hopes and convictions, let God's people sing *Aleluya*!

Byron Spradlin came to Manila as stage director. When other people went off to lunch and conversations and much-needed naps, he stayed behind in the hall and attended to the many details of planning and coordination so necessary and yet often assumed or overlooked. He blocked the stage, placed furniture, and timed movements. He coached plenary speakers on the platform hurdles—to know how to find the access stairs, the rooms backstage, and the right seat on the platform. He arranged to have the lectern stands at the correct heights. He checked for clear eyesight communication between himself and platform people. He gave himself without reservation to making things run as smoothly as possible.

From past experience, he knew that speakers are the worst offenders of program planning. They ignore the clock. Byron came prepared to deal with that problem. He made huge red and white "time cards" and flashed them before the speakers, sparking most of them to stay sharp and on time. Those cards cost him $110.

More importantly for me, he helped, as he said he would, fit the strange and the unexpected art forms to fit into plenary sessions with ease and appropriateness. He describes that role as "sculpting the event." I will always be grateful for his insight and sensitivity, his energy and selflessness.

Beverly Vander Molen was assistant stage director. She acquired that role at the opening plenary session because Byron had not yet arrived. He was unable to depart from Los Angeles on July 7 because of confusion over his plane tickets and hotel accommodations. He spent two days trying to get things straightened out and did not arrive in Manila until July 11, the second day of the Congress.

Beverly stepped into the gap, put on headphones, and became a connecting link between technicians in the communication booth, located high above and at the rear of the auditorium, and people on stage. She had recommended this role for herself months earlier in our planning discussions because of her need to enable Ken to fulfill his role successfully.

She never got ruffled. On opening night, when Ken forgot to give time for the Filipino choir to sing and instead began a hymn introduction for the entire assembly, she quickly removed her headphones, ran up the steps to the piano, and whispered in Ken's ear. He immediately stopped and apologized.

The next day, Beverly taped a little two-way intercom to the left side of the piano so she could communicate directly with Ken and forestall any further scheduling mishaps. Whenever he heard the intercom crackling he knew she had a message for him, one he would need to get his ear down to hear.

As Ken's assistant—his eyes—and as assistant stage director, she sat through every plenary session, always keeping her sense of humor, always exuding calm in the midst of intense pressure, always enabling Ken to be ready for the occasion.

Not until after the Congress ended did I learn what went on between Beverly and Ken and the technicians in the communication booth during the last session. Just as all of the other four thousand participants were doing, I was giving my full attention to the closing ceremony, happy to be coming to the end of an exhausting yet joyous time. What none of us knew, including Byron Spradlin, was that Beverly had become the target of "the most colossal joke of all time," as Ken later described it.

The technicians, Bill Thatcher and Scott Wilson, had decided to tell Beverly that at nine o'clock, just as the final session of the ten-day Congress was coming to an end, the Filipino union workers planned to walk out on strike. At that time, both sound and lights would cease. With the stage full of people and the auditorium jammed to capacity, she would be the one to handle the emergency.

The schemers set their plan in motion by asking Beverly to put the headphones on Ken for a few seconds, just prior to the beginning of the last session, when he and Beverly were seated together in the front row of the auditorium. Over the headphones, Bill told Ken what he intended to tell Beverly and asked that Ken act as though he knew nothing. Ken managed to keep his composure and returned the headphones to Beverly. She put them on. Bill told her. The final session was just beginning. She had no chance to do anything but tuck this startling new information into a corner of her mind as she tended the platform.

As the evening progressed, the two technicians kept reminding Beverly of the impending crisis. Bill to Beverly: "Do you think people will be able to handle it?"

Scott to Beverly: "Well, we really don't have to worry too much because I know where the sound board is and I know where the lights are. Even if everything goes dark, I can probably get things back on."

Ken interacted from his position at the piano by asking Beverly over his inter-com, "Have you heard anything yet?"

Beverly relayed the question to Bill: "Have you heard anything yet?"

Bill to Beverly: "No, they're still negotiating. They're negotiating. Keep your eye on how many people are up on the stage."

Neither Scott nor Bill knew how they were going to fess up to this prank when the appointed hour arrived. In the meantime, they continued pressing against the outer edge of Beverly's unflappable calm.

She watched people going out into the hall and thought, Oh, those poor people—they're going to be stuck in the bathroom and the whole place is going to be dark. She constantly watched to see where people were on the stage so that if they had to be rescued she could give instructions on how to get to them.

She kept watching for nine o'clock. At five till, she alerted Ken: "We have five minutes to go. Be prepared."

At nine o'clock Bill came over the headset: "Beverly, it's nine o'clock. Everything's going out!"

Beverly: "You're kidding me!"

Bill: "Y—ES!"

Beverly started laughing and totally forgot her responsibilities. Ken was onstage leading three hundred people in singing "Alleluia" as the closing song of the Congress. He went on verse after verse after verse, seemingly ad nauseam because Beverly did not give him the signal he was waiting for. By the time Bill got through to her that it was time for Ken to STOP, the batteries in Ken's intercom had gone dead. She had to send a runner up the steps to whisper in his ear.

Ken and Beverly have told this story to producers and stage crews everywhere. They begin by saying, "Have you heard the story about Manila?" As with all oral stories, it builds and builds. Ken cannot wait to hear what it will sound like in ten years. He is sure it will become an epic.

One of the special delights for me in planning special events is watching the people I have invited and the plan I have shaped pick up creativity and momentum and go beyond my original design. My partners for the challenge at Lausanne II were not only capable, they were fun!

Tensions

The Lausanne movement is unique. It is not tied to any particular church identity. It sees its mission as the whole Church taking the whole gospel to the whole world. Participants who attended the first Lausanne Congress included Pentecostals who came and worked and worshiped alongside Presbyterians, Baptists, and Anglicans, to name just a few of the denominations represented.

Since 1974, the charismatic movement has swept the globe. Now the largest churches on nearly every continent are charismatic churches. An uncomfortable dilemma permeated the planning for Lausanne II, namely, how could the Congress program integrate the charismatics and the non-charismatics? The tension involved everyone on the program committee, but I felt particularly on the spot, being the program associate for worship.

I have always enjoyed visiting different kinds of churches. When my husband pastored, vacations were our only free times for worshiping in other churches. One Christmas Eve, when my family gathered in the

Ozarks and finished with gifts in the afternoon, my husband and I went to three different services: the Lutheran service from 9:00 to 10:00, the Episcopalian service from 10:00 to 11:00, and the Roman Catholic mass from 11:00 to 12:00 midnight. We left each service five minutes early and arrived at the next five minutes late.

When I taught church music at Moody Bible Institute, I required my students to attend a variety of churches to experience different styles of church music. I considered myself quite ecumenical.

In September of 1987, I participated in an ad hoc meeting preparing for Lausanne II. During an informal session, when the chairman put aside the prepared agenda and invited general concerns, Floyd McClung spoke up: "I'm sick and tired of hearing people say, 'What are we going to do with the charismatics?'"

With a guilty feeling, I realized there was a part of the Church I avoided, an increasingly significant part at that.

My thoughts went back to the Ozarks and the little community church where my mother and we four children walked when my father traveled long distances on Sundays, tending his rural Sunday schools. Lay preachers provided the sermons at our little community church. Amy Driscoll came once each month. On those Sundays I wanted to melt through the cracks in the floor. She started calmly, but I dreaded what came next. She got louder and louder. By the time she finished, huge purple veins stood out in her neck. I could scarcely bear to look at her. She called herself a Pentecostal. I determined to avoid Pentecostals.

When I grew up and could make my own choices, I gravitated toward liturgical worship, perhaps unconsciously making my way to the opposite end of the church spectrum. Whenever I encountered charismatic worship, I cautiously kept my distance. Floyd's comment made me squirm. How could I be worship coordinator for Lausanne II with my bias against charismatics?

When the meeting adjourned, I made an appointment with Floyd for breakfast the next morning. I confessed my lack of appreciation and experience on the charismatic end of things and asked how I might quickly educate myself. He told me about an Episcopal church in Darington, Connecticut, which combined liturgy and spontaneity in the most delightful mix he knew.

When I enrolled for classes a few weeks later at Chicago Theological Seminary, I asked permission to design an independent study course for myself in charismatic worship. Although Chicago has twelve seminaries, none of them offered a course of this kind. I decided the only valid way to learn about the subject was through actual personal experience. I would have to go to charismatic worship services. I made a list of churches to attend, including churches in places I would travel to in the coming months as I prepared for Lausanne II. I wanted to be open to the total experience, including the unexpected, and not make judgments ahead of time.

My most immediate need was to discover the kind of music distinctive to these worship services and include it in the Lausanne II hymnal. I collected praise and worship tapes and listened. I collected praise and worship songbooks and sang. I collected suggestions from charismatic friends and prayed. I soon realized that the matter was critical. If the hymnal did not include their songs, the charismatics would not feel included.

After hearing of Floyd's enthusiasm for a charismatic Episcopal church, I decided to ease into these experiences through the liturgical church. Saint Patrick's Episcopal Church in Atlanta, Georgia, permitted me to attend their renewal weekend planned for delegations from other Episcopalian churches wanting to learn about renewal through the Holy Spirit. Everyone who came stayed in homes of the members. I stayed with Adelaide Beall, director of the prayer ministry.

Both staff and laypeople taught the classes we attended. They followed up instruction with opportunities to observe and participate. They moved the midweek service to Friday night so we could attend as part of our seminar course. The instruction that day included explanation and history about the phenomenon of being "slain in the Spirit." That evening I saw it happen with my own eyes.

Sunday morning I attended both services, the 9:30 and the 11:00. At the end of the second service, determined to participate in the experience up to the end, I went forward to be prayed over by the prayer ministry team. I told them that I was scheduled for eye surgery the next morning. Cataract removal and lens implant on my other eye had required two separate surgeries. Looking forward to another bout with my eyes filled me with apprehension. How would the surgery go this time? Coming to this church had also filled me with apprehension. What was I getting into?

As they prayed, the clouds parted and a ray of sun streamed through the sanctuary window and rested on the troubled eye. In that instant of warmth, God gave me peace for both my surgery and my charismatic adventure.

I continued through the list. I went to an Assemblies of God church in the Ozarks while on a trip to visit my parents; to Faith Tabernacle in Chicago, not far from my home; to the Church on the Way (First Foursquare Church) in Van Nuys, California, while attending a program committee meeting; and to the Vineyard Fellowship in Evanston, a suburb of Chicago.

My last visit took me to the Vineyard Fellowship in Anaheim, California, on October 22, 1989, just days after the San Francisco earthquake. The morning's teaching continued the series from the book of Joel:

> And it shall come to pass afterward
> That I will pour out My Spirit on all flesh;
> Your sons and your daughters shall prophesy....
> And I will show wonders in the heavens and in the earth:
> Blood and fire and pillars of smoke (Joel 2:28–30 NKJV).

The text fit like a glove. No one moved. At the conclusion of the one-hour-long presentation, the teacher gave an invitation:

> You may have felt a witness in your body about this last-day ministry—a tingling around your mouth, a tingling in your ears or your hands, or your heart raced very fast. Come and we will pray for you.... There is a distinct group that God wants to touch this morning.

I was sitting in the front row where I could position my small stereo microphones on the floor for recording the service. Many people came forward, filling the space between the first row and the low platform.

A large woman stood directly in front of me. Her hands trembled. In a few minutes her entire body shook as though she were standing on a vibrator. Suddenly, without any warning, she fell backwards onto my microphones and my foot. I did not move a muscle but watched incredulously. Her head had landed so that my ankle formed a cushion.

I feared for my microphones and pulled them out from under her. She did not stir. The couple seated next to me tended her. Eventually she got up and told them she did not know what had happened. At that point I felt free to move my foot.

The first church provided the theory. The last one provided the practical application. Of the six churches, Saint Patrick's Episcopal in Atlanta and Vineyard Christian Fellowship in Anaheim formed a perfect combination to begin and end my experiences in charismatic worship.

Floyd's comment set me on a course which continued after my duties as program associate for worship were finished. In December of 1989 I completed the independent study course. The paper I wrote for Dow Edgerton, my advisor and professor for this special course, included the goal I had set for myself:

> In encountering the six charismatic churches of this paper, I tried to be objective and not let my early childhood experience prejudice my thinking. I struggled to see beyond the immediate responses my personality leaned toward, for, according to the Myers Briggs Type Indicator, I am an INTJ (Introverted, Intuitive, Thinking, Judging). My husband has been very helpful in pointing out when and where I've lost the struggle and assisted me in getting on course again.

When the special Congress issue of *World Evangelization* arrived, the editorial page had a photograph taken in Manila. It showed people standing, singing from the Congress hymnal. But what thrilled me most about that photograph was the hands up in the air. I hope Floyd McClung also felt comfortable, in that great hall, to be charismatic as he worshiped.

Now that I have done my homework, I have far more understanding for the charismatic tradition of worship.

Decisions

Decisions are not fun for me. Worry, procrastination, and lack of certainty lengthen the process, spending my energy and emotions. When decisions remain unresolved and lighthearted alternatives come along, I welcome the excuse to put hard choices on hold even longer.

Shortly after being appointed program associate for worship, I found myself with a difficult decision to make regarding the Congress. While the matter was still undecided, a personal incident diverted my attention. The prior obligation lost ground to the personal and, as a result, I ended up handling both in regrettable ways.

The story goes like this. On August 9, 1988, Ed Dayton called me to discuss the matter of a master of ceremonies. He highly recommended Graham Kerr for a number of reasons. (1) Graham was Australian, not American. Lausanne II needed to find non-Americans to be in leadership positions. (2) Graham had an excellent public personality. He had a television background as the "Galloping Gourmet." His sense of humor and impromptu style would liven up the audience in Manila. (3) Graham could bridge between different worship leaders. (4) Ed found Graham easy to work with. Ed suggested I call Graham and explore the possibility of his being emcee at the Congress.

The next day, I called Graham at his home in Tacoma, Washington. After a brief get-acquainted conversation, he explained his idea of a balanced ministry where men and women share the leadership. He had observed that, at times, women in leadership roles were not relaxed and therefore did not present themselves well. At the same time, he realized that women never would develop the facility to communicate effectively if they were not given opportunities necessary to gain experience. Therefore, he wanted to share whatever came his way with his wife Treena. They were a team.

I asked whether they could send me a video to introduce themselves and illustrate how they might work together. They had one which involved both of them but not as cohosts. The video came and I found myself drawn into their story of fantastic success and crushing failure. They spoke separately and together, sharing their personal faith in Christ which had enabled them to confess and forgive and bring healing to their marriage.

Ed and I talked some more. He had no objection to including Treena and having two people jointly lead the Congress as cohosts. Adding Treena could bring the positive element of more platform involvement for women. He suggested that I try to meet them and, if I felt good about inviting them, to go ahead with the informal invitation. Graham and Treena were scheduled to come through Chicago on Sunday morning, October 2. They had nearly an hour layover. We agreed to meet at the airport.

Several days prior to October 2, a letter arrived from Anchorage, Alaska. Mickey Templin wrote to say that her daughter Andria was coming for a friend's wedding. For several years, my husband had had a warm spot in his heart for Andria Templin, wishing he could introduce her to our son Brian. Mickey Templin also had this same wish. When her note arrived, the matchmaking wheels began to turn.

I called Mickey and got Andria's schedule while in the Chicago area. The only available time to plan any kind of social occasion was early Sunday morning. We decided that I would invite Andria's brother and his wife to bring Andria and come for breakfast. I would also invite Brian and his roommate, Jonathan, for breakfast. The Templins agreed to come.

Jonathan could not. Leery of telling Brian what was up, I omitted all mention of the other guests.

It was not until late in the evening Saturday, October 1, that I realized what I had done. The next morning was Sunday, October 2, and I was due at the airport to meet Treena and Graham at 9:00 A.M. There was no way I could host a breakfast at 8:00 and be at the airport at 9:00. I would have to cancel one of those engagements. Which?

It was nearly midnight. I agonized over my dilemma. I could not call at midnight and cancel breakfast, nor could I call at 7:00 the next morning as they were leaving and cancel. I had no choice but to proceed with the breakfast. Sunday morning, I would call the airport and page the Kerrs, thereby canceling our 9:00 appointment. I had made a miserable mess of things and I knew it.

Ray was not at home.

In the morning, I called Brian just before he came over and told him about the other guests. His anger flared immediately. He agreed to come, but as he was, wearing his dirty, smelly work clothes. He'd gotten up very early that morning to finish the cleaning at Epworth United Methodist Church, where he worked as custodian to help finance his budding career as an artist.

When the clock hands moved to the arrival time of Treena and Graham's flight into O'Hare, I excused myself from the breakfast table to call the airport and page them. They were disappointed. They had been looking forward to our meeting and were excited that they had even more layover time than when we first set up the plan to meet between flights. I am sure my vague explanation—that I would not be able to make it—left them wondering, especially since it had been my idea.

Brian did the dishes that morning. I could see his anger grow. I had done this once before, introducing him to a girl I especially liked. The repercussions then were mild compared with this time: He told the girl he was dating all about it later that day. Things went from bad to worse. She took it very hard and Brian tried to console her. Did this mean we did not like her?

I repented to both of them. I bought flowers and went to see Lisa at her apartment and make amends.

Ray was still not at home.

Brian took action against what he labeled a premeditated deed. He grounded his parents for one month. We could not see him or talk with him or come to his apartment (eight blocks away from our home) or send him any communication. And, of course, he would not come or call.

I could not spend all my energy on the new problem because I still had to make some kind of decision about Treena and Graham. There would be no further chance to meet them before Ed expected word from me. I wish I had done nothing, just stalled until after the ad hoc meeting scheduled for October 26 and 27. But Ed wanted them to be at that meeting if we decided to go ahead with them. Nobody else was even being discussed. Also, the Kerrs needed to know soon. The possibility of their being involved had been dangling since August.

The decision weighed heavily on my mind. I felt as if I was stuck in a quagmire, and it did not help a bit that it was of my own making. Usually I openly discuss problems and seek advice before making decisions, but this was one of those times when I lost patience and moved ahead without assistance. Unfortunately, it was a time when I really needed help, as I was out of my field of expertise.

I rarely watch television. My inexperience in this medium made me ill qualified to evaluate people whose context and perspective is television.

My understanding of cohosting reflected this gap in my awareness. When Graham explained that he wanted to cohost with Treena, I thought that meant they would alternate on the platform. In my own experience, when my husband and I do something together we take separate pieces of the task and do them independently. We do it this way largely because we have different styles. So, for instance, in our home, when he washes the dishes he prefers that I leave the room and do something else. He turns on the radio to his station, to his volume level, and does the job from start to finish. That is how we work together at household chores. Our roles in public are much the same. When he attends an event which places me on the platform, he is in the audience, and vice versa.

Added to my television gap and the independent work style which Ray and I use in our married life was the perspective of the seminary. Women who anticipate going into pastoral ministry expect to preach, teach, and counsel as individuals in their own right regardless of whether they minister alone or as part of a multiple staff.

Up to this point, I had talked with Graham a number of times by phone. On one of those occasions, he invited Treena to get on the line also. She was battling a fly as we talked. It had gotten into the house and was annoying her. I found her to be vivacious and talkative. That had been my only opportunity to talk with her.

The evening of October 3, one day after the breakfast and the cancellation at the airport, I decided to act. Anxious to get out from under the burden of this dilemma and eager to pass the ball back to Ed, I called Graham and extended the informal invitation to cohost the Congress.

Ed wrote them a letter on October 12:

> It is with a great deal of delight that I invite you to co-host our Lausanne II Congress in Manila July 11–20. . . . We will be having a meeting of an Ad Hoc Planning Group at the Quality Inn at L.A.X. on October 26 and 27. We think your participation in that would not only help us shape the program, but would also help you and Corean Bakke, our worship coordinator, to complete some of the planning.

We met at the October 26 meeting. Graham was very suave. Treena was just as I had expected from that one telephone conversation: dramatic and animated. Graham often interpreted her responses. She did not function apart from him even in our small group. I wondered about the appropriateness of their style for an international event.

At the ad hoc meeting, Ted Ward was very diasppointed that platform leaders had already been selected, thereby preempting any input from the committee. He disengaged himself from Lausanne II at the conclusion of that meeting and did not attend the Congress in Manila.

The Kerrs and I met repeatedly as the ad hoc planning committee worked through thirty-three plenary sessions. I discovered they were consistent, effervescent charismatics, not only in private but also in their public lives. I rationalized my frequent embarrassment over their emotionalisms as my problem.

From the beginning, Treena appeared to feel uneasy about her role. She repeatedly questioned Ed Dayton about the advisability of her being involved. She also questioned how her primary concern, to facilitate worship, could be accomplished, especially when she saw how tightly everything was being planned and timed. Where was time for the Holy Spirit to work? How could she lead people into praise and confession if she were continually bound by the clock?

Ed assured her that she would do a great job.

The matter of style continued to nag me. Would Graham and Treena's style intimidate non-Westerners? They had definite ideas and were not timid about expressing them. I found it difficult to raise alternative ideas in conversations. In an international context, would others also struggle to share ideas and be themselves?

The cross-cultural issue emerged. It seemed that the Kerr's experience omitted much of the non-Western world. I began to realize that, although Graham was Australian and Treena was British, they were very Western.

Finally, I discussed some of my apprehensions with Ed. He planned to visit his daughter in Tacoma over the holidays and would attend the Sunday school class which Graham and Treena team-taught to see how their practice of team leadership actually worked. It seemed all right to him. His daughter, who knew the Kerrs, did not dissuade him. She only suggested they be given strong direction for their participation at the Congress, something I also would have needed and wanted for myself had I been in their shoes.

But as the months passed, I felt more and more guilty over the way I had bungled my role by not meeting them prior to making the decision to invite them. I wished I could roll back the clock, visit with them in person, think through the situation for which we needed platform people, and not feel pressured into a decision.

I decided to call Ed Dayton and ask him to reconsider the invitation. Ed did not hear me out totally. He interrupted by saying that they were still the best solution. He had no problem with uninviting them if he thought it necessary. In either event, he wanted to take it out of my hands and discuss it with the highest level program committee. Apparently, the committee concurred with Ed, as nothing more was said. I ceased debating the decision.

When we arrived at the Congress, a national leader had been chosen to host each morning's activities. The Kerrs primarily did announcements, with great humor and wit and "showbiz." They also led some of the charismatic-type audience responses during worship.

In the planning stages, Graham and Treena were very supportive of having Ken Medema lead the Congress worship as both song leader and primary accompanist. I needed and appreciated that support especially when Gary Clark, assistant program director, voiced his conviction that Ken would not be an effective song leader.

Graham and Treena stood solidly with me, maintaining that Ken could do it. Their solidarity came at a time when I sorely needed it.

Ed gave Treena the additional responsibility of introducing all the artists. I was to give her biographical information on each of them so she could prepare her comments. This is where I let Treena down. I failed to prepare that information before leaving Chicago. After arriving in Manila, my responsibilities escalated, making it even more difficult to put that task into my schedule.

Treena kept asking for bios on the artists. At that point, all I could do was suggest that she talk with them personally, or have a steward do this. I told her where they sat during all the plenary sessions, in seats right behind hers. I had myself to blame when she struggled to pronounce names and organize introductions from the information she finally got.

My husband reminds me from time to time that I am not culturally in tune with American life as we approach the twenty-first century. My preference for less rather than more probably had a lot to do with my discomfort when her introductions tended toward the dramatic and resembled television-style hostessing: And now help me welcome ———!

Treena wrote me a note on her flight from Manila:

> It was an experience that both taught us, stretched us and changed us. . . .
> Thank you for your patience with me at the beginning. I learned—!

The personal crisis at the Bakke household had nearly run its course by the time the Congress concluded. My husband and I endured the grounding imposed by our son and had no contact with him for one whole month. He sent his girlfriend over once during that time to pick up something he wanted but, according to his own rules, could not come and get.

Andria Templin got married two years later in Anchorage, Alaska. Lisa, the girl for whom I bought flowers, is now my daughter-in-law. She and Brian were married three years after that ill-fated Sunday-morning breakfast in October 1988.

Kay sang at their wedding.

An International Hymnal
The Plan

A special hymnal for Lausanne II in Manila seemed critical. I could not imagine any other way to conduct corporate worship for four thousand participants who spoke many different languages, without a hymnal made for the occasion, a hymnal with musical notation. Others disagreed.

On May 24, 1988, Ed wrote a memo to the program committee and ad hoc planning committee:

> I'm attaching a copy of a letter from Corean Bakke dated May 1, in which she outlines at considerable length, some ideas for the design of the worship program, including the publication of a hymnal. . . .
>
> How do you feel about the general idea of having a hymnal for the Congress? What are your feelings about the tension between having people learn a number of new songs and hymns versus having them be able to sing songs for which they might have some knowledge (but would obviously all be Western)?

On August 2, Ed wrote me after receiving feedback on this memo:

> The program committee has basically said that we should not put energy into a Congress hymnal, though they have no objection to such a hymnal being available in time for a Congress. Our current thinking is that the Congress hymns should be part of a Congress book that contains the programs, etc. However, I can easily see how we would make a decision to split the hymns into a separate booklet. It's a question of logistics, costs and the final analysis.

The "no objection" clause encouraged me. They were not willing to put energy into a hymnal, but I could! They said nothing about unwillingness to put funding into a hymnal. Perhaps they would.

The idea of having a worship section with hymns in the participants' notebooks became less and less desirable as I lugged my oversized loose-leaf notebook to all the program planning meetings. I could imagine others feeling the same way at the Congress. When it came time to worship, I thought we should feel free to empty our hands of all that information, kick it under the seat, and enjoy the sweetness of our time with God. Ed agreed. Again, I was encouraged.

The next hurdle in making a hymnal was the song leader. I hesitated to move forward, knowing that song leaders must have a say in the songs they will lead. I learned about the critical relationship between song leader and songs at Urbana, a huge student missionary conference, where I watched a song leader pick and choose from a specially prepared hymnal. He seemed to definitely prefer some songs over others.

In trying to analyze the situation, three potential combinations of song leaders and hymnals emerged: (1) Song leaders as bringers of songs. They provide all the songs for the occasion, often many of their own. (2) Song leaders as selectors of songs. They choose from a body of available songs, any of which are possibilities for the occasion. (3) Song leaders as partners with the songs. They bring commitment to the songs chosen for the occasion.

Having already experienced the difficulties of the first two options in Stuttgart and at Urbana, I wanted to go with the third, a song leader who would be part of a team. We would choose the songs together and then trust the song leader to use them in the best possible way.

In August of 1988, Leighton Ford, chairman of the Lausanne Committee for World Evangelization, sent a memo to Ed Dayton, program director, and Saphir Athyal, chairman of the program committee:

> May I make one urgent recommendation. . . . Concerning the worship, I think it is of great urgency that an early recommendation and decision be made on who will be leading the music. Musicians—good ones—have their schedules filled at least a year ahead of time. It may be almost too late now. I don't think you can wait until December—in fact, I'm not sure you can wait longer than September to make that decision.

Leighton's memo to Ed and Ed's memo to me regarding my appointment to be program director for worship crossed in the mail. The matter of song leader remained unresolved. In September, Ed raised the question again in preparation for an ad hoc meeting. Would we want to consider having "one or more song leader/music director on the platform"?

At the time, I did not realize how seriously the indecision over the song leader would delay the making of the hymnal. Between my silence about any other possibility for song leader and no one else's strong recommendation, Ken gradually emerged as the song leader for Lausanne II. This process took time, and not until January could I speak of Ken as the song leader. Again I was encouraged, because he would have no stylistic limitations. The Congress hymnal could reflect the diversity of the Church around the globe and Ken would teach and lead those songs.

Next I went to work on themes necessary for the Congress hymnal. On December 31 I wrote letters to all the plenary speakers scheduled to speak at Lausanne II:

> I am writing to ask your assistance in putting together a hymnal for Lausanne II. Do you have a particular hymn or song which you would recommend in connection with your topic....
>
> If the song you recommend is in a language other than English, please send the indigenous language plus a singable translation in English. We cannot promise to include all suggestions as there are many factors to consider in making a pocket hymnal. The committee hopes to include hymns and songs from around the world as well as Western ones....
>
> We hope to plan the hymnal and the worship at the conference to be relevant to the people and the concerns they raise.

As editor, I decided the hymnal also needed to reflect all nine official languages chosen for the Congress: Spanish, Portuguese, Arabic, Chinese, Japanese, Russian, German, French, and English. I wanted the non-English representation in the hymnal to be authentic. I looked for hymns originating in the official languages. This part of the plan came into focus gradually after I realized that a general search for hymns did not produce anything in Portuguese, Arabic, Russian, Chinese, and Japanese.

It seemed appropriate to go beyond the nine official languages and include hymns from additional languages. The reasons for making these choices took shape as the plan progressed.

As a final consideration in shaping the hymnal, it seemed that these new hymns, unknown to the majority of the participants, should be balanced with traditional Western hymns for conservatives, and contemporary Western choruses for charismatics. Everyone would have to learn in order to participate, but they would have the advantage of a hymnal with the musical notation, and the advantage of a strong male vocalist leading the way.

With a plan to accommodate diversity of style, themes, languages, and ecumenical preferences, a new international hymnal was off to a good start, but I had not yet begun.

The Process

I had never made a hymnal before. Here I was, attempting a complex one with multiple languages and expecting to take it from start to finish in a matter of months. I had no idea what I was getting into. Armed with innocence, a certain measure of arrogance (that no other hymnal would do), and determination, I began looking around for help.

Ed Dayton suggested asking Word Publishers whether they would be interested in publishing a Lausanne II hymnal. Ken's involvement might be a lure to securing their involvement. I called Word in Waco, Texas, and found I could not speak to a person, only to answering machines. I left several messages.

I did not know who our publisher would be, but I knew it would not be Word.

John Wilson, an instructor at Moody Bible Institute when I was a student there, now worked at Hope Publishing Company. I called him. After listening to a few of my questions he suggested that I talk with the president. George Shorney was most kind. He listened. He advised. And he said, "If you need any more help, give me a call."

The matter of a typesetter weighed heavily on my mind even though the music had not yet been selected. George gave me two names, but neither person had time to take on a new project and finish by June 1.

Not knowing what to do, I turned to another task. I called Harold Best to confirm his availability for the hymnal selection committee. He asked how things were going and I told him my dilemma. He put me on hold in order to bring a third person into the conversation. Tony Payne, composer and arranger, had just discovered the possibilities of writing music using computer software. Harold wondered whether I would be interested in having Tony come to our April 3 meeting and bring a sample of his work.

Tony brought "Amazing Grace." This was my very first look at music desktop publishing, and to my eye it looked as fine as anything I'd ever seen printed. We made an appointment to meet the following week and discuss a cooperative working arrangement for a hymnal which would bypass typesetting and permit far more flexibility, something this complicated hymnal would need.

After gathering songs for several months, I scheduled the first and only hymnal selection committee meeting of seven people. We had to accommodate ourselves to Ken Medema's schedule. On April 3, less than two months before the camera-ready manuscript would need to leave for publication in the Philippines, we met in Ken's hotel room at the O'Hare Hilton: Harold Best, dean of the Wheaton Conservatory of Music; Tony Payne, assistant dean at the Wheaton Conservatory; Ted Ward, professor at Trinity Seminary; Ken Medema, who would lead the singing at the Congress; Beverly Vander Molen, his assistant, who would teach him all the music; and myself.

Prior to the meeting, Ed Dayton requested that I include a charismatic person on this committee. I arranged for Anthony Powell, song leader at Faith Tabernacle in Chicago, to meet with us. I had visited his church as part of my charismatic worship course. He and the music director had already assisted me with copies of contemporary praise and worship songs to be considered for the hymnal. Our meeting fell on Monday, his day off. He looked forward to coming.

At the last minute, he could not come. His pastor called and preempted those plans by asking him to edit tapes for their television programs on Monday. It was too late to find a replacement.

Each committee member had three stacks of songs: (1) traditional hymns, (2) contemporary Scripture and praise songs, (3) and songs originating in non-English languages. Harold suggested we begin with the songs most often neglected, the third stack.

We examined the music itself, looking for cultural identity and distinctiveness, hoping in every case to choose songs well known and used by the churches of that culture. In many cases, these songs had never been sung in English. If we chose any of them, we would have to get translations made. Although there were nine official languages, English would be the primary language.

The largest stack, traditional hymns, required the most selectivity. Most hymnals, even those in other languages, concentrate on these songs. We hoped to have a balanced hymnal, giving about the same amount of space to all three categories of songs. We tried to choose carefully as we selected traditional hymns.

The contemporary praise and Scripture songs presented the most difficulty. They were the most difficult for me to gather and I went to other people for assistance, asking for the best examples of this kind of music, the songs which they thought would still be around in ten or twenty years.

The committee evaluated each song in category two according to theology, musical composition, length, and suitability for four thousand people to sing together. Unfortunately, only a few Scripture and praise songs survived this kind of scrutiny.

Tony and I met weekly in April, either in his office at the conservatory or at his home. As a church musician and leader of worship, he saw the importance a hymnal committed to integrating the two main streams of church music in the United States—traditional hymns and contemporary praise and Scripture songs—with indigenous music from other cultures and languages. Our combined firm commitments to produce such a book drove us forward and impelled us to resolve each problem along the way.

I sent all over the world for permission to use songs and hymns. Publishers in the most faraway places were among the most cooperative. English-language publishers and copyright owners presented the most difficulty. They were very particular, very protective, and (some of them) very slow.

Tony hired a helper, Howard Beno, a senior student in composition at the conservatory. Together they compiled all the songs on Graphic Notes Music Publisher Software, both music and words. Tony was patient and understanding with the process. He knew that I would not be able to give him an exact list of the hymns to be included, at least not right away. He and Beno worked through the inexact list, doing many songs which were never used.

We struggled to find the best way to put eighteen different languages into the hymnal—the nine official languages of the Congress: Spanish, Portuguese, Arabic, Chinese, Japanese, Russian, German, French, and English; and nine additional ones: Creek (Native American), Swedish, Thai, Swahili, Zulu, Korean, Cambodian, Balinese, and Tagalog (Filipino).

We wanted each song presented in its original language in addition to an English translation. Tony knew of a program which would enable us to print in other scripts, but it proved too costly for this venture. As it turned out, we spent more money going alternative routes. The Slavic Gospel Association in Wheaton allowed us use of their Cyrillic type font, but it developed a glitch and would not cooperate. We used typewriters for the Japanese and Arabic and handwritten characters for the Thai and Cambodian. The Chinese and Korean were done at print shops. Tony wrote all other languages with the software, adding extraneous markings by hand as required.

The Congress executive committee arranged for a publisher in the Philippines to handle all printing needs: Oversees Missionary Fellowship Literature, Inc. (OMF). All manuscripts were to be prepared in the United States, then shipped in camera-ready condition to the Philippines.

Rey Halili, managing director for OMF wrote Ed on April 3:

> ... concerning Lausanne Hymnbook ... We need camera ready and cover art work before end of May. . . . We are scheduled to reprint *Hymns for Worship*. . . . We could shelve this project and shift to the Lausanne Hymnbook.

Ed called toward the end of April and suggested the hymnal project be dropped. He worried over two approaching deadlines: (1) completion of the camera-ready manuscript on time, and (2) printing and delivery of the hymnals by the printer in Manila on time. Ed knew that I was cutting the time factor very close. He also knew about Filipino time, which is always later than the scheduled time.

I consulted with Tony on how to respond to Ed. Tony, who has a doctorate in composition from Northwestern University, is very articulate and responded with this list of arguments for the hymnal:

1. We would not have started if we could not finish.
2. We know we will be pinched for time.
3. It is a window of opportunity that we do not want to miss.
4. We like the challenge.
5. The hymnal will have a lasting impact.
6. Technology is on our side.

The hymnal project continued. I hope Ed put his worries away. I never admitted to him that I did not. Sunday morning, May 21, the start of the final working week on the hymnal, with company coming to my home and so many things still to be finished, I went to Ebenezer Lutheran Church for the morning service. It was only two blocks away, much closer than my own church. In the middle of the service, fear and worry grabbed me in the pit of my stomach. I walked out and went home to continue working on the hymnal.

Every time I met with Tony, I drove eighty miles round-trip from Chicago to Wheaton and back. Roosevelt Road, the principal route, was under construction. I always arrived late for our appointments. The drive back home to Chicago and north on Lake Shore Drive became an inspiration as the countdown became tense. As I admired all the skyscrapers, each one different from the others, I imagined the problems which must have accompanied their construction. How many times did the plan to build them just about come apart? Who was it that always hung in and refused to let the project collapse?

The Lausanne II hymnal became like one of those skyscrapers, a project to protect and complete. Two of us stood between success and failure. We had so much left to do and we were so tired.

Completion

We needed a few more days. I called Rey Halili in Manila and asked for an extension. He agreed to receive the manuscript the first week in June. We worked frantically, barely getting any sleep during those last few days, still compiling, still preparing translations, still waiting for permissions to use copyrighted songs.

The major frustration was copyright holders/owners who sat on things and did not respond until it was too late. A publisher in Chicago verbally gave permission and agreed to the wording of the credits, then later sent a letter stating that, for publication outside the United States, I would have to contact a publisher in France. I was able to resolve that by fax and sent the change to the publisher after the manuscript had already left for the Philippines.

I requested permission from Maranatha! Music for five songs. Unknown to me, two of the songs needed British permission for publication outside the United States. That word was slow in coming. After we rerouted that request, the British publisher did not respond at all, and we withdrew "Bind Us Together" by Bob Gillman and "May the Fragrance of Jesus Fill This Place" by Graham Kendrick.

The most frustrating experience of all involved the hymn "Sing Alleluia to the Lord," whose copyright was held by New Song Ministries. Their response arrived June 2, a day after the deadline. The publishing agreement they sent had no phone and no address. Just a post-office-box number. Tony was especially sorry to remove that song. He liked it and was very pleased over the way he had been able to format it on the software.

Another last-minute change involved "Shalom Chaverim." We wanted to include a Hebrew song and thought this was a folk song available for anyone to use. Two days before the manuscript was finished, on a holiday weekend, I discovered a copyright attached to this song. We did not want to risk the possibility of a legal suit, so Tony removed it and renumbered all the songs accordingly.

The copyright permission for "Alleluia," the first song in the book, was still in the negotiating stage when we went to press. Correspondence got misplaced at Manna Music and did not surface for months. Not until August of 1990, over a year *after* publication, was everything settled between us and that copyright owner.

All the way through the process of making the hymnal I kept in touch with Beverly and Ken as songs were added and subtracted. Keeping in touch meant calls between my home in Chicago and all points of the United States. I could always get a telephone number for them through their Briar Patch office, and Beverly always faithfully returned calls.

The night before taking the finalized selections to the printer to make the camera-ready copy, Beverly called and we went over the index I had sent her. She pointed out a significant omission: We had four days of Bible study on sin and not one song on sin.

At our first hymn selection meeting, Harold Best had promoted "What Can Wash Away My Sin?" saying it was a gem of a song. Its melodic and harmonic simplicity and form made it very well suited for cross-cultural use.

I had never liked the song. It was too simplistic, too repetitive, for my tastes. At the last minute, when choices had to be made to keep the hymnal within specified boundaries, I had seen my chance to get rid of it. Now, at the last minute, Beverly was saying we needed it. Meekly, I put it back, displacing a different song.

Tony and I titled the book together. I wanted a one-word title, understood by all. *Hallelujah* was a universal worship word, but I preferred the simplicity of the Spanish spelling, *Aleluya*. Tony wanted the title to identify the event for which it was prepared. He added a subtitle: *The Music of Lausanne II*.

Tony asked a friend of his, Tim Ward, to design the cover, and talked me into accepting whatever design Tim sent us. Tony called ABS Printing in Addison, near Wheaton, and asked whether Susan Lauer, Harold Best's daughter and a graphic designer, might help us prepare the manuscript to be camera-ready. We took it to her on May 31, wishing we had another day to proofread, evaluate, and refine, but the time was up. Susan worked with us for much of two days until the manuscript was boxed and ready for DHL Worldwide Express pickup.

We corrected errors right up to the last moment. Just as the manuscript was ready to box, I glanced again at the cover design. The word *Lausane* caught my attention! We had not thought to proofread the cover!

Before putting the manuscript into the mailer, I made copies of each page in order to have a master copy, something to duplicate and make into notebooks for the small ensemble.

When DHL picked up our package that afternoon the label read "DATE 6/1/89; TIME 349PM." I sent a message to Rey Halili at OMF Publisher in Manila:

> The hymnbook manuscript is due to arrive on Wednesday June 7 via DHL. . . . I am suggesting that you deliver 5,100 copies to the PICC Lausanne II office the afternoon of July 7.

Tony and I were finished! We knew it was not a perfect job, but for the moment we did not let that diminish our gratefulness.

My last errand with the hymnal came ten days later. I arranged to meet Beverly and Ken at the Holiday Star in Merrillville, just across the state line in Indiana, to give them their loose-leaf copy of the hymnal. I never got there.

The combination of construction and heavy stop-and-go traffic caused many accidents. During a "go" period, I gathered too much momentum while casually watching an accident on the other side of traffic. I could not stop our heavy Volvo and smashed into the rear of a camper.

The state police came immediately, from the other side of traffic. The camper was unharmed, but the collision cracked my radiator. Water spilled all over the roadway. The police radioed for a tow truck and I terminated that final journey in the parking lot of a service station. Instead of celebrating the completion of our hymnal over lunch at Beverly and Ken's motel, we met at a truck stop across from the service station. I rode back to Chicago in the cab of a tow truck with my crippled Volvo trailing along behind.

Usually my husband takes care of all matters related to the car, but as he was traveling during much of June, I had to take care of this emergency myself. We held our breath for fear our insurance company would refuse to accept the claim because of our car's advanced age and mileage. It was a 1980 model with nearly 200,000 miles. I prepared to fight it out, to say that a diesel engine cannot be compared to a gasoline engine and that its mileage simply showed how well it continued to function. That *was* our car. We had no other.

State Farm honored the insurance claim. When I drove our newly repaired car back home, Ray congratulated me. There had been a hole in the radiator for some time. He thought it absolutely brilliant of me to get a new one installed for no charge.

In paging through my loose-leaf copy of the hymnal, my eye caught mistakes, but relatively minor ones, the kind where the computer spaced wrong or a simple word was misspelled. However, on my way to Manila I discovered a preposterous mistake in the acknowledgements. I did not know whether to laugh or cry. The letter *g* had been omitted from the word *singing*, turning it into *sining*:

> CALLED AS PARTNERS IN CHRIST'S SERVICE: Words © 1981 Jane Parker Huber; from *A SINING FAITH*. Used by permission of Westminster/John Knox Press.

There was nothing I could do.

Use at the Congress

On Saturday, July 8, I arrived at the Lausanne II offices in the Philippine International Convention Center. Gary Clark greeted me with the gift of a freshly printed hymnal, then escorted me to the storage room to see five thousand more. I wished Tony could have been there to see them. I savored that happy moment for both of us. They had arrived right on schedule, one of the few things that did during the course of the Congress.

One of the most delightful experiences for me as program associate for worship was to see the hymnal in use. I had many memories of nearly every song, such as where I got it, how it survived the committee decisions, and how it actually made it into the hymnal. At the Congress, when I saw how the hymnal functioned far beyond our expectations, I realized God had guided our work even when we were not consciously looking for assistance.

Many stories could be told about the hymnal. These are a few of my favorites.

O for a Thousand Tongues

Joni Eareckson Tada was the first plenary speaker to answer my letter asking for recommendations for the hymnal. As a quadriplegic universally acclaimed for her ministry called Joni and Friends, she would speak on evangelism in connection with disabled persons. She wrote:

> Since my talk will focus on social concerns, I have enclosed the words and music to "O for a Thousand Tongues." I have checked off the first and fourth verses that I would like to have included.

I read through both verses, but not until we sang it at the Congress did I see the significance Joni had in mind when she sent me her choice.

> Hear Him, ye deaf; His praise, ye dumb;
> Your loosened tongues employ;
> Ye blind, behold your Savior come,
> And leap, ye lame, for joy!

We sang with fresh understanding as Ken, blind from birth, led us, and as Joni, her helpless body strapped into a chair, sang with us. When Ken took his fingers off the keys at the close of the hymn, he flung both arms overhead, adding a physical exclamation point to verse four.

What Can Wash Away My Sin?

The hymn which I tried to leave out of the hymnal led to another exquisite moment. When it came time to sing "What Can Wash Away My Sin?" Ken, seated on the piano bench, asked the question, "What can wash away my sin?" There were a few sputterings here and there. Ken asked the question again, louder: "What can wash away my sin?" The response grew stronger.

The third time, Ken shouted the question: "WHAT CAN WASH AWAY MY SIN?" The firm, clear response came from all over the great hall: "NOTHING BUT THE BLOOD OF JESUS!"

As we sang, I watched in astonishment as tears rolled down Ken's face. The singing of my least favorite hymn, the one Harold Best had praised and called a gem, became one of Lausanne II's treasured moments. I repented of my dislike for that hymn.

Our Cities Cry to You, O God

Every song in the hymnal was scheduled into the Congress program, but not every song was sung. Worship time, conveniently expendable, was often shortened to make room for additional program items. Participation time decreased as program time increased.

One song—the result of considerable search by the Lausanne urban associates office in Chicago and therefore the focus of great expectation by Ray Bakke, senior associate for large cities—was withdrawn from the participation category, meaning the time spent actually singing together, and placed into program, meaning time spent observing others perform the songs.

"Our Cities Cry to You, O God," the only urban hymn in the hymnal and the best urban song found during the search, was scheduled to be sung at the conclusion of the video: *God Is Building a City*. The program director, determined to keep the session from running over as previous ones had done, made a decision during the plenary to have the hymn read instead of sung. Reading would take less time.

All five of the speakers in that plenary carefully planned and rehearsed their participation to fall within the time limits. At the conclusion, a surprised Ed Dayton looked at his watch and said, "What happened? We're four minutes ahead of schedule!"

The plenary production time sheet listed length in minutes for the video *God Is Building a City* at eighteen. It took only fourteen. Ray's disappointment over not singing that hymn, with four thousand participants focused on urbanization, has not diminished.

Paglilingkod

Priscilla Pascual, my friend at Northen Baptist Theological Seminary, helped in the search to find a Filipino song for the Congress hymnal. She had me contact Melba Maggay, the director of the, Institute for Studies in Asian Church and Culture (ISAAC). Melba sent three songs published by ISAAC and a letter:

> nthusiastic about Lausanne, as I could more or less predict that it will be just another American extravaganza, with the West projecting their own notions of where the churches of the rest of the world are at this time. However, for the sake of our friendship with [Priscilla] and the rest of the Body of Christ, we are prepared to be of help in any way we can.

From the songs Melba sent, the hymnal selection committee chose "Paglilingkod," a Tagalog song. Harold Best affirmed the choice by saying we needed to include a song in the hymnal to represent the host country. Priscilla made a literal translation into English.

My limited experience had proven that the most successful way to get a singable English translation was to ask an American, someone for whom English was the mother tongue. I made some phone calls, hoping to find an American fluent in Tagalog. I made an appointment with a retired former missionary to the Philippines. However, very soon in our conversation I realized he had no idea how to set words to meter. Time was running out.

I went to a poet friend, Sharon James-Ledbetter, showed her the music and the English meaning, and asked whether she would write a poem expressing the Tagalog idea with meter to fit the music. In order to have enough words to fit the tune, she would have to substantially embellish the original meaning because Tagalog words have far more syllables than English words. The song had four verses.

Sharon had never before attempted such a thing. She invited Jackie Whowell, a musician friend, to help. They struggled together for several days, getting very little done. I reviewed their progress and made some suggestions. A few days later, unable to sleep, Sharon got up, went to work, and by morning finished all four verses. Nothing had to be changed.

On opening night, after Leighton Ford finished speaking, Romulo's choir returned to the stage and sang "Paglilingkod." They sang all four verses in Tagalog and then the first verse in English:

> What service can I do for you?
> What off'ring shall I bring?
> What worthy praise is due to you,
> My Father and my King?
> What can I give, what holy gifts are worthy of your Name?
> For by Your will all things were made,
> By Word creation came.

The song was far more beautiful than I expected. All the memories of getting ready for that moment returned and mixed with the sounds. I remembered how Sharon and Jackie had struggled to write those very words, and I wished they could have been there to experience that exquisite moment. I was grateful to have a recorder in hand.

One of the first things I did after returning home to Chicago was make tapes of "Paglilingkod" for Sharon and Jackie. I will never forget the joy of playing that tape for Sharon. My kitchen became a sacred place as we listened together.

Blessed Assurance

This song was used in two ways at the opening ceremony of the Congress: as congregational hymn and as postlude.

The congregational hymn began after Ken sang an introduction in the style of African song leaders who have no instruments to play an introduction. Not until verse three did he introduce any instruments.

The postlude involved Ken Medema on the keyboards, Pedro Eustache on the flute, Ren Merry on the guitar, and Steven Agyaku on the drums doing a jazz improvisation of "Blessed Assurance." This delightful surprise alerted music lovers to expect the unexpected in the coming days of the Congress.

Songs Used but Not Found in the Hymnal

The commitment to make a hymnal involved a lot of time and money. The hymnal selection committee, Tony, and I went to great lengths to bring together a body of songs to suit all the needs of the Congress. It therefore seemed appropriate that we use the hymnal for all our singing and not bypass it with other songs people might want to include.

It was agreed: no songs were to be used that were not in the hymnal. This agreement was broken two times.

On day two, Treena Kerr impulsively requested that everyone sing "Happy Birthday" to Deyanira Toruño, who had just finished singing "Cantad al Senor." That impromptu congregational song preempted the hymn scheduled to precede Bible study that morning: "Blessed Jesus At Your Word."

When Ken Medema inserted "Jesus Loves Me," Beverly Vander Molen turned to me and said, "He cannot function without that song." We ought to have put it into the hymnal, but I was uncertain about its origins. It has a pentatonic melody. Does the tune trace back to China? I did not have time to search for the answers.

Songs Suggested but Not Used

Several days before the Congress closed, Ed Dayton brought me a song, saying that he had been given four thousand copies. It was entitled " 'Proclaim Christ until He Comes,' Hymn for Lausanne II in Manila and the Philippine Congress on World Evangelization. Music by Citas Cabildo; Lyrics by Arcadio Cabildo."

A note at the bottom explained:

"Proclaim Christ until He Comes" was especially composed for Lausanne II in Manila and the Philippine Congress on World Evangelization. It reflects the message and objectives of both Congresses.

Ed Dayton asked, "What shall we do with this?" I answered, "We're committed to using the hymnal. We cannot use it."

There was another reason why we could not use it. It would not have been fair. Another song had been submitted the previous October as a theme song for the Congress: "If God Be for Us," written by Robyn Claydon. The hymnal selection committee decided it did not meet the criteria necessary for the Congress hymnal, even after careful revisions.

On day two, Lee Yih, a businessman from Hong Kong, livened up the Congress by comparing evangelists to frogs and lizards. Frog-like evangelists, the professionals, sit and wait for events to bring people to them. Lizard-like evangelists, the non-professionals, cannot afford to wait but go looking. His illustration continued to reappear, day after day, as other speakers referred to frogs and lizards, sometimes identifying themselves as one or the other.

Toward the end of the Congress, in a relaxed and mischievous mood, I wrote a note to Beverly Vander Molen during one of the plenary sessions: "We should have a song about frogs and lizards."

She consulted with Ken, who could have improvised such a song, and then wrote a reply: "It's not in the hymnal!"

The unexpectedness of getting trapped by my own rule added to the merriment of the moment.

. . .from A SINING FAITH

Not until the end of the Congress did I get up the courage to again read the page in the acknowledgements with the words "Sining Faith," and when I did, I had to look closely to believe what I saw ". . . from *A SINGING FAITH.*"

Rey Halili not only graciously gave Tony and me an extension on getting the camera-ready copy to him but also took the time to do some proofreading. He found that preposterous error and corrected it.

I began the task of making an international hymnal alone and ended up with many skillful helpers. Together we completed a formidable task.

An International
Worship Team

When the ad hoc committee approved my idea for a small ensemble under Ken Medema's direction, they gave me permission to find a guitarist, a flutist, a drummer, and a female vocalist. None of these four musicians could be "white faces" because Ken already was. They were to be a microcosm of Lausanne II, representatives of the world Church, not the American church.

The other members of the worship team—soloists, artists, and choirs—were also to be representative of the world Church. In both areas—the small ensemble and the larger worship team—I had to look beyond people I already knew and find non-Americans.

The difficulties of my idealistic plan became apparent. I was totally dependent on recommendations from other people. That was only the beginning of the problem I had given myself. Once recommendations arrived, I had to find a way to evaluate the contributions each person could bring to the international worship team. I hoped, when the team was completely formed, that each contribution would complement the whole and that the whole would reflect the global diversity represented at the Congress.

I could not rely on written or verbal recommendations. That did not mean that the sources were unreliable. It meant that people have different ways of describing sounds. Only after personal, firsthand contact with each recommendation could I make a decision. Tape recordings provided that firsthand contact.

I collected dozens of tapes as I put together an international worship team.

Naga Guitarist

In June of 1988 a letter arrived from Nagaland, India, from Margaret Shishak, director of music at Patkai Christian College. She was looking for a way to enable one of the Nagas to continue with master's level studies in order to return and teach at Patkai. She knew of my involvement with two young women students from Nagaland while on the music faculty at Moody Bible Institute and hoped I might be able to find the necessary financial backing:

> I am writing you today about a third Naga young person who has also just graduated from Moody with a major in guitar: Mr. Ren [Renthungo] Merry. He has expressed a desire to teach at Patkai, and what could be more appropriate for us than a guitar teacher? Guitars are easily available, pianos are not. . . . Ren has applied to the American Conservatory for his master's. . . . He would study with his former teacher. . . . I have written to Ren today to contact you and come to see you personally. . . . I am sure you can find out a lot about Ren from Gerald Raquet.

56

I knew about the pianos in India. All of them are imported. Most arrived with the British and struggle with the hot and humid climate. Newer ones often come into the country to serve the musical needs of foreign embassies.

My experiences in India changed earlier misconceptions about the piano being indispensable and foundational to all music study. In many countries it simply was neither practical nor economically accessible. I agreed with her 100 percent.

How amazing that she would write me about her concern for a guitarist when I was looking for one! Her letter was the first recommendation. It precisely suited the ad hoc committee's requirements for a non-American, and it made my job of establishing contact very easy. Ren was just a half hour's drive away. Although at that point I had not yet been appointed program associate for worship, I was already looking for potential worship team members.

I called Gerald Raquet, the head of the sacred music department at Moody Bible Institute, as Margaret had suggested. He gave a tremendous recommendation. When Ren had arrived four years before, he scarcely knew English. But with his quick ear, he soon picked it up. He played classical, rock, and folk music. He accompanied and improvised. I was advised to contact Ren's music theory teacher, David Smart, if I needed another reference.

I made the second call. David Smart's comments reinforced those of the department chairman. He told me how Ren had successfully worked to overcome great odds and fulfilled all the Institute's requirements. He was a natural leader, well liked by the entire student body. And he was an outstanding performer.

I made a third call, this time to Ren, to introduce myself and set a date to get acquainted. We met in the lounge of the men's dormitory, mostly deserted during that first session of summer school. He told me about touring India with the New Life Singers, a contemporary Christian group, and with the Billy Graham Evangelistic Association Evangelist Robert Cunville. He told me about his master's degree in English literature from North Eastern Hills University in India and his one year of teaching before coming to the United States.

I inquired about his church involvement and learned that he accompanied the worship music at a very small Bible church. Although the church had a piano, no one could play it. He served as both song leader and accompanist. I made arrangements to attend one of those services and make a recording.

When I inquired about his classical music performances, he gave me a tape of his senior recital at Moody. He offered another tape of his accompaniments for a male vocalist, including some of his own compositions. Those three tapes of Ren's playing were the first of many tapes I gathered in preparation for Lausanne II.

On the first of November, I wrote to Ren saying that the committee had approved him to be the guitarist for the small ensemble that would lead worship at Lausanne II. The others—a flutist, a drummer, and a female vocalist—were yet to be found. None of them could be white Westerners. All of them, like Ren, were to be from other cultures and other races.

One difficulty after another pursued Ren in the months between November, when he was selected to be the guitarist, and July, when the Congress began.

His father sent money for him to come home for Christmas. Ren had not been home to Nagaland for four years. He was torn between accepting this gift and postponing the trip to a less hectic time for him personally. I was relieved when he did not go.

Because of his student visa, Immigration required Ren to take four classes during the spring semester of 1989. He enrolled in four major courses at Moody Bible Institute: youth ministry, educational psychology, biculturalism, and marriage and the family. These four courses consumed most of his time. In addition to class attendance and preparation, Ren worked eighteen to twenty hours in the library each week.

His experience of church music was limited to the Baptist church in Nagaland, the Billy Graham evangelical crusades in India, and the Leavitt Street Bible Church. Musically he was as Western as an American. He grew up in a country where the newly born church tossed out indigenous music and culture to enthusiastically and obediently embrace everything Western. He came to Moody with a background of Western rock and folk music, Western hymns, and contemporary Christian songs.

When spring semester began, I explored the possibility of a specially designed course for Ren to broaden his musical experiences. Chicago had all the necessary resources: every kind of church and countless opportunities to encounter ethnicity from around the world. Such an arrangement would have to be supervised by a faculty person and approved by the school.

There was no way to work it out. He took the four classes, he worked in the library each week, and on Sundays he went to the Leavitt Street Bible Church in fulfillment of his practical ministry assignment for that semester. That left little time for practice.

In March, he dislocated his left elbow playing soccer, terminating all practice.

Knowing my concern over his limited knowledge of global music, he attended two performances of non-Western ethnic music: a sitar recital and a concert of Russian music including the balalaika. Eventually his elbow healed and he could practice again.

Ren completed his course work at Moody Bible Institute in May and joined the small ensemble at Lausanne II in July. He brought one guitar, his classical guitar, as I requested.

One of my regrets as program associate for worship is that I did not sufficiently discuss Ren's need for a particular microphone ahead of time with the person in charge of sound resources. It is possible we could have given Ren adequate amplification for the vast plenary hall.

As it was, Ren had difficulty being heard. The less delicate instruments in the small ensemble, drums and flute and piano, were easy to amplify, and the synthesizer which Ken Medema used in combination with piano had unlimited volume. But the type of microphone Ren needed to project his classical guitar into the hall was not available. He had to work with a less-than-satisfactory substitute.

His solo, "Jesu, Joy of Man's Desiring," beautifully played and accompanied lightly on the synthesizer, helped redeem this problem. His quick ear and improvising skills complemented the other members of the small ensemble. His amiable spirit came through in all the complexities and difficulties. Every time we talked, he told me how much he was gaining from the experience.

When the Congress finished, Ren went home to Nagaland, I returned to Chicago, and another letter arrived from Margaret Shishak, director of music at Patkai Christian College. She reminded me that I had not yet given any attention to the initial request which had introduced me to Ren fourteen months earlier:

> A lot has happened during the past year, and now Lausanne II is history. Ren Merry came to see us on July 24, just after arriving from Manila. . . . Did he tell you he has been accepted at American Conservatory and has been offered a $3,000 scholarship (yearly, I presume)? But in order to get

his I-20 form, the institution requires him to provide $13,000 yearly for himself (rather to prove that he has resources equal to that); he needs $10,000 more a year.

Her reminder propelled me into a new venture, that of assisting Ren to continue his education. In August of 1993, Ren completed his master's degree in guitar and returned to Nagaland to teach guitar and music theory at Patkai Christian College. At the time of this writing, he has fifty private guitar students.

Venezuelan Flutist

I left the ad hoc meeting in October of 1988 knowing that somewhere I had to find a versatile flutist, one who improvised in addition to playing the classical repertoire.

Friends suggested I check with music schools in Chicago as a starting point. Chicago had many international students studying music. But that approach presented a critical problem. How would I be able to ascertain the Christian commitment of any flutist found in this way? The criteria for being part of the small ensemble involved two equally important considerations: musicianship and discipleship. I could not see my way clear to pursue this uncertain route.

Several weeks later, after having done nothing about the problem except pray and wait, the phone rang as my husband and I prepared to eat our evening meal. My husband answered. When it immediately became apparent that the phone call was for me, I grabbed pen and paper and took the call in his study, away from noises in the kitchen.

It was Sam Olson in Venezuela. He was returning home from a Lausanne-related meeting in Los Angeles where he had heard about my

61

need for a flutist. As soon as his plane landed, he headed for a phone. He had a suggestion.

He suggested I contact Pedro Eustache, a young man from the church he pastored in Caracas. Pedro had studied flute in Venezuela and Europe and was now continuing his flute studies in the United States. He spoke three languages: Spanish, French, and English. Sam gave me the phone number in Los Angeles where Pedro and his wife were staying with relatives.

I could hardly believe my good fortune. When I called Pedro, we talked at length on the phone. He seemed to be the answer to my prayers.

He had earned a graduate degree in flute performance in Caracas, Venezuela, where he had also played with the symphony for two years. He had studied with teachers in Paris and Switzerland. Now he was in the United States studying jazz flute. He acknowledged that God had given him a special gift.

Although Pedro sounded like exactly the person I was looking for, I had to be consistent and ask him to send an audition tape. He was very busy and this was not easy to squeeze into his schedule. I told him it did not have to be polished and the quality of the recording was not important.

In January, on my next trip to Los Angeles, he came to meet me, carrying a duffle bag. He explained that his instruments were safer when they could not be recognized. He brought four that day, the ones he recommended taking to Manila: a soprano saxophone, a concert flute, a bass flute, and an Indian flute made of bamboo. He told me about his flute collection, the flutes he has collected from around the world and the ones he hopes to someday add to his collection.

Pedro had definite ideas about the kinds of instrumental music appropriate in the worship context. The only classical composer he approved of in worship was Johann Sebastian Bach, because Bach was a born-again believer. To illustrate the limitations of this conviction, he said he could not bring himself to play Mozart flute solos in worship services because he did not think Mozart was a believer.

He had several Bach pieces he could perform at Lausanne II. He also had some hymn arrangements which followed the theme and variation form, and numerous improvisational possibilities using Negro spirituals. He thought it especially important to share with me his feelings that instrumental music in worship be respectfully appropriate and at all times excellent.

He also shared with me the tragedy which he and his wife had experienced since coming to the United States for his studies. Their baby daughter had become ill with cancer at home in Venezuela. After much prayer, she was healed and they proceeded with plans to leave home for more study. Shortly after their arrival, the cancer revived and she died. I hurt with him as he described their agony and loss.

In March, after getting the audition tape from Pedro, I officially invited him to come to Manila to be part of the small ensemble which would lead the worship.

His jazz skills made a colorful addition to the music of Lausanne II, particularly in the context of urban themes. For his solo spot on the program, during worship, he chose to play a sarabande for unaccompanied flute by Johann Sebastian Bach, when he could have opted for a dramatic and flashy arrangement or improvisation.

I never knew which instrument to expect. He kept all four of them ready, lying on the floor under the grand piano, and let the context and his own feelings dictate the choice.

Of all the musicians who came to Manila, he was most obviously energized by the exotic and unfamiliar instruments. When he had time off, time when he could nap or sightsee, he often reappeared to spend time with musicians from Bali and Thailand to learn from them and play their instruments, and, where possible, arrange to add to his own musical instrument collection.

Pedro was definitely not Western. He was Latin through and through. He was as extroverted as Ren was introverted, as exuberant and flamboyant as Ren was reserved and politely cautious.

The sounds of a flute ornamenting the singing of the congregation and interweaving with the melodies of soloists will always be associated with the music of Lausanne II. In private conversation he told me this was the first time he and his wife had been separated since they lost their little daughter. No one hearing his playing could guess how much he was still grieving. As part of the small ensemble, he exuded joy and praise!

In my thank-you letter to him I wrote:

> You brought many things to Manila—many instruments, many musical experiences, much talent, and personal tragedy. . . . I hope that you were able to take much away, helpful things for in the future.

I started out hoping to find a flutist with a flute. I never expected to find a flutist with a bag full of instruments—many more than I thought we could even use.

I wanted a flute to reinforce the melody, especially on new songs. I got a flutist who played melody and harmony and counterpoint, slipping effortlessly from part to part.

I needed to find a non-Westerner. I got a South American who spoke three languages.

I hoped for someone who would work with me in choosing appropriate music for solos during the Congress. I got someone who already had convictions about suitable music for worship.

I hoped for a flutist who could adapt to the different styles of music in our hymn book. I got one who already played in many different styles, with appropriate instruments to suit each musical style.

I got far more than I ever hoped for.

I cannot take credit for finding Pedro. I simply acted on the recommendation of a friend who heard of my need and made an international phone call at his own expense to tell me about a flutist he knew. Sam Olson's gift gave me a welcome break in the countless hours of work involved in putting together an international team of artists.

Traditional African Drummer

I have always associated drums with Africa. As a child I heard missionaries tell stories of the drums and how central they were to African life. As an adult I read stories about the power of talking drums and how early American slave owners were afraid to have drums around.

As program associate for worship, needing to represent Africa in the small ensemble and wanting to represent it through the instrument so basic to Africa, I began looking for a drummer. My dream was to find a traditional African drummer and use traditional African drums in the worship at Lausanne II in Manila. I assumed it would be no problem to find someone. I was wrong.

Finding an African drummer was like looking for a needle in a haystack. The drummer I was looking for, one who played in the traditional African style and could do this as accompaniment to hymns and songs in Christian worship, turned out to be almost nonexistent.

The search became less general and more focused in January when Roberta King and I met for lunch. She had worked in various African countries as an ethnomusicologist/missionary under the Conservative Baptists. When I told her my hope to find a drummer who would be able to play in the traditional African style to accompany singing at Lausanne II, she told me to find a Ghanaian drummer. In Ghana the people have come a long way toward reclaiming their traditional art forms. She suggested that Dr. Appianda Arthur, a Ghanaian ethnomusicologist and head of Prison Fellowship International in Accra, might be able to suggest a drummer for me.

I sent word to Dr. Arthur. I also shared my need for a drummer with a Ghanaian doctoral student at Northern Baptist Theological Seminary, Emmanuel Amponsah-Kuffuor. He had links to many Ghanaians in North America. Through him I learned about two Ghanaians in Toronto, Canada. One of them had been in Toronto for twenty years, going back and forth to Ghana. The other had spent two years in Jamaica before going to Canada, where he was waiting for his work permit and could not travel. Neither seemed right. The African drummer I was hoping for would be a drummer in Africa, not one who had emigrated to the West.

On February 1, a telex message arrived from Dr. Arthur:

I CAN CERTAINLY FIND A DRUMMER FOR MANILA BUT PLEASE EXPLAIN WHETHER DRUMMER IS TO PERFORM ON TRADITIONAL AFRICAN DRUMS OR REGULAR WESTERN DRUMS. ALSO INDI-CATE WHETHER DRUMMER WILL BE REQUIRED TO BRING ALONG OWN DRUMS.

I sent back word:

SEND AUDITION TAPE OF TRADITIONAL AFRICAN DRUM PLAY-ING. IF SELECTED, MUST BRING OWN INSTRUMENTS.

In February, I went to Manila to get a firsthand look at the venue for Lausanne II and arrange for Filipino participation. Just as I was planning the trip, a brochure arrived announcing "Artists' Experience in Bali," February 12–22, 1989. This little gathering involved artists from around the world. Perhaps if I went to Bali I would find some artists to include in the worship that I was organizing, which had to represent so many different parts of the world.

I had heard that Wilcox World Travel and Tours, the official travel agency for the Congress, might be able to route me to Manila via Bali. I called Susan Holt, the Lausanne II project coordinator at Wilcox, and requested a ticket. After checking with Bill Ditewig, her liaison with the Congress planning staff, she sent me a ticket. My husband, helping me get ready, got out my passport. Happy to have one less detail to take care of, I stuck it in my purse without opening it.

I flew Northwest from Chicago to Minneapolis and then on to Los Angeles. From there I flew Garuda Indonesia to Hawaii. At Honolulu, I got off the plane just briefly while the crew cleaned. At the next stop, Biak, a northern island of Indonesia, I asked to remain on board during the cleaning. I was too tired to move.

As we approached Denpesar, Bali, I got out my passport and began filling out the immigration forms. When I went to write the date of expiration I made an alarming discovery. I had the wrong passport! Ray had given me the temporary one from summer of 1987 when the Nigerian embassy held up our regular passports and we got temporary ones in order to leave the United States on schedule. It had expired in October of 1987. There was nothing to do but pray. I purposed to be as charming and cooperative as possible.

The immigration official read my documents and then, leaning forward and speaking softly, discreetly asked whether I knew my passport had expired. I explained that I had just discovered it moments before as the plane landed. He asked why I had come to Bali. Fortunately, I had the brochure in my purse, not in my suitcase. He read:

ARTISTS' EXPERIENCE IN BALI
A 10 day seminar-cum-worship for committed
Christian artists and craftspeople world wide

As he escorted me to claim my suitcase, he said, "You are a Christian. It'll be okay." He left me at the immigration office to await the arrival of the official who would review my situation and make a decision.

The new official told me to have the director of the conference come to the airport. I called Bruce Nicholls. I had read Bruce's writing with great interest and looked forward to meeting him, but not under these circumstances.

After waiting two hours for Bruce to return home from Sunday morning worship, I reached him by phone. He was most gracious. He came and offered to give up his own passport as security for me. They settled for a letter on Bruce's official stationery guaranteeing that I would get a proper passport and present it to them at the airport.

Leaving the right passport at home is not a simple situation to correct. Indonesian officials wanted the number of the left-at-home passport. That evening, from the hotel in Denpesar, I called Ray in Chicago, waking him up with the request to find my valid passport and call back with the number.

On Monday I took the information to the United States consulate office, a room attached to the private home of the consulate officer, in Bali. She applied for a new passport. The process took all week. On Saturday my new one arrived by boat from a neighboring island, and I picked it up that evening.

I did not go to the airport until time for departure for fear I might be detained or shipped out ahead of schedule. When I left two days later, I simultaneously immigrated and emigrated. That page in my passport contains a full page of Indonesian writing besides the official stamp.

While all this was going on, I participated in the Artists' Experience in Bali, excited to discover two artists from Ghana, a painter and a dancer. On the final day of my stay, all the artists spent many hours on charter buses, traveling a long distance to experience Sunday morning worship in a beautifully designed Balinese church.

On the return trip, I sat with Seth Newman, the dancer from Accra, Ghana. I explained my need for a traditional African drummer and that I had been advised to find a Ghanaian.

Seth taught traditional African dance in the University of Ghana's School for Performing Arts. A pastor in Accra, Enoch Agbozo of the Ghana Evangelical Society and Medina Presbyterian Church of Ghana, a church of about five hundred, had asked Seth to train some of the church's young people in the traditional arts and incorporate those arts into the congregtion's worship. Eleven people were now in Seth's group. A drummer in that group might be a possibility for me. When he returned home from Bali, Seth would give special assistance to that drummer in case I should need him.

I told Seth about my attempt to find a drummer through Dr. Appianda Arthur. He told me Appianda had only been back in the country for one year and was not working in music now. I told him about the drummers in Toronto and my apprehension that Ghanaians who had left the country might no longer be truly African in their style of playing. Seth told me that if they had been professional drummers before leaving they would be all right.

We talked over the various kinds of drums, I needed to know, once I found a drummer, the names of the drums that person should bring to Manila. Seth recommended four drums. and I asked him to sketch them as I had no idea what they looked like. It was not easy to draw pictures while riding that bumpy bus, or even to write. When I left Bali the next morning, I was grateful to be taking with me information about a drummer.

In March, back in Chicago, Emmanuel Amponsah-Kuffuor's contact led me to a Ghanaian music educator in Evanston. Kwasi Aduanu invited me to his home to visit. He told me that my request—African drumming to accompany hymn singing—was most unusual. The new generation of musicians do not know how to do that. They are into popular music.

He mentioned the Spiritual Churches, begun about fifty years ago, which are reviving the use of the drum in worship, but many unfortunate associations have to be overcome. He remembers when children at Ghanaian missionary schools were punished for being interested in the drums. They were not even permitted to touch the drums.

Western missionaries took this harsh stance because of their convictions that Christianity and traditional African drums stood against each other. To them, the drum represented pagan practices, and as missionaries, they were there to rescue people out of paganism.

I asked Kwasi whether he knew Seth Newman. He did! Seth had been a student of his in Accra. He told me I would not go wrong with Seth's recommendation. Kwasi showed me his drums and recommended three. I wrote down their names and descriptions and drew their pictures.

It was now April 1989. Six months earlier I had envisioned the task of adding a drummer to the small ensemble as that of selecting one drummer from among many drummers. With time running out, the task became that of connecting with the only drummer I knew about. At this point I concentrated on trying to reach Seth Newman to see whether the person he was training at the church could come to Manila. Although I had a phone number for Seth at the University, I could not reach him there. Time was too short to rely on letters. There had to be another way.

I had been to Ghana several summers earlier with my husband. We had visited the World Vision office where I met a Philemon Quaye. Perhaps he could help me.

I called Philemon at World Vision in Accra. He remembered me and was willing to help. I asked for assistance in contacting Seth Newman to give him word that I needed the name of the drummer he had recommended in Bali, some idea of his availability for Manila in July, and an audition tape from that drummer. Remembering that Dr. Appianda Arthur might have a recommendation, I also asked Seth for assistance in contacting him.

Early in May, a tape and letter from Seth Newman arrived at my door via DHL, sent by World Vision International in Ghana. The letter read:

> It has not been easy getting things organized here. . . .
> I have still not been able to get in touch with Dr. Appianda Arthur, but I just met a friend this week who told me Dr. Appianda Arthur had complained to him of finding it difficult getting some drummer. . . . I therefore suspect that he is yet to get someone. . . .
> The name of this drummer I have got is STEPHEN AGYAKU.
> He says he will be willing to come to Manila from July 11-20.

The tape included an African song in call-and-response style and "How Great Thou Art," both accompanied by traditional African drums played by the drummer whose name I now had.

A telex arrived on May 22:

> Send formal letter of invitation.
> Steven Sarge Agyauku
> Agric. Development Bank
> Head Office
> Box 4191
> Accra, Ghana
> Best Regards, Seth Newman

Every time a communication arrived about this drummer, his name was spelled differently. But at that point, correctness was the least of my concerns.

The morning of June 2, as I pulled old wallpaper off my kitchen walls in readiness for a crew to begin some remodeling, the phone rang. It was Steven calling from Ghana! He wanted to let me know he had been getting the messages and was very happy to come to Manila!

On June 9, DHL World Wide Express picked up a package for Steven: a letter of invitation, a looseleaf copy of *Aleluya*, program information about Lausanne II, and two of my audio cassettes of Ken Medema. I sent the tapes so Steven would have some acquaintance with Ken before arriving at the Congress. All other members of the small ensemble were able to meet Ken and listen to his music before Lausanne II. However, Steven would not meet Ken until he arrived in Manila. I estimated the value of the package to be $15. DHL charged $124. to pick up and deliver.

On June 22, Philemon Quaye at World Vision in Ghana sent a cable for me to World Vision in California:

> PKG BY DHL FOR STEPHEN RECVD ON MONDAY JUN 19, '89. AND DELIVERED TO HIS OFFICE SAME DAY. UNDERSTOOD STEPHEN WAS ON LEAVE. TRYING MY BEST TO TRACE HIM FOR HIM TO TAKE DELIVERY OF PKG. WILL INFO U WHEN DONE.

One day earlier, Ed Dayton had sent me a message with a copy to Bill Ditewig, the person in charge of travel arrangements:

> Subject: COREAN'S DRUMMER
> THERE'S NO COACH CLASS OUT OF GHANA FOR THE DRUMMER
> SO I AUTHORIZED BUSINESS CLASS. HOPE HE'S GOOD!

I hoped so too!

I asked him to bring the instruments recommended by Kwasi Aduanu: *dondo*, a drum in the shape of an hourglass, held under the arm and played with a curved stick; *apentema*, a tall drum played with the hands; *atumpani*, a pair of talking drums resembling kettle drums; slit bells, made of metal; and rattles. I also requested he bring traditional Ghanaian cloth (national dress) to wear. World Vision staff, many of them also traveling to Lausanne II, assisted Steven onto the plane with his drums and managed to avoid overweight baggage charges.

Together, Steven and Ren and Pedro brought the drums to the plenary hall, carefully making their way through the crowded lobby with a fully loaded hotel cart. The drums were an astonishing sight. Steven had added a fifth: *brekete*.

When the Congress began, the African drums and the colorfully dressed Ghanaian drummer caught everyone by surprise. His five drums—the tall rhythm drum made from a tree trunk, the wooden frame holding two talking drums at an angle toward the audience, and the two lightweight drums—occupied an entire section of the platform next to the grand piano and synthesizer. His presence symbolized an entire continent. The rough wooden drums, so obviously handmade, and the African drummer, so joyful and delighted to be part of an international worship team, constantly reminded participants that non-Western forms of worship bring richness to the whole. Steven played his drums for all the singing, and one day, during the worship, he performed a solo combining drum and dance.

I had not anticipated the photogenic dimension of the drums. Throngs of photographers maneuvered to get pictures. Interest did not wear off. We finally installed barriers to keep cameras at an appropriate distance and assigned stewards to keep sight lines to the platform clear of photographers. The last day, realizing that I had no pictures of the drums, I became one of those photographers.

When I found that Steven was scheduled to return home through Amsterdam, I explored the possibility of getting permission for him to stay there a few weeks. Floyd McClung sent a message to Youth With A Mission in Amsterdam to send a formal letter of invitation to Steven which could be taken to the Netherlands embassy. Getting a tourist visa for a Ghanaian was extremely difficult. The visa was granted.

I looked for people to buy the drums so Steven would have some spending money in Amsterdam. He had a wife and child at home in Ghana and of course wanted to take them gifts. Everything except the talking drums were sold. They had been borrowed and were not for sale. Two drums went to California and one to Wheaton; the rattle went to Wisconsin, and I purchased the bells. Steven wrote me a very long letter in September after returning home to Ghana:

> Dearest Mother Corean,. . . . I joined a Christian rock band to Rotterdam for a concert after which we witnessed to the people. We had a talent show where I joined Sister Rita . . . (the Ghanaian from Canada), sang worship songs in "Twi" our local language and danced in our costumes. . . . It has been from dream to dream. I went to the ARK . . . and even to the LOGOS boat for lectures. . . . I want to attend a Bible School in America where I can be nearer to you for guidance in the music . . . so please arrange that.

I wrote to Steven to encourage him to stay in Ghana:

> You are in a good place. The kind of musical skills you are developing could not happen anywhere else in the world.

I wrote to Seth to thank him for providing a traditional African drummer for Lausanne II:

> It had been so difficult to find a drummer that at times I almost gave up trying. . . . Communication was so difficult into Ghana. Everything about it was difficult. . . . I realized that at so many points, the whole sequence of events which led up to Steven being on that platform at Lausanne II could have fallen apart. The odds against him being there were tremen-

dous. We can only say that it was God's plan.

My final letter of appreciation for the traditional African drummer went to Susan Holt at Wilcox World Travel and Tours:

Just a couple of days ago, a friend sent me a tape prepared for the Chapel of the Air. That particular fifteen minute broadcast began: "When my wife returned from the Lausanne Congress in Manila, she brought a drum." That drum was one of Steven Agyaku's drums, the drummer from Ghana. The entire broadcast was constructed around the experience of being led in worship by a man and his drums from Ghana and how that turned up-side-down my friend's youthful understanding of missions, an understanding which rose out of her home church where the missionaries they supported were always white.

I remembered all over again the whole sequence of events which led to that drummer coming to Manila and realized I had overlooked an important link in that story—your part.

Steven was there because I got to go to Bali on that ticket which you came up with at a quarter of the normal cost. . . . Thank you, Susan, for your part in assisting the Lausanne Congress in finding a drummer from Africa.

Nicaraguan Vocalist

The small ensemble, as I first envisioned it, included Ken as vocalist and instrumentalist, plus drummer, flutist, and guitarist. In October, the ad hoc committee requested the addition of a female vocalist. Their request set in motion a most dramatic and suspenseful series of events.

Never suspecting how difficult the job would be, I began by gathering a few tapes of female vocalist possibilities, non-American vocalists per the committee's requirements. Ken listened. He wanted a different kind of sound.

January 23, 1991: I said to Ken, "If you could pick anyone you wanted, who would it be?" He replied, "Deyanira Toruño." She was Nicaraguan, a choice the ad hoc committee would approve. He had met her while doing a concert in Nicaragua. He liked her natural, folk-style voice and manner of singing, free of affectations and sophistication.

How could we find her?

It so happened that on the previous evening, at Northern Baptist

74

Theological Seminary, the seventh annual mission conference had begun: "Mission in the Context of Oppression and Violence." Dr. Gustavo Parajon, a pastor from Nicaragua, came as one of the speakers.

Ken knew Dr. Parajon. I called the seminary from Ken's room at the O'Hare Hilton where he and I and Beverly Vander Molen were working, and presently Ken was talking with Dr. Parajon. It also just happened that Dr. Parajon had been Deyanira's pastor before she left Nicaragua City. He gave us his son's phone number in Ohio. David Parajon would know how to contact Deyanira.

Since Beverly and Ken knew her, I suggested they be the ones to contact her and find out if she was available. February and March passed. Beverly was unable to make even an initial phone contact with David Parajon. I decided to try. I had more time flexibility and could make that task a priority.

David Parajon directed me to Mike Thompson, Deyanira's brother-in-law. From him I learned that she was in the United States with a temporary visa and had requested political asylum. Her appeal was in process. Although she wanted to go to Lausanne II, if she left the country she could not reenter. Only if her case was processed and resolved favorably could she obtain the necessary documents to return to the U.S. after the Congress.

April 11: I wrote:

> You cannot imagine how excited I was to hear that you are available and willing to come. . . . We began our search for a female vocalist during the fall, and our search for you in particular in January. It was a long search.

In that same envelope, I sent an official letter for the U.S. Department of Immigration explaining about the Congress and her invitation to sing. In addition:

> I would be available to give whatever assistance might still be required in order for Ms. Toruño to secure the necessary documents for her reentry into the United States. She will conclude her contract with us in Manila on the evening of July 20, 1989, and would need to reenter the United States shortly thereafter.

I did not understand all the complexities of her situation. Her English-language skills were not adequate to explain the technicalities. This much I did understand: the State Department lawyer thought her case might come up for review between June 15 and July 9. But that was not certain.

I proceeded as though she would be coming. What else was I to do? We had no other person in mind to fill her spot.

June 7: I wrote to Deyanira:

> As I write this I again pray that God will provide a way for you to get to Manila, that your court case will be resolved before time to leave.
>
> The hymnal is finally finished and I am enclosing a xeroxed copy for you. . . . I have scheduled you for a solo on day 2, July 12, at the 8:30 worship and Bible study. . . . You have a three-minute time slot for your solo. I don't want to confine you to the hymnal, but yet at the same time let me give my reasons for wishing you could use it. There are two Spanish songs which people will enjoy very much and you might introduce them that morning as solos. . . . Could you phone or write me your solo selections by the end of next week (June 17)?. . .
>
> Again, many of us are praying about your court case.

When I discovered that she did not read music, I made her a tape. I went through the entire hymnal, first giving the song number and title, then playing the melody on the piano. She told me a musician friend from Nicaragua would work with her on the music.

I worried. What would we do if she could not come? Beverly was sure we could find someone at the Congress who could become part of the small ensemble.

No one connected with Deyanira seemed able to make anything happen. Her lawyer, the key person, was in Louisiana and difficult to reach. The latest word from the lawyer was that the immigration office had said it would study her political asylum case in August. She had applied in May of 1988. I could not understand why this was taking so long. The answer—because political asylum needs time and research.

The frustration over nothing happening finally got to me. Maybe something could be done from Chicago. I would not know until I tried.

June 26: On Monday evening I began. It was not a likely choice of a time to get anything going, but I felt compelled to get started. I called Chris Gutierrez, whose husband, Juan, is Puerto Rican. Juan said to get in touch with Travelers Aid.

I went to the attic where my husband was painting a ceiling and wishing I would not start a new project at this time of day. I asked whether heknew anyone connected with Travelers Aid. He knew a Craig Darling who was connected somehow with immigrant travel aid.

I called Craig, who told me to call two persons: Elana Segura-

VanTreeck, connected with the Episcopal diocese, and Phyllis Goldman, a lawyer. Both women were away for the evening at meetings, but their husbands expected them back by 9:30 or so. Neither husband seemed annoyed that I was calling for assistance at that time of evening. Neither did the women. They both returned my calls that evening, did not hesitate to talk with me, and counseled me so I would know where to go next.

I soon had something specific to do: get the name of the lawyer in the town where she had applied for political asylum. Which town in Louisiana might that be? Phyllis Goldman suggested it probably was New Orleans. I needed to talk with people in New Orleans, and she gave me a list: someone in Catholic Charities, someone in the archdiocese of New Orleans since they actively assisted Central American immigrants, a good attorney, and someone in immigration.

I went back up to the attic, to where my husband had about finished the ceiling, with another question:

"Who do you know in New Orleans?"

"Bill Brown. He directs Trinity Christian Fellowship and knows everybody."

"Can I call him now?" It was going on 11 P.M.

"Yes. It's never too late to call Bill Brown."

Bill was just getting into bed, but he answered the phone. As I told him the list of persons who needed to be contacted so as to jar the State Department, he supplied the names. Catholic Charities? Sister Anthony, head of Catholic Charities. He knew her well. The archdiocese office? He knew the archbishop. An attorney? John Volz, very influential and experienced in immigration cases. Someone in immigration? John Caplinger, district supervisor of immigration. He also thought Tom Finney, editor of the *Clarion Herald*, a New Orleans newspaper, might be helpful.

Before going to sleep that night, Bill thought through the various options for the next morning, looking for shortcuts. There was no time to go through Catholic Charities. Nor was there time to go to John Caplinger, district supervisor of immigration. It might take several days just to get an appointment. He would have to work from the top down. He later told me of thinking, I don't know whether we can pull this off or not; the time is so short.

June 27: Bill had a doctor's appointment at 9:00 in the morning at the Ochsner Clinic. The doctor always kept him waiting. He made calls as he waited. The staff at his own office, Trinity Christian Community Church, met for prayer at 9:30. He called and asked them to pray. I called Beverly and Deyanira and asked them to pray. In Chicago, I prayed.

Bill started at the top by calling the U.S. attorney of Louisiana's office. Florence Onstad managed that office. For several years she had been part of a weekly Bible study group Bill taught. They knew each other well. He called from the clinic, "Florence, we've got a real problem."

With that as an opener, he described the whole situation: If she leaves the country, she will lose status on applying for political asylum. It's now been pending for a year and a half. This is a straight number. The girl is a key player in an international music group. She will come right back.

John Volz was away in Washington D.C., but Florence said he called his office every day. She would tell him about this case. She reassured Bill, "John Volz knows you and who you are."

That afternoon Bill returned to his office. As he sat at his desk, wondering what to do next on Deyanira's case, the phone rang. John Caplinger, district supervisor of immigration, was on the line. He called directly, without secretarial assistance. "I understand you have a real problem. I got a call from John Volz. He told me I should help you. So whatever you need, let me know."

Bill went right over to the immigration office. John Caplinger assigned an agent, Miss Dugas, to work with Bill and arrange, as quickly as possible, temporary exit and reentry documents for Deyanira.

Bill had been "running around the courts" for years. He already had a lot of experience with attorneys and judges and knew how they think. Attorneys liked to extend cases and get larger fees. They like to "sit on things." The call that morning from John Caplinger surprised him. For some unexplainable reason, John Volz was not sitting on this one. Nor was John Caplinger.

That afternoon, less than twenty-four hours after beginning with Travelers Aid in Chicago, Bill called me, and in a very laid-back, nonchalant southern drawl he said, "Well, they're going to let her go."

Had I heard right? After six months of waiting and nothing happening, his words put me off balance. I needed a moment to recover. I wanted to hear the news again.

But Bill went right on to the next order of business. He had a job for me. I was to contact Deyanira and tell her to send three pictures to his office: regulation-sized passport pictures in color. She was to send them by express mail, not registered mail.

June 28: Bill contacted Deyanira's own personal attorney. Bill went to see the attorney to acquaint her with what was going on. The attorney objected: "I don't know about this. I think it might prejudice her case."

Bill countered, "How in the world would this prejudice her case? It would strengthen her case, not weaken it."

June 29: Before leaving that day for South Carolina, where he was scheduled to perform a wedding on Saturday, Bill called Deyanira in Ohio to explain the urgency of getting the photos taken care of immediately: "You cannot sit on this now. Immigration needs it right away." From South Carolina he kept in touch with his staff to make sure the photos arrived.

July 1: Saturday evening, Bill returned to New Orleans and went to his office to make sure the photos were there.

July 3: Monday morning, Bill took the photos to the immigration office.

July 4: Holiday. I called Bill from Washington state to inquire about how things were going. Again speaking in his laid-back, nonchalant southern drawl, he said, "You asked for a miracle. You got it."

July 5: When Bill arrived at Immigration, everything was ready to go. He then took the packet of travel documents to an overnight delivery service. As his final part in this drama, he called Deyanira to say her documents were on the way. She could expect them the next morning.

July 6: Travel documents arrived in Ohio from New Orleans.

In the meantime, the matter of getting a plane ticket to Manila needed urgent attention. I called Bill Haire at Wilcox World Travel and Tours first thing on Wednesday morning, June 28, and asked if he could arrange something for her at this late date. He kept me on the line while he checked. I was to fax him the necessary information for making out her ticket, such as birth date, passport number, place issued (Managua), and full name the way it appeared on her passport (Deyanira del Rosario Toruño Revera de Gonzalez).

Wilcox scheduled her to leave JFK Airport in New York on Northwest flight 17 at 11:20 A.M., July 8. I worried about her connecting flights: Toledo to Dayton and Dayton to JFK. Ray did not trust our own connections. If we arrived in Seattle late and missed our overseas flight, there would be no other space for us. The planes to Manila were filled to capacity. We flew to Seattle several days early and spent time with relatives.

I asked Wilcox to get Deyanira to New York a day early to be sure nothing happened to delay her at this point. René Gorbold, at Lausanne Urban Associates in Chicago, arranged hotel space for her at the Mid-Way Hotel, a Best Western, four miles from JFK. The reservation was made with a Lausanne Urban Associates credit card. But the hotel would not accept payment without a card in hand. They called René who creatively solved that problem by faxing details of the credit card account to the hotel and allayed their fears of not getting paid.

July 8: Deyanira boarded Northwest #17 for Manila, due July 9.

July 9: She did not arrive.

July 10: She did not arrive.

Where was she? Had something happened? From Manila I called her brother-in-law, Mike Thompson. Had she left as planned? So far as they knew, she had. She had called them just as she was about to board to say everything was "A-OK."

The news alarmed the Thompsons, who began checking on their end. Her sister, Sandra Thompson, immediately began to fear the worst, putting together her fears of New York City and Deyanira's vulnerability. Sandra considered Deyanira too friendly for her own safety. She talked to everyone. Maybe she had been raped or murdered and was now in some garbage can!

Northwest Airlines would not give out any information, would not confirm whether or not she got on flight 17 at JFK Airport. The only way they would release any information would be to the police in the case of a missing person. The Thompsons called the police in Maumee, Ohio, to report that Deyanira was missing. The Maumee Police Department contacted the New York City Police Department who then contacted Northwest Airlines who then confirmed that Deyanira had left on flight 17.

July 11: Very late on day one of the Congress, about midnight, Beverly Vander Molen called my room to say that Deyanira had arrived. I got into my bathrobe and went to welcome her, to meet her for the first time, and to discuss her solo, scheduled for the next morning during worship and Bible study at 8:30. There was no time to hear the full story of why she had been detained. She needed to get to bed and so did we. Ken suggested postponing her solo, but she would not hear of it. She wanted to sing as scheduled.

July 12: She sang her solo as scheduled: "Cantad al Senor," from the Congress hymnal. Only Ken and Deyanira had rehearsed early that morning, but when she began singing, Pedro, Ren, and Steven joined in. She sang the three verses through slowly and expressively, with subtle melodic inflections. All the non-Spanish-speaking participants heard the words clearly.

Then Ken, with Pedro taking a strong lead on his bass flute, quickened the tempo as she sang all the verses through a second time. After an improvised interlude by the small ensemble, she sang all three verses a third time. That simple song, sung each time in Spanish, was exquisite.

Time, the most critical element in her story, stood still for me that morning as I drank in the scene on stage. I wished Bill Brown could have been sitting next to me. Only he and I knew the incredible story of the last few days.

But why had she arrived late?

In the press of time at the Congress, I never got the full story. Months later, as we discussed the matter by phone, I tried to fill in the missing pieces. The flight she had boarded in New York did not leave as scheduled due to engine problems. All the passengers, including Deyinera, were put up overnight at the Hyatt hotel.

Why did she not let anyone know?

It seems there were two reasons: exhaustion and possible misunderstanding. She said they were not allowed to make calls from the hotel. Perhaps she did not understand how she might have called her sister collect.

When the flight made a layover in Seattle, it apparently was grounded with engine trouble again, causing another four- to five-hour delay.

Hoping to get full details of the story directly from Northwest Airlines, I contacted customer relations in Saint Paul, Minnesota. I asked for the actual flight schedule from JFK to Manila for flight 17 and whatever other flights might have been involved. Melissa Howland responded with a fax:

| Flight # 17 | JFK to NRT | 11:20a | 2:05p |
| Flight # 3 | NRT to MNL | 7:00p | 10:20p |

JFK = New York
NRT = Tokyo, Japan
MNL = Manila, Philippines

Her response included no dates and no indication of anything amiss. I sent a to Melissa Howland at Northwest Airlines:

I need something a bit more detailed. The passenger who flew NW to Manila did not arrive until two days late. The details of her story for the two weeks prior to getting on #17 were dramatic beyond belief.

My letter went unanswered.

In view of all the successful, even miraculous, phone calls beginning on the evening of June 26, I could afford to lose this last attempt to get information. As Bill said, "We scored on every phone call."

Egyptian Singer

My interest in the Arab world began some twenty-five years ago when I met Gina and Daryl Erickson. Daryl, just finished with medical school, was an intern at Swedish Covenant Hospital in Chicago, preparing himself to serve in the Arab world as medical doctor and surgeon.

In 1982, at the completion of my first trip to Asia, I returned home through Amman, Jordan, in order to spend time with them. They were studying Arabic at the special school run by Martha and George Kelsey. When Gina and Daryl completed their language study, they moved to the Oasis Hospital near Abu Dhabi in the United Arab Emirates. In 1984, my husband and I visited them at that hospital.

I was already committed to including the Middle East on the worship team at Lausanne II. The general neglect of the Arab world by Christians and my strong relational ties with the Ericksons motivated me to find an Arab musician for Lausanne II.

The search began one evening in October with a call to my friends the

Ericksons, who no longer lived in the Middle East but in New Hampshire. When I explained my need for an Arab musician, Daryl suggested I call Yousef Hashweh, a Jordanian currently studying at Nyack College in New York State. Daryl knew of numerous music groups, but if I was interested in a single musician, one who played an 'aoud, I should ask Yousef about Nagieb Labeb.

I had never met Yousef. Daryl immediately called Yousef to tell him about me. I was told to wait fifteen minutes. If Daryl did not call back, I should assume that he had successfully communicated with Yousef. At the appropriate moment, I dialed Nyack, New York, and began a conversation with a person I had never met before, the first of three such calls I would make that evening.

Yousef told me about three different possibilities. He told me about the Hashweh quartet. It included him and three other members of his family. They sang many styles of music and played guitar, accordion, and piano. Next he told me about a professional group in Egypt that performed most-ly Western music. Last of all he told me about Nagieb Labeb, a folk-style singer who knew all kinds of Arab music. He played an 'aoud, a guitar-like instrument long associated with Arab music. As a traveling musician and evangelist, he sang all over the Middle East.

Nagieb sounded like the person I had hoped to find; however, I need-ed to get a tape recording before making any decision. Yousef had several tapes of Nagieb. In fact, he had tapes of each group. I asked whether he could send me copies. Yousef sent me his own personal tapes.

But one thought troubled me. If Nagieb traveled so much, he might already be scheduled for July. I could not risk waiting for the tapes. I should call immediately and find out whether he was available.

Yousef had no phone number for Nagieb, but he did for the president of the Baptist church in Jordan, a man who could tell me where to find Nagieb. Yousef cautioned me to wait until ll:00 P.M. before calling, until folk in Jordan finished their night's sleep.

I busied myself until the appointed hour, then called Amman, Jordan. Rev. Omaish answered the phone and gave me the number where Nagieb could be reached but told me to wait another hour. It was still very early there in Jordan.

After another hour, I called and found it was still early for Nagieb. My call woke him up. I tried to explain who I was and why I was calling. He was very gracious and told me he had those dates free. We would keep in touch. I went to bed, delighted with the evening's accomplishments.

The tapes arrived. I listened to the Egyptian group. They sounded like an American group except that they sang in Arabic. The Hashweh quartet was more versatile, singing both Western songs and Middle Eastern songs. As for Nagieb? I wrote my response to Daryl and Gina:

> I received tapes from Yousef and was thoroughly charmed by Nagieb Labeb. He is precisely the kind of musician we are looking for at this conference, someone who uses traditional music to do evangelism. He is available to come to Manila and it sounded as though he has not been invited before to participate in this kind of an international event.

Later Daryl told me more about Nagieb, calling him the Amy Grant of the Arabic world. He told me that Nagieb is Egyptian and his music is distinctly Arab, much of it his own. He is appreciated by all who hear him. It sounded as though Nagieb was the right person to represent the Middle East in the worship at Lausanne II.

In November I wrote to Nagieb asking whether he was still free to accept an invitation to participate in Lausanne II. I also asked for detailed information about his songs:

> I need to know your repertoire in order to schedule you into the program. I need titles in English with a brief description of what the song is about, plus approximate time it takes to sing that song. . . . Would you also have a hymn or two to give us for the conference hymnbook, Arabic songs which could be translated into English? We are putting together a special hymnal for the conference. We will print both words and music so I need a musical copy of any song you would send.
>
> One section of this hymnal will be indigenous hymnody. Each of these will have two languages given along with the music, the original language plus a translation into English.

In December, Nagieb called to accept the invitation and to tell me his songs, as requested, were being prepared. Later that same month, thirteen songs arrived from Martha Kelsey at the language school in Amman:

> A few of us have tried to help our good brother, Nagieb Labeb, to get off the music requested for the Manila conference. He spent hours working on it before he left for a campaign in Iraq, where a most responsive crowd is attending meetings for the first time since the war.
>
> First are the four songs he chose to have translated to English according to meter and tune. . . . Nine others are summarized in English or have

the corresponding Scriptures copied from the NIV.... Tomorrow we have a traveller leaving, which is faster and safer, so we will send on that which is complete.... If there is something you would like done differently, let us know that too.

Each song came in a standardized format:

English Title
Subject
Writer and Composer
Time required to perform
English meaning, typed
Music, either xeroxed or handwritten
Arabic script

Half of the songs were notated as handwritten melodies. I suspect they were written out for me by Martha Kelsey. I thanked her in a letter:

Dear Mrs. Kelsey, . . . I cannot suggest how you might have improved on what you did. This must have taken you a great deal of time. It is clear and complete and carefully done. Thank you very much. I hope that there is some benefit for you as well in doing it.

When the hymnal selection committee met, it chose one of the hand-notated Arabic songs for the hymnal, the one titled "Bless the Lord." The English meaning read:

Praise the Lord, O my soul;
  all my inmost being, praise his holy name.
Praise the Lord, O my soul,
  and forget not all his benefits.
He forgives all my sins
  and heals all my diseases.

Psalm 103:1-3

The next step was to prepare an English version which could be sung. Presumably the song had never been sung in English, always in Arabic. Since time was slipping away and it was now already April, I called Amman with my latest request. The translation arrived accompanied by a letter from Martha:

Several of us got our heads together to get Psalm 103:1–3 from Arabic into singable English, and we felt that our friend Bob Robertson came up with the best, which I enclose.

I gave the translation to Tony Payne. Some of the accents in Bob Robertson's English translation failed to match the musical meter. Tony made some revisions and gave it back to me for approval. I went to work on the lines:

> *He heals your sicknesses,*
>   *your sicknesses,*

While these words suited the meter and included all the necessary syllables required for the melody, I wanted to avoid repeating *sicknesses*. A phone conversation with poet friend Sharon James-Ledbetter helped. She suggested:

> *He heals your sicknesses,*
>   *gives you new health,*

A curious dilemma emerged around the use of the words *praise* and *bless*. Which was more suitable, or did it make any difference? The song arrived with *bless* in the title and *praise* in the English meaning, taken from the New International Version of the Bible. Tony removed *bless* from Bob Robertson's translation and put in *praise*. Ought not a Scripture song use the words of Scripture?

But maybe those who knew Arabic knew something Tony and I did not know about those words. To be on the safe side, I removed all the *praises* and put *bless* back, hoping for a chance at a less hectic time to examine these two words and find out whether I had made the right decision.

I asked Martha how I should go about getting permission to use the Arabic song in the hymnal. She wrote back:

> Nagieb himself passed through Amman and I asked him about the permission from Boulos Bushra. He said, "I heard about this permission business in Europe but we don't have that concept here. At any rate tell Mrs. Bakke to print it on my responsibility."

Nagieb came to the United States in June on his way to Manila. I sent him a loose-leaf copy of the hymnal. I also sent his assignments for the Congress. The program planning committee had scheduled him to sing four times: to introduce the Arab song in the hymnal and help teach it, to sing a solo in the plenary session titled "The Church in Challenging

Settings," to sing a solo in a morning worship time, and to sing in the closing celebration.

He asked whether I expected him to sing in English. If so, he would have to relearn his songs. I told him we wanted him to sing in Arabic, that we would work with him on appropriate ways to introduce his songs so non-Arab people would know what he was singing about. He learned our English translation for "Bless the Lord" and sang that one song in both languages.

His 'aoud, which resembled a pregnant guitar, could not adjust to the wetness and humidity of July in Manila. On the final day of the Congress it came apart. I sent a steward out to buy glue in a desperate attempt to put it back together, but our efforts failed. Nagieb sang that last evening at Lausanne II accompanied by the small ensemble, while his now pathetic 'aoud sat in pieces backstage.

I wrote him following the Congress:

> I hope that your 'aoud is safely repaired and playable again. The climate there in Manila was about as opposite to Jordan as one can get. No wonder it had problems.

Nagieb was a delight to work with:

> I so appreciated your graciousness when the scheduling became chaotic and you had to wait, and then get canceled as happened that one day. You were wonderful to work with and I hope we can work together again some day in some place.

Nagieb played a strategic role in the worship team at the Congress, giving all of us a greater appreciation for the sounds of the Arabic language and its indigenous music. He demonstrated the generosity and sensitivity of the Arabic peoples and their willingness and availability to help.

The first page of *Aleluya* shows the theme of Lausanne II, "Proclaim Christ until He Comes," written in all the official languages of the Congress, including Arabic. To have integrity as the music of Lausanne II, Aleluya had to have an Arab song. It would have been much easier to do as most other international hymnals do and omit anything Arabic. Not one hymnal in my collection included an Arab song. Fortunately, we did not have that option. Aleluya has one because Nagieb and Martha Kelsey spent many hours in Amman preparing songs.

In the month following Lausanne II, a worship publication arrived at my door with an article on Psalm 5 titled "The Grind of Discouragement."

The author, Chuck Swindoll, connected discouragement with minor keys and wrote, So many folks I meet are playing out their entire lives in a minor key.

Because of my experience with Nagieb and his songs, and because of similar comments from other Christian friends, I felt strongly motivated to respond. I wrote a letter to the editor:

> Mr. Swindoll brings two assumptions to this article: (1) that music is a universal language; and (2) that Western music is the best expression of it.
>
> Lausanne II in Manila, a large international gathering of Christians, brought musicians from around the world to lead the worship. The American missionary to Thailand who came with Thai musicians and dancers told how that music was like noise to him when he arrived in Thailand. He would not support any notion of music being a universal language with innate capability to say the same things to all peoples everywhere.
>
> I have heard many people, particularly Christians, equate major and minor keys with joy and sadness, but that is a cultural association. Much of the world's music sounds more minor than major, including the music of the Middle East. Twenty songs were submitted by an Egyptian singer for possible use at Lausanne II. Seventeen of them sounded minor and included such topics as the attributes of Christ, joy and confidence, victorious living, the Lord's Prayer, praise for salvation, and praise songs from the Psalter. The Arab song from Psalm 103, "Bless the Lord," became a Congress favorite.

"Bless the Lord" was one of those seventeen songs which sounded minor but it was not an expression of discouragement.

Apart from my friends the Ericksons and their connections with Arab Christians, how would I have found Nagieb Labeb? Looking back, I realize that the Arab singer and the Arab song were a direct result of that friendship begun over twenty-five years ago in Chicago.

The chance to look once again at the words *bless* and *praise* came four years later when an Arab musician and church historian arrived at my home. Habib Badr approved my choice of *bless*, surprised that there was even a question. In Arabic, as in Hebrew, the word used in Psalm 103 is *bless*, not *praise*.

Filipino Choir

The Congress began on July 11, 1989, at 7:00 P.M. with a three-hour opening ceremony. It symbolized the culmination of months and years of hope and hard work for hundreds of people. In anticipation of the grand occasion, the program planning committee asked me to find a large choir.

I consulted with Priscilla Pascual, student at Northern Baptist Theological Seminary, who loaned me cassette tapes of groups she knew in Manila. After listening to them all, I chose His Sounds, the a cappella choir founded and directed by Romulo Pizaña. The choir members, between thirty and fifty young Filipino men and women, were from many different churches in the Metro-Manila area. They primarily sang Western choral literature but also indigenous Filipino hymns.

When I arrived in Manila in February, Cristy Ticlaw, associate director of communications, arranged for me to meet Romulo. She escorted me from the Lausanne II office at the Philippine International Convention

Center (PICC) to our meeting place in Quezon City. It was a long, slow ride through dense traffic.

I told Romulo how much I admired His Sounds from listening to Priscilla's tapes. I told him about the Congress coming up and asked whether he would consider bringing his choir to participate. After sharing with him some of my ideas regarding music for the Congress, we set up another appointment.

Cristy suggested Gene's Bistro for our next meeting, a restaurant located conveniently for both Romulo and me. I walked there from Carol Herrman's place, where I was staying in Quezon City, and felt like an executive taking a business associate out to dinner.

I told him as completely as I could what I hoped he could do at the Congress: (1) bring a large choir to open the Congress and take a significant role that evening; (2) lead singing on opening night as a stand-up-in-front traditional song leader, something Ken could not do; (3) arrange for a brass group to play a grand processional and postlude for opening night; (4) bring his choir back again for a pre-evening-session half-hour concert; (5) bring the choir to be part of the closing-night ceremonies; (6) look into the possibility of an ethnic Filipino instrumental group.

We discussed the costs he would incur, such as fees for arranging the music needed for opening night, payment for assistant conductors to help rehearse the two hundred singers he hoped to recruit from churches in Manila, food needed for those singers during the rehearsal snack time, copying music needed for a megachoir, personal expenses, and honorarium. We agreed on prices and tasks and the next day I returned home.

Joining a choir in Manila is a major commitment. Romulo's choir members generally leave for work at six in the morning. Many of them work in banks in Makati, the financial district for Metro-Manila. They travel by two different buses and arrive at their jobs just before eight o'clock. At five o'clock, they leave and begin the long ride back home.

On days when the choir rehearses, members try to get a quick bite of supper along the way at a McDonald's or Jollibee because it takes just as long to get to rehearsal as it does to go home from work. Rehearsal lasts from 7:30 to 9:00, concluding with snacks which Romulo provides: soda and biscuits, better understood by Americans as pop and cookies. Travel time back to their homes and their waiting suppers takes another hour and a half to two hours.

After staying for one week in Manila, I saw how traffic shapes people's lives. Preparing a large choir gathered from the Metro-Manila area would be far different from doing that same job in Chicago. After Romulo described a day in the lives of his choir members, I understood why he included food as a budget item. I also understood why we had eighty-five singers at the opening ceremony of the Congress instead of the two hundred Romulo had originally hoped for. I vowed, while in Manila, never again to complain about traffic in Chicago.

Romulo needed to know what music to prepare for the opening night of the Congress. He understood that the choir would function in two ways: by performing and by leading the participants in singing from the new hymnal for the first time. At no point was Romulo free to move ahead and make selections independently.

The committee wanted the choir to perform three times on opening night. I asked Romulo to have the choir sing the Tagalog song from the hymnal as one of those three. That left Romulo with two more program slots to fill. Knowing my bias toward indigenous music, he chose a setting of Psalm 147, "Purihin Si Yahweh" written by a Filipino composer. His second choice was "Gloria," from an Asian musical setting of the Mass done in the original Latin. I took those choices to the committee, holding my breath over the Latin piece. Both were accepted without any questions.

Next, the congregational songs which the choir would lead had to be chosen so the choir could learn them as well. Again, there would be three songs. The ad hoc committee worked through the choices, beginning with the final hymn which would follow the opening-night speaker, Billy Graham. "Blessed Assurance," long associated with the Billy Graham Association, seemed the most appropriate choice to conclude the evening. Ed Dayton wanted to introduce one of the new songs in the hymnal on opening night. Here again, the speaker guided the choice of song. "Dieu A Tant Aimé le Monde," a French song based on John 3:16, written for the 1986 Graham Crusade in Paris, became the choice for the congregational song located midway through the opening-night program.

The last of the three congregational hymns was the most difficult to select. It would function also as processional. The many people involved in shaping the opening ceremony complicated the choice. Dale Kauffman, involved with special programming of youth on opening night, suggested "Crown Him with Many Crowns." We accepted that choice and I put it into the hymnal.

The second part of Dale's suggestion was more problematic. He knew of a taped orchestral accompaniment, which, if used as the first thing on the program, would be very impressive. Ed Dayton hesitated over having the Congress begin with a professional, prerecorded sound. It might make everything which followed anticlimatic by comparison. I jumped in on his uncertainty and offered to get an arrangement specially written for brass, choir, and congregation. I knew Tony Payne would be interested in writing it. The committee approved my idea.

Tony began immediately. With each verse, he changed languages. The choir learned Spanish for verse one, German for verse two, and French for verse three, all sung as they processed into the hall and onto the stage. The final verse, in English, was for congregation and choir together. The accompaniment was written for brass choir, beginning with a fanfare introduction. On June 14, Romulo asked whether the arrangement could arrive the next week. Tony got it off by fax on schedule.

With the choices made, some of them later than Romulo would have liked, I considered my decision-making duties for opening night finished. That suddenly changed when a fax arrived from Cristy Ticlaw on June 30:

> Romy called up today and asked me to fax the following to you. . . . He wants you to know that he is getting at least five dancers to interpret the song "Gloria" during the opening night. The dancers will come from the Cultural Center's BALLET PHILIPPINES and the professional fee will be very high. But they were able to negotiate the price and obtained discount. . . . Please let him know if he should go ahead with this.

This time I hesitated, very uncertain how to respond. While I enjoy dance immensely, many Christians do not. I was not afraid to schedule folk dance from Thailand on the opening ceremony, but classical ballet was an altogether different matter. Did we want both on the same program? Gatherings such as the Lausanne Committee for World Evangelization normally do not have dance at all. I sat on the decision because I had many questions. In a few days I would be in Manila and could discuss it in person.

On July 6, the night I arrived in Manila, I called Romulo to see how things were going. The brass ensemble was not what he had hoped. They were not professional players but students at the University. They were having trouble with the high notes. However, he thought that with a couple more rehearsals they would be fine.

Then he brought up the subject I still was unsure about. I had no answer ready, but I did have many questions.

"Do you like my idea about using dancers with the choir?"

"How would they be dressed?" I had gotten into big trouble once by putting a dancer wearing flesh-colored leotards into a worship service.

"In white dresses. No shoes."

"How would we pay them?" I had already strained the budget.

"If the money is a problem, I will pay it myself."

"How can we possibly fit choir and dancers both on the stage?"

"The choir will stand at the very back, on the narrow upper stage. They will be crowded but it will work. The main stage is big enough for the dancers."

"Where would this fit in the evening program?"

"The choir and dancers should come just before the evening speaker."

I was nervous. He was asking for the choicest spot! How would the speaker feel coming in on the heels of a dance performance by the Philippine ballet?

The opening ceremony had gone through many changes, including a change of speaker. Billy Graham had extended his crusade in London, leaving no time to come to Manila before getting to his next commitment in Budapest. Leighton Ford was now scheduled as the opening-night speaker. I went to Leighton and asked how he felt about following dancers. He had no problem with that. Ed Dayton had no strong feelings either way. I gave Romulo the go-ahead.

The ethnic Filipino instrumental group, the sixth item on the list when Romulo and I met in February, had been dropped. It was one thing too many to add to the schedule. Romulo's addition of another group, the Philippine ballet, which required no additional program time, was the far better suggestion.

But decisions for opening night were still not over. At dress rehearsal the night before, the brass players arrived late, possibly aggravating their musical struggles. Romulo was too busy with his choir to discuss the situation. It did not look good.

The program committee decided to cancel the brass choir and replace it with Ken Medema. Fortunately, I had a copy of Tony Payne's processional with me. I had made a special point of getting it before leaving home. Beverly Vander Molen took the score and played it for Ken, teaching him the music.

I called Romulo the next day to say we wanted to cancel the brass ensemble. He said there was no way to reach them before they arrived at the PICC for the final rehearsal and performance, but he would meet them upon arrival and tell them of the change in plans. However, he still wanted to pay them. As a professor at their university, he needed to settle this matter without destroying relationships.

Ken, with his synthesizer, took on an additional role that evening, that of brass ensemble and choir accompanist. He did it with all the fanfare required for the grand occasion.

The dancers, accompanied by the choir, were the high point of the evening for many people. Cameras captured their exquisite movements from many angles. When the special Congress edition of *World Evangelization* arrived, the ballet dancers were on the front cover in color and on the index page in black and white. Among many other pictures of the Congress, the editors included a large, two-page photo of the hall with the dancers on stage. I was so glad Romulo had refused to be talked out of having them.

On day two of the Congress, Bryant Myers stopped by my PICC office to talk. The dancers had capped the previous evening for him. He was still ecstatic. Seizing the opportune moment, my husband explained to him about the fee. Bryant took out his checkbook and paid the bill right then and there.

Later in the week, when the choir sang their concert, Romulo again demonstrated his skill in programming. The final song, "Light of a Million Mornings," with soprano soloist, required an encore—which, of course, he had all ready.

The choir won everyone's affection. They gave us music as long as they were around. The first night of the Congress, while waiting for their departure bus, they sang in the lobby, directed by one of their student conductors. The sounds of their unaccompanied voices floated through the entire massive complex. As tired as I was, I lingered, not wanting to walk away from their music.

The final evening, they repeated the Tagalog song from the hymnal. As people walked out of the plenary hall for the last time, the choir, seated on the grand staircase in the lobby, sang to them. They had an extensive repertoire and knew it all by memory. They generously gave far more than we asked.

The day after the Congress finished, Romulo and I had a leisurely conversation over lunch. I learned about all the different hats he wears: evangelist, lay preacher, soloist, conductor, lay theologian, InterVarsity staff person, counselor, lecturer, professor, mathematician, and doctoral candidate.

I remembered Ed Dayton's consternation when he discovered, prior to the beginning of the Congress, that Romulo, the man I had chosen to be a primary musician at the opening ceremony, was not a professional musician. I had discovered that for myself in February, but it made no difference. He had a good choir.

Following the Congress, a letter arrived from Romulo:

Department of Mathematics
College of Science
University of the Philippines
Diliman, Quezon City

Dear Corean,
The group has been tremendously encouraged after Lausanne. I must say that there is still a lot of work I have to do. . . . I guess there is no limit in our quest for beauty and excellence for the Lord.

The Congress choir director did not intend to rest on his laurels.

Filipino Singer

With artists coming from all over the world to be part of the worship team, I did not want to exclude local artists. We could not accommodate multiple artists; I would have to choose one. How to make that choice and how to stand firm in that choice were problems I struggled with as program associate for worship.

Again I went to the one person close by who knew about artists in Manila, Priscilla Pascual. She wrote out a list of them for me complete with addresses, phone numbers, and descriptions of their art. She had neither address nor phone number for Gary Granada, the second person on her list. She suggested getting it through the Institute for Studies in Asian Church and Culture (ISACC) in Quezon City. Priscilla had formerly worked at ISACC as personal secretary to the director, Melba Maggay. Through a careless oversight, when preparing the list of people to meet while in Manila planning for the Congress, I omitted Gary's name.

While in Manila in February, I talked with people about singers and listened to tapes of singers recommended to me by the Far East Broadcasting Company (FEBC), looking for the one who would best fit into the type of program being designed. Fred Liongoren, visual artist on Priscilla's list, told me about Gary's song "Bahay" (the house), written to challenge the social status quo. He told me of the powerful impression that song makes on audiences of all kinds. He told me how that song affected him personally. Arlene Villaver, another visual artist, gave me her own personal copy of Gary's album so I could listen for myself.

From the start of my work for Lausanne II, I tried to avoid primadonna types, artists with big egos and inflexible styles. Every person on the team had to be willing to adjust as needed. No matter how well prepared we might be, in July we still might encounter surprises. I did not want personalities complicating an already very complex program.

On my last evening in Manila, while Romulo and I conversed over dinner at the Bistro in Quezon City, I brought up the matter of a Filipino artist for the Congress. Romula heard me out, then said Gary Granada was the person I was looking for and gave me his phone number. I called Gary that evening. He said he would be happy to help out in the Congress. I regretted having no time left to meet him.

Back home in Chicago, I went to Melanie Monteclaro, a Filipino friend, and asked her to translate "Bahay" into English so I might understand the words. Perhaps this was the song we should fit into the Congress program.

About this time, the Lausanne program office began putting pressure on speakers who had not yet submitted their plenary session texts. That included my husband, Ray Bakke. He had no text to submit because he intended to divide his plenary time of twenty-eight minutes into interviews with four strategic urban people. Together, the five of them would work out the details in Manila. The only thing Ray could supply in advancew as the names of those people.

After returning from Manila in February, I went to my husband with what has to be one of the most presumptuous requests I have ever made. I asked him to include Gary Granada as one of the four people he would interview in the urban ministry plenary on day three of the Congress. He already had many people in mind to choose from, people he personally knew. Neither of us knew Gary. I suggested he ought to consider including an artist (I am always looking for niches for artists) as they are among the most strategic of urban people. Continuing to press my case, I gave him the newly prepared translation to read while he listened to "Bahay."

Ray has always been willing to take risks. He agreed to include Gary. In April I wrote to Gary:

> Ever since hearing. . . . your song on the tape, I have been looking for a way to include you in the Congress. The third morning . . . looks like the right time. . . . The 9:30 plenary is titled: "Good News For The Poor." The following plenary at 11:00 is titled: "Urban Evangelism." . . . Ray Bakke is putting the second plenary together. He wants to do it by selecting a number of persons from around the world to represent distinctive issues in the city. Together he and they would script out brief interviews of 2–3 minutes each which would be done live in that plenary. I have asked him to use you as the person he interviews concerning housing for the poor and then include your song,"Bahay." . . . Would it be possible for you to do this? A song in Tagalog presents problems for all of us non-Tagalog speakers and I'm struggling with ways to solve this.

Gary's disappointing response came by phone through another person. I went to my desk and wrote a letter dated May 25:

> This morning Amanda Bueno called me with the message that you will not be able to accept the invitation to sing at Lausanne II. She mentioned two reasons why you are declining the invitation: (1) Because you were not recommended by the FEBC, and (2) because Lausanne II is not the right audience for you.
>
> Your response surprised me because of our telephone conversation in February. . . . You said you would be available to help out at the Congress. Therefore I did not anticipate the news I received this morning. Your name was on the list of musicians I gave the program committee to be included in the handbook. I will owe you an apology if that has already gone to the printers.
>
> When Amanda and I finished talking, I immediately called Priscilla Pascual to ask a number of things, including the meaning of the FEBC. Whenever I talk with her and other Filipinos, I struggle to understand which organizations are referred to when the speaker uses the abbreviated form of the name. As Amanda talked with me, I was thinking FEBC referred to the organization of Evangelicals in the Philippines. I had not received any list of recommendations regarding musicians from them. When I realized, talking with Priscilla, that it was the Far Eastern Broadcasting Company, then I began to put together some of the pieces which helped me understand what might have led to your response. . . .
>
> When I arrived in Manila, a number of people were contacted to meet

me and discuss possible musicians. Everywhere I turned, people had musicians to recommend. Even the missionary I stayed with wanted to invite a married couple to breakfast for me to meet, because she thought I ought to know about them and consider them for Lausanne II. It seemed reasonable to listen to some of the musicians being recommended, and at FEBC they had many tapes at their finger tips. I spent time there listening and left with a tape of several different musicians.

Over the next couple of days, I kept listening to what people said about the various musicians, trying to determine who might be the best soloist to work with the musicians already invited to the Congress. One of my dreams has been to get musicians together from various parts of the world to hear each other and to provide the opportunity for their talents to blend together in imaginative ways. One of my convictions is that musicians from different parts of the world need encouragement to speak in the musical language of their country and not feel pressured to imitate Western singers and instrumentalists. Therefore I looked for musicians who speak with the authentic voice and instrument of their people. As I shared these dreams with various people, it was your name which emerged as the musician I should invite. . . .

I am aware of some of the tensions which must have led you to reply as you did—to the long history of injustices inflicted by Americans to your people, to the present tension between ISAAC and the Evangelical leaders in Manila and between Roman Catholics and Protestants. When the call came this morning it seemed to point to something which I didn't understand so I have written this letter to try to tell you about my position in the Congress and why I invited you to be part of it. If you are still unable to accept the invitation, we will have one less musician. I will not replace you with another.

The plenary leader for the day you were invited is . . . Ray Bakke, a person very sensitive to international and ecumenical issues and a current professor to Priscilla Pascual. I think I can safely say that you would feel very comfortable being part of what he plans to do in that plenary.

I sent off the letter with a tape of Ken Medema's, "Is Your Phone Ringin'?" and a prayer that God would resolve this impasse. Word came from Romulo Pizaña that both he and Gary's wife were hoping to get Gary to change his mind. I waited apprehensively. As a member of the ad hoc program planning committee, I understood the dilemma of time running out with a still-uncommitted plenary person.

Gary's next response, dated June 20, arrived as a strong personal statement and story:

I believe I owe you some explanation in my decision not to participate in the Congress particularly in the session you have indicated in your letter.

My wife, Susan, and I have been involved in development work for the past ten years. We had the privilege of learning from fishermen, peasants, migrant workers and women in rural plantations. As Evangelicals, we decided one day to put what modest experience we had to use in the context of mission. Sooner or later we would find out that political advocacy was not exactly in the agenda of Philippine evangelicalism. We regard the brethren highly enough not to push the issue unnecessarily and decided to work directly with local congregations instead of councils or conferences, whether evangelical, ecumenical or even Roman Catholic. Please keep it to yourself that while we never softened in the task of evangelism, we honestly believe that the work of proclaiming Christ until He comes is shared by sincere Christians of all traditions. This too was my understanding of the international Congress. And in discussing the issue of urban power I firmly suppose such a premise requires affirmation.

Gary continued his letter by telling a parable:

Once upon a time, a farmer and his family lived peacefully in a peaceful land. One day a wounded hunter came to the farmer's hut and asked if he could stay for a few days until he was fit to go on his journey. The simple farmer immediately summoned his wife and children and instructed them to prepare a meal for the stranger after which they were to vacate the only room in the hut to accommodate the guest. When the sumptuous food was served, the visitor noticed that the farmer had neither plates nor spoons nor forks. The following morning the stranger went around the village and came back quite excited, "I think I like your place enough to make me want to stay for a long time," he told the farmer.

"But you're not a farmer. How will you survive?"

The stranger then brought out a set of shining chinaware from his bag and showed them to the farmer who examined the objects carefully and was left speechless. "Let's make a deal. We'll open a village restaurant. I'll provide the plates. You provide the food and we'll split the profit."

The restaurant prospered quickly until one day the stranger hid the plates and took the food and sold them secretly. Moreover, he accused the farmer of stealing the chinaware and his wife and children of eating the food. And so the farmer started paying for the plates by working harder and harder. The incident happened a second time and the farmer had to sell his land to the stranger, himself becoming the tenant.

Finally, the stranger decided to do the trick a third and last time, calculating that this time all that was left to the farmer would be his. But the farmer caught him in the act of hiding the plates. He grabbed the fragile plates and smashed them one by one on the stranger's head.

I would like to add a middle chapter to this my friend Paul's tale. After the second set of plates were "lost," the stranger suggested to the farmer that perhaps they should work together in finding better ways to make the land more productive so he might be able to pay his debt faster.

Corean, you would of course understand that it is very difficult for me to imagine people coming together to take an honest look at poverty when the organizers come from a position of strength. Since 1974, the First Congress has yet to comfort one family whose father was tortured and killed in the interest of the national security of the US-Marcos government; has yet to protest against the Mendiola massacre under the present administration which claimed the death of many peasants, none of whom I suppose was an evangelical. To discuss cooperation at this time is out of context. Our colonizers cannot but merely theologize on the question of justice, otherwise the global order which ensures the agenda of their political and religious institutions could be undermined. Praise be to God that our people have begun to outgrow the orthodox theology of free salvation through costless faith, not to mention our oppressor's latest trick: prosperity gospel. One can do better than a token gesture of allotting one morning to discuss our social responsibility. Taking an open stand against your own military bases or urging your missionaries not to lord it over our congregations and live modestly could be more credible. I know that there are many first world Christians who are genuinely concerned about poverty and injustice, but don't you think you should police your own ranks first? For our part, we are prepared to say we do not need your generosity to continue our advocacy in behalf of the overwhelming majority of our rich but robbed people. But then again our very own Christian leadership is not prepared to openly say so. This I think is the other premise to a better understanding of poverty.

Corean, believe me, we are on your side. We also think you are on ours. I also know that you have worked so hard in trying to make the most out of the little token space set aside. If only for solidarity with the work you are doing, I am willing to participate. . . . I am so sorry for the insensitivity. I shall be there on the 13th, unless of course you find my sentiments more hurting than helping.

Two days before the Congress began, the four of us met: Gary and

Susan, Ray and I. We asked them to take us to Smokey Mountain, the noto-rious garbage community where the fires burn day and night. They did, in their little Volkswagen. We got out and walked around in the mud and rain as household dogs protested our presence. We asked questions and lis-tened to stories of their involvement with the poor and the powerless in Manila. When it became too dark to see, Gary drove us back to our con-spicuously comfortable hotel. He seemed increasingly open to the idea of working with Ray and the other three persons chosen to present their urban ministries to the Congress. He agreed to meet the next morning to begin the work of shaping their individual and collective contributions to Lausanne II.

Ray scheduled Gary last, after interviewing Jember Teferra from Addis Ababa, Viju Abraham from Bombay, and David Ngai from Hong Kong. Gary revised the English translation of his song and prepared his response with great skill. He closed with the strongest statement made in that ple-nary, perhaps of the entire Congress:

> Unless and until we resolve to resolve this aberration of our faith, we cannot be surprised if the people of the garbage dumps of the cities of the world will think of our message as just another piece of trash.

Everyone sat in stunned silence, watching Gary prepare to sing. As he fumbled to lower the microphone, he spoke off-script, "Sometimes I seri-ously wish I were tall [more fumbling], instead of good looking!"

The heavy silence gave way to laughter. Gary was very much at home on stage and in front of cameras. As long as he occupied the PICC plat-form, he was determined to have everyone's attention.

Gary sang "Bahay" in Tagalog. Each verse began with Ray reading the English translation accompanied by Gary on his guitar, followed by Gary singing:

One day I visited a "house" on the garbage dump
Squeezed inside was a household of fifteen people,
Enduring a small, makeshift, brokendown shanty
While a nearby mansion was almost empty.

Imprisoned inside wooden slabs and corrugated boxes
Shaded by rusting zinc sheets and worn-out tires
Mended together by scraps of trash and held down by stones
I could not understand why such a thing is called a house.

I decided to write a story about what my eyes saw
And even made a song that others may hear and know
I painted what I felt and put up a simple play
And asked knowledgeable people what they can say.

A famous senator was the first person I came to see
And then an expert professor of a prominent university
And a blessed businessman, and the newsman and the pulpitman
And they all agreed that indeed it was a house.

Day and night they scrape off the mountain of trash
And eat like chickens on the floor as they squat
And force their bodies to sleep on an old torn bed
Far better is the resting place of the dead.

And if one day you'll accidentally pass by that place
And feel and hear and smell and see them face to face
I do not mean to deride, I leave it for you to decide
Do you think that in the eyes of the Creator this is a house?

For days after, people requested copies of the English translation. When the first supply ran out, we made more.

Gary's involvement at Lausanne II cost me many hours. He was so close, yet so out of reach. I hardly knew how to describe my feelings when he held that huge audience in the palm of his hand. His presence, his words, and his music magnificently exceeded my expectations.

Balinese Artist

During a meeting of the ad hoc program planning committee in late April, we worked on the communion service for day four of the Congress. Sometimes we got inspired to go off the beaten track. It happened that day. We started talking about the possibility of finding a way to communicate the transforming power of the gospel in a nontraditional, nonverbal way.

In a whispered aside, Eric Miller told me about Nyoman Darsane's mask dance at Artists' Experience in Bali. I had missed it by leaving three days early. The dance portrayed a person before and after coming to Christ. The mask symbolized life before Christ; the removal of the mask, life with Christ. The astonishing thing about this dance, in the context of Bali, was the removal of the mask. Dancers *never* remove their masks on stage. They protect themselves from vulnerability by hiding behind masks. Eric suggested we consider incorporating the mask dance into the communion service.

I remembered Nyoman. For Balinese Night, he brought a gamelan orchestra of fifteen musicians to accompany a biblical dance/drama. Those of us from the rest of the world sat spellbound as we watched the exotic dancers in their Balinese costumes and masks and listened to Balinese musical instruments. All the performers were from the Protestant Christian Church of Bali.

I reflected how far removed they were from the bathrobe-style biblical dramas of American churches. Every Sunday school Christmas play, from my childhood up to the present, has Joseph and the shepherds wearing bathrobes. Why? I suppose because, once upon a time, a Sunday school Christmas play producer decided there was a connection between Palestinian peasant clothing and American men's bathrobes.

The exotic quality of Balinese biblical drama is intentional. In 1972, after missionaries stripped the Protestant Christian Church of Bali of its Balinese culture, the church leaders met. In their deliberations, they decided to express their faith using Balinese traditions. As a result, biblical plays are staged with Balinese costumes and masks and music. Christ might dress like a warrior in batik and turban and move about the stage in stylized Balinese dance movements, looking nothing like Sallman's *Head of Christ*, the painting which has become the standard representation of Christ around the world. Even though I went to Bali deliberately to experience the creativity of artists from other parts of the world, Balinese drama continually astonished me.

The committee accepted our idea and slotted the mask dance into the communion service on day four. It was up to me to work out all the details.

First I had to reach Nyoman. It was now May. There was no time for letters, just phone calls. Eric had a phone number for Bishop Wayan Mastra, a theologian in Denpasar, Bali, and from him I got Nyoman's number. Nyoman spent most of his days and many evenings in his art studio, making it difficult to reach him.

When I called the second time, after he had a chance to discuss the matter with Dr. Mastra, he gave me a verbal acceptance. Yes, he would come. He would come for the entire length of the Congress.

On June 8, I faxed World Vision Indonesia requesting them to add Nyoman to the ticketing list. On June 12, a message came back: "Thanks for your fax of June 08, 1989. . . . We have already put him in our list."

A second problem emerged. I did not feel comfortable asking him to come for just one dance. What else could I suggest? He had only a short time in which to prepare. Decisions needed to be made quickly.

I learned that whenever he prepared dance/dramas, he consulted with Dr. Mastra. The two of them, artist and theologian, made a very effective team as they found ways to bring Balinese culture into the church.

Bill O'Brien, former missionary to Indonesia, was scheduled to speak on day nine in the plenary titled "Cooperation in World Evangelization." This was a natural place to include Nyoman. I called Bill and inquired about his choice of biblical text. He planned to draw from the story in Luke where Jesus healed the paralytic man whom friends lowered through the roof. Could Nyoman tell that story with puppets? I would find out.

The committee decided to also put drama into day ten, just prior to Luis Palau, the morning plenary speaker. I went ahead and offered all three spots to Nyoman. The last spot was the most difficult to plan because the speaker had not chosen, or at least not sent us, a biblical text. All we had was the subject and the title. I sent word to Nyoman through Rev. M. S. Anwari on June 19:

> On day ten, in a morning plenary titled "Looking to the Future," there is a space for a 7 minute drama. This time slot could be shortened according to what would be appropriate. The speaker's message is titled: "Don't Be Afraid of the Future," and he will challenge people to not be afraid to let God use them. The drama comes just before the speaker. I have not been able to get any biblical text from that speaker. Mr. Darsane thought that he could also do something here if you and Dr. Mastra provided some guidance in what he created.

Three days later, June 22, Rev. M. S. Anwari from World Vision of Indonesia sent word, "I have met Dr. Mastra and have made confirmation that the third drama will be based on Matthew 6:24–34."

I got out my Bible to see why they had chosen that text—because it commands the reader to not worry about tomorrow! I marveled over the appropriateness of their choice and looked forward to the dramatic presentation.

The biggest challenge still lay ahead, that of incorporating Balinese dance/drama into a program of mostly Western elements. We needed to rehearse each drama and carefully consider the best way to make it work in the context of Lausanne II. Rehearsal time became the biggest problem of all. Everything scheduled to take place on the platform during the Congress had its own scheduled rehearsal slot in the hall, time when the persons involved met, discussed the logistical details, and walked through their parts. Byron Spradlin, the platform director, worked out all the kinks ahead of time to eliminate fumbling and delays. These rehearsals often ran overtime.

Nyoman needed some helpers for his mask dance, people to join him in a dance of celebration following his conversion, the time when he removes the mask. He wanted people of wide diversity to show the internationality of the Church. I assured the people I asked that we would rehearse and they would know exactly what they were going to do. Everyone sat waiting for the scheduled rehearsal to finish, freeing Byron and the stage for our special rehearsal.

Just as it finished, a new person appeared to work out Leighton Ford's platform details individually with Byron. Leighton had not come to that now-finished rehearsal.

Not all of the volunteer drama team could continue to wait. They had other commitments. I had never seen this dance, just heard about it. Talking it through was not sufficient. When the platform space and Byron were finally available, we had too little time to adequately prepare. Not knowing what else to do, we programmed it for the full eight minutes Nyoman said it took. As eight minutes was the maximum time available to us, we omitted any introductory comments.

After the Congress a description appeared in *Asian Church Today*:

> Half way through the Congress, a Holy Communion Service was held for 3,300 participants. It started well with singing and the reading of Scriptures. Suddenly, the lights in the Auditorium went out. The spot light was on a horrible creature dancing on the 'holy' platform. The programme Committee tried to make the dance meaningful, but the tragedy is that creature seemed to be a 'monkey god'! It shocked me to see the creature catching lice from its head and fleas from its side.
>
> Next moment, the creature unmasked before the Lausanne Logo and became a handsome person. It was totally out of place before the preaching of God's Word on 'Holiness'.

Almost immediately, Byron and I realized what we should have done: edit the dance down to a shortened version and prepare an explanation to be presented first. Then people would have understood that the "horrible creature" was meant to be horrible. It was a sinner.

I neglected to ask Nyomen ahead of time what props he might need. We should have had a cross on the platform for this dance. Then the horrible creature could have unmasked before a universal symbol of God's power to transform, instead of unmasking before the Lausanne logo, our only alternative.

We should have explained the Balinese reluctance to appear on stage unmasked and the powerful symbolism of a dancer who accepts the vulnerability that unmasking brings. The "horrible creature" turned "handsome person" was a sinner transformed into a saint, totally appropriate "before the preaching of God's Word on 'Holiness.'" Had everyone had the simple explanation ahead of time, they could have translated Nyomen's Balinese symbol for conversion into their own cultural understanding. But it was not understood.

Bill O'Brien came to the rescue for day nine's drama. He and Nyoman and I spent several hours working out the details of the shadow-puppet drama. We decided to include a brief introduction of Indonesian puppetry to give the audience some preparation for what they would see. Bill was exactly the right person to help turn the earlier experience around. He knew shadow puppetry from his days in Indonesia and he was as interested as I in using indigenous art forms, including exotic art forms of Asia, to communicate the good news unique to Christianity. He prepared and gave the introduction.

Indonesian shadow puppets are flat figures attached to long handles. Only their arms move. The puppeteer sits on the floor and introduces one character at a time, then moves it aside and thrusts it upright into a puppet stage in front of him while he brings out the next character. Puppets already introduced, off to the side of center stage, remain part of the drama. The audience continues to see them.

Nyoman told me he needed a banana-tree trunk to make his puppet stage. He wanted to keep the puppetsthat were not actively performing vertical by plunging their bone handles into the soft trunk.

I asked Grace Agtani, one of the Filipino stewards who had been assigned to help me, where we could get a banana-tree trunk. She did not know. Nyoman agreeably assured me he could manage without. He could lay the out-of-action puppets down on the stage rather than stand them upright, but of course no one would see them lying down. Grace and I both understood the need. I understood nothing about banana trees.

The next morning, before breakfast, the phone rang in my hotel room. Grace excitedly reported that she had a banana-tree trunk. She remembered a friend with a banana tree growing in the back yard. She bought the tree from her friend and secured a taxi to bring it to the PICC. I owed her a total of 135 pesos: 115 for tree, 20 for taxi.

Nyoman needed it cut into three parts: two short pieces to raise and stabilize a longer piece where the drama would take place. I sent a request to the cafeteria for a large knife. The manager accompanied knife and messenger back to the plenary hall to take full responsibility for this lethal weapon. With practiced aim and experienced eye, Nyoman quickly and efficiently converted the banana tree trunk into his portable stage.

Next we organized who would carry what. The stage and puppets all had to be put into place on the platform during the singing which preceded the drama. And once the drama finished, all the pieces had to immediately disappear. In a most interesting and totally unforeseen way, that plenary on cooperation became one of the most cooperative productions of them all.

People loved it! They understood from Bill O'Brien's explanation what was happening and were intrigued with the puppets. Afterwards they crowded around Nyoman, wanting to see the different characters up close and wanting to have their pictures taken with the puppets and the puppeteer.

As we prepared for the final drama, about a shepherd and a lost sheep, Byron Spradlin took the lead in editing Nyoman's longer drama into a shorter and more accessible version. Froilan (Froji) Cruz, the Congress mimer, assisted by playing the part of the lost sheep and hid under one of the platform ferns. Nyoman, the shepherd, wearing exotic Balinese clothing, began by playing his flute, a Balinese bamboo instrument. He strolled about the platform in a relaxed mood.

Suddenly, he discovered one sheep missing. He darted everywhere looking for it, to the accompaniment of recorded Balinese music. When he found it (Froji, under the platform fern), he carried it home on his shoulders, possible because Froji was short and slight, and "home" was only the length of the platform.

I held my breath wondering how Luis Palau would respond to a Balinese shepherd and sheep act coming just before he spoke. Afterward he interrupted a video taping to thank me for the drama.

The Filipino sound technicians excitedly told me what they had learned: that common things found in their own environment had great potential. Nyoman, sitting up on the platform behind his banana-tree-trunk stage telling a Bible story to four thousand international participants, inspired them to think more positively and creatively of the resources in their own culture.

In addition to being a composer, musician, and dancer, Nyoman was also a visual artist. He brought some of his batiks, and early in the Congress he gave them all to me to select one as a gift. I chose the one of Jesus opening the blind man's eyes. Nyoman had painted that story in Balinese style, with both figures seated on the ground.

I wrote him in August:

> Thank you so much for coming to Manila and giving us a glimpse of Balinese art. Thanks for your willingness to adapt the extended dramas into those tiny little moments.... I was thrilled to see you up on the stage in costume along with the speakers in their formal Western dress. You brought internationality and cultural distinctiveness to that platform and modeled pride in not being Westernized.... In Bali you are so much ahead of many parts of the world. You know how to share the gospel to your culture without preaching.

The ad hoc program planning committee, back in late April, had wanted a way to communicate in nontraditional, nonverbal language. We found it, thanks to the efforts of Wayan Mastra the theologian and Nyomen Darsene the artist, and their determination to let the church in Bali be Balinese.

Filipino Mimer

The program planning committee returned again and again to the problem of communication at the Congress. How could we most effectively plan so that people who spoke nine different languages would all understand?

We recognized the danger of verbal overload, especially in a program organized around words: words from introducers, words from plenary speakers, words from video narratives. Additional words from program people about buses and housing and meals and identification and security and umbrellas and headsets might go unheard and unheeded.

Mime came up from time to time as we struggled with the problem of effective communication. We discussed the advantages of bypassing translation by having a nonverbal person reinforce announcements through body language. The more we thought about it, the more it seemed like a good idea.

The mimers known to the committee were either American or United

112

Kingdom people. Here, as in most other aspects of choosing personnel, we tried to find a non-Western, nonwhite mimer.

In February, at Artists' Experience in Bali, I met Froji Cruz, a Filipino mimer from Manila. We talked briefly about the Congress coming up, and I gave him some information. He sent me a letter in April:

> Regarding the talk we had . . . I just want to know of the developments. Lausanne II is just 2 months hence. Please let me know of your plans so I can prepare.

When his letter arrived, I was swamped with the hymnal and set aside the letter, unanswered. It was not until the final planning meeting of the program committee, in June, that we decided to go ahead with a mimer if I could come up with one.

At that point I began looking for Froji and learned, to my dismay, that he had left Manila and was in Indonesia. On June 26, I sent a letter by fax to Rev. M. S. Anwari in Indonesia.

> Could you assist me in locating Froilan G. Cruz? He offered himself to the Congress to be a mimer. I failed to confirm as I ought to have and I hear he has now departed Manila for Indonesia. . . . He was working with YFC in Jakarta. . . . I hope to find him and get a response this week before I leave the country on July 5.

Two days later, word of his discovery arrived. I responded through World Vision, Indonesia:

> The program committee has these requests (1) That Froji assist the MC couple in making announcements . . . (2) That Froji be available to assist Mr. Darsane if he needs help . . . (3) Optional: That Froji perform during box supper in Reception Hall or other times/places that seem [like good] possibilities—be the Congress strolling dramatist.

Graciously, he came, and I apologized for not answering his letter.

Onstage, he assisted Graham and Treena Kerr in making announcements and he assisted Nyoman Darsane in two dramas. Offstage, in the reception hall, he found places and times to mime, at times inviting other worship-team members to assist him. He also kept meticulous records.

I wrote him in August:

> Things kept changing at the Congress. The original plan to make a big thing out of the announcements changed. Graham and Treena Kerr thought they would MC most everything. Then chairmen of the day were

added, to properly give representation to other parts of the world on the platform. They took time giving their unique input. It became a problem of too much. We were over-programmed.

When I realized you were on the losing end, I began praying that in some way the Lord would minister to you as you sat through the sessions day after day. My prayer for all the musicians and artists was that they would inspire and learn from each other. But my prayer for you went beyond that. I prayed that you might find a very special message from God for your life through the Congress. . . . I ought to have written down the times you planned your solo performances. At this point I don't remember how many it was. Could you write and remind me of what you did? . . . The dramas you did, their names, the length of each one, what kind of props you used, where you did them, when you did them, and an estimate of the number of people you think watched . . .

In September, Froji wrote a lengthy letter:

Regarding Lausanne II, I would say gathering together the Christian theologians and thinkers; planners and preachers; educators and evangelists; authors and artists from all over the world was a tremendous success and achievement in itself. And as I sat through the sessions, the dynamic spirit of Lausanne gradually absorbed me or should I say it was irresistible! Well, in spite of the problems we ran into, the Congress served as a channel for a breakthrough in Christian performing arts which eventually led to Christian worship taking on a new form with distinct features. Now, about the performances. On July 17 (Monday), at the Reception Hall, I performed the following sketches before an audience numbering 60–80:

1) "The Fruit of the Spirit," a mime-dance presentation
About: Galatians 5:22, 23
Music: Taped Sundanese music using the *kacapi*, a stringed
  instrument, and the *suling*, a bamboo flute.
Duration: 5 minutes and 40 seconds
Note: The Sundanese live in the western part of Java Island in
  Indonesia. They are a predominantly Muslim ethnic group.

2) "The Temptation of Jesus," a mime presentation
About: Matthew 4:1–11
Music: Taped Sundanese instrumental *degung* (wind and
  percussion).
Duration: 4 minutes and 30 seconds

3) "Tightrope Walk—to Year 2000 and Beyond," a mime
 presentation
About: Christian with vision, courage, and commitment
Music: Taped Western light classic
Duration: 2 minutes and 10 seconds

But prior to this, on July 14 (Friday), at the same hall just beside the stairs going to the 2nd floor, I had the opportunity to do mime and dance antics in the street theater tradition. Three Thai musicians assisted me. They used their traditional musical instruments. In the span of 20 minutes, we managed to" attract" 80 persons. Most of them were transient spectators. But we had real fun.

At the Plenary Hall, I mimed 2 strings of announcements. One was on July 12 (Wednesday) and the other on July 14 (Friday). I assisted Nyoman Darsane on July 14—served as one of the four dancing Christians in "The New Creation"; July 19—served as a tapper for his abridged *wayang kulit* presentation; July 20—performed the role of sheep in "The Lost Sheep" with Darsane acting as shepherd. Finally, on the last day of the Congress, I interpreted in movements Nagieb's song interpretation of "Bless The Lord O My Soul."

Not a single prop was utilized in all the mime and dance performances. Due to time constraint, the use of the *ligay* backdrop or scenery became inevitable. But it added an Asian dimension to "The Fruit of the Spirit." Oftentimes, the spotlight was there to help in the aspects of visibility and creation of mood. Mime technique used is patterned after the Modern French Technique with dashes of movements inspired by Javanese *wayang kulit*, Balinese dance, and Chinese martial arts. In a sense, the technique is a fusion of Western realism and Eastern expressionism. Make-up and costume is basically Asian Indian/Chinese/Southeast Asian.

So, how's life after that historic Lausanne II in Manila? I hope everything is fine. Corean, thank you very much for giving me a role in the Congress. Its benefits and blessings were and are enormous. Regards to Ray. Standing beside Mr. Urban Missions himself was a privilege indeed.

God Bless! *Mabuhay!* [Long-live]

He included in the letter a gift of photographs for me, pictures taken with his camera at the Congress. He had an amazingly complete visual record of his involvement as a mimer.

In October I wrote again:

Thank you for your beautifully written letter with all the details of your performances. . . . And thank you for the pictures, including the description on the back sides. You did a good job of making a photo journal of Lausanne II, something which I was unhappy not to be doing for myself. I had a camera along but with all the tasks to be done, I gave up taking pictures even before I started. . . . Thanks again for your cooperative spirit at Lausanne and for your performances. I continue to see new write-ups about the worship and drama and dance at the Congress. Ray just returned from Finland, bringing with him a Finnish church publication with four photos from Lausanne II. Of the four, two were of the worship team.

For a word-centered event, the number of photographs featuring the worship team on covers and front pages of Congress reports surprised and delighted me. The possibilities of body language, although risky in multicultural contexts, deserve much more attention.

Thai Troupe

When I began the task of finding people from around the world to become an international worship team, the only group I already knew who fit the requirements was the Thai Folk Drama Troupe. All other groups and all other persons, outside of Ken Medema, were discoveries along the way to the Congress.

I first heard about the Thai troupe in 1980 when my husband returned from Pattaya, Thailand. He watched them perform and became an enthusiastic supporter. A few years later, when the troupe came to the Chicago area, I went to their Easter Sunday morning performance. Never before had I experienced exotic Asian costumes, makeup, body gestures, and musical instruments played by performers seated on the floor. They performed in Thai superbly translated, simultaneously, by Joan and Allan Eubank. Soon after being named program associate for worship, I contacted Allan Eubank in Chiang Mai, Thailand, with an invitation to bring the troupe. Together we initiated an intensive cooperative effort, determined to move aside every barrier that stood in the way of getting the troupe to Manila.

The primary difficulty involved finances. Allan suggested different possibilities to make their coming possible. They could come with as few as five for an economy-priced performance. However, twelve would be much better. But, given the grandness of the occasion, sixteen would be the best. That would enable them to have the full number of actors and musicians needed for their dramas. Airfare was relatively inexpensive between Manila and Bangkok, but food and housing and surface transportation added a prohibitive amount.

On the second day of my February visit to Manila, Cristy Ticlaw, from the Lausanne II office at the Philippine International Convention Center (PICC), arranged for me to meet Mrs. Anita Teh. She had her own film distribution business: importing, exporting, producing, and distributing films. She wanted to get involved with Lausanne II.

Viggo Søgaard, friend and communication specialist from Denmark, and a local pastor, Richard Mirpuri, met with Mrs. Teh, Cristy, and me. We strategized together and came up with a plan which would enable the entire Thai troupe and other performers to come to Lausanne II, thus enlarging cultural representation on the worship team beyond the small ensemble.

Mrs. Teh suggested we house performers in homes, saying, "The Filipino people are known for their hospitality." She offered to coordinate the arrangements! This was an astonishing offer. We discussed the details. I should send her photos and descriptions of each person, such as name with pronunciation helps, age, occupation, sex, marital status, nationality, customary foods, and size. She wanted to make sure the bed sizes matched the people sizes. Families with telephones and cars would be sought in order to help facilitate rehearsal and performance schedules.

She also had an idea for raising money to take care of airfares—concerts outside Lausanne II. In this way, the church people of Manila could be given opportunities to benefit from the musicians and artists from other parts of the world.

The news of our conversation encouraged Allan Eubank, and he went ahead with plans to bring the full troupe. I sent Mrs. Teh photos and names of the Thai troupe and suggested combinations for housing per Allan's suggestion.

Females	Males
Mrs. Tida Prasitbureerak	Mr. Jamlong Singhkan
Mrs. Somkit Chaitwat	Mr. Prapun Pochai
Miss Laksana Tavichai	Mr. Somnuk Munyoo
Mrs. Venus Vannarattanarat	Mr. Vinai Srirat
Miss Supah Srisangjun	Mr. Sujinda Chaiyagunsarakorn
Mrs. Yuriam Im-ote	Mr. Archib Kongchai
Mrs. P-Wongdguen Yontararak	Mr. Manop Suriyakham
Ms. Siriporn Suriyakham	Mr. Prayong Muangta

I had no pronunciation guide to send along.

Next, Allan and I began working on specific performances. He needed the program planning committee to identify, as soon as possible, the specific dramas and dances we wanted for the *ligays*, traditional Thai dance-drama, based on biblical stories; two modern Thai dramas; ten dances with a Christian message. All the dramas were long but could be shortened to thirty minutes. Each dance took three minutes.

Allan called attention to the selections he thought might be particularly fitting for Lausanne II. "Prodigal Daughter," their first drama, was the most popular of their *ligay* dramas. It could be shortened from ninety minutes down to fifteen minutes. They had a short dance titled "Flower Blessing Dance" which Allan suggested could be used to welcome all the participants to the Congress.

The ad hoc committee accepted Allan's suggestion and scheduled the troupe to open the Congress with its "Flower Blessing Dance." Props for this dance included five golden bowls and a generous quantity of pretty flower petals. The dancers would sprinkle the flower petals around on the platform and, as they moved out into the audience, on the participants.

In addition, the committee scheduled the troupe to perform in conjunction with two Bible study sessions, doing a song with an accompanying dance and performing the fifteen-minute version of the "Prodigal Daughter." The troupe would have an evening slot of twenty-five minutes in which to do a variety of traditional dances plus another abbreviated

Finally, all these times were finalized. I sent Allan the schedule:

Three minute dance—opening of Congress	Day One
Ligay in morning Bible study	Day Four
Evening performance at 6:30	Day Four
Dance and Thai song in morning Bible study	Day Eight
Closing ceremony	Day Ten

My job in getting this schedule worked out had to take into account commitments outside the plenary hall, including a workshop on day seven, and two thirty-minute performances in the reception hall on days three and seven. In addition, they wanted to schedule some performances apart from the Congress in the Manila area. Moving a troupe with costumes and backdrops and orchestra required significant packing time, travel time, and setup time. The planning had to be meticulous.

In Thailand and on tour out of Thailand, the troupe always performs with backdrop scenery. Allan sent me a description of the kinds of pipe he would need to purchase in order to make a portable frame to hold the backdrop sceneries: three-fourths inch light steel pipe or water pipe and sixteen feet of four-inch plastic water pipe.

He would also need a vehicle to bring the piping back to the PICC. Would he be able to sell the piping when he left Manila and recover any of the cost? I would check.

The committee, after discussing all the possible ways to set up and quickly remove backdrop scenery, decided it would not work on the main platform in the plenary hall. The only time the troupe could use backdrop sceneries would be for performances in the reception hall and in the churches.

The matter of excess baggage came up. The troupe would come with two bags each (150 pounds) plus backdrops and tubes weighing five hundred pounds. He would bring the following musical instruments, also adding to the baggage problem:

Ranad (a Thai xylophone)
Circle gong
Glongtat (pair of drums)
Tapong (drum)
Flute
Ching (finger cymbals)

In the past, whenever the troupe traveled, Allan had always been able to get the airlines to validate an allowance for excess baggage. He would be willing to advertise for Philippine Airlines in exchange for such arrangements. This required much negotiation between Bill Ditewig, the Lausanne II person who arranged for all the transportation, and Wilcox World Travel and Tours.

On the day before the Congress began, I began assembling golden bowls and flowers for the opening dance of the Congress. I asked the Filipino stewards what kind of flowers we should use. They suggested the *sampaquita*, the national flower of the Philippines. That sounded appropriate. I got my husband to donate the funds needed and sent a steward to order the flowers.

The troupe was due to arrive that same day, July 10. At the appointed time, their hosts and hostesses arrived at the PICC. After waiting a long time, we learned that the plane from Bangkok had been rescheduled for the following day. I apologized and they turned around and went home, a major portion of their day spent driving in Manila traffic and waiting at the PICC.

The flowers arrived about noon the next day. I opened the bag, found little hard balls, and panicked. The flower blessing dancers could not throw these hard little things onto the platform and into the audience like so many hail stones! People would feel pelted, not blessed!

A young Filipino woman in a neighboring office saw my dilemma. She said the flowers had to be soaked in water to open up. She took the bag and promised to take care of them for me, to have them opened up for the 7:00 evening performance.

The plane from Bangkok kept getting delayed. Finally, it was scheduled to arrive in Manila at 4:00 P.M., exactly the time when rehearsal began for the evening's complicated sequence of staged events. I tried to think of everything I could do by phone to assist the troupe at the airport, enabling them to clear customs and arrive at the PICC as soon as possible.

I arranged for a Lausanne II bus to be at the airport to meet them and for Lausanne II hostesses to meet and escort them through customs, help them get their baggage, and run interference for them through the throngs of waiting people inside the airport and through the throngs of determined porters outside the airport. I stayed by my phone until I got word that the plane from Bangkok had landed. Then I went to the plenary hall and asked that rehearsal plans be rearranged, putting the Thai troupe at the end.

When sixteen Thai dancers processed down to the stage of the PICC an hour later, loaded with musical instruments and costumes, I wanted to applaud. Allan told me they went through customs so fast that he had to turn around and go back at one point, because he had hurried past a necessary step in the immigration procedure.

I relaxed and joined in the mounting excitement as opening hour approached. At 5:45, a preopening session began—a session to brief the participants; introduce key personalities for the ten days, including Ken Medema; rehearse two of the hymns for the grand opening celebration; and prepare ourselves for celebrating the culmination of months of hard work by many, many people.

Suddenly, I remembered the flowers! Where were they? I had promised Allan to have them ready at 7:00! But I did not want to leave my seat! I might miss something!

Duty prevailed. Apologetically, I squeezed myself past people seated between me and the aisle and hurried through the dimly lit passageway to the doors.

At the entrance to the plenary hall the flowers met me, carried by the gracious young woman who had spent her afternoon soaking them, coaxing them to open. Their damp fragrance filled my nostrils. They truly were beautiful. Gratefully, I sent them backstage to the waiting dancers. Only a few of us knew how close we came to not having petals to fill the golden bowls that evening.

The dancers were very tired. They had been on their way since the day before when they left Chiang Mai, Thailand, at 7:00 A.M. They traveled by bus to Bangkok to meet their 7:00 P.M. departure for Manila, a flight of less than four hours. Philippine Air canceled that flight and put them up in the airport hotel, where Allan arranged rehearsal time for them that night in the unoccupied hotel night club. The next morning they got up at 3:00 A.M. in order to arrive at the airport by 5:00 A.M. for their four-hour flight which arrived in Manila eleven hours later.

Not until after the dancers had carried all their luggage and performance equipment into a room backstage, rehearsed, then got into costumes and makeup, and opened the Congress at 7:00 P.M. with the "Flower Blessing Dance" could they relax. Their performance took three minutes. The grand opening session of the Congress lasted three hours. Afterward, I waited in the lobby with the weary travelers, reluctant to leave until Filipino hosts claimed them all. It was well past midnight by the time they were settled for the night.

Caring for the troupe became a full-time job. I assigned one of my stewards, David Padil, a Filipino-Canadian, to work exclusively with them.

Finances cropped up again. The plan for them to eat at the homes of their hosts and hostesses was fine except that they got hungry during the day while at the PICC. My husband helped. When he discovered Donald McGilchrist, international director for Navigators, in the hotel, having a lunch meeting with ten other Navigators, he interrupted by saying, "Excuse me," and shared the needs of the hungry Thai dancers. Everyone gave a generous donation.

When he saw how effectively his strategy worked, he repeated it. For days, at lunchtimes and in the hallways, Ray interrupted conversations and meetings to ask for money for the troupe. He frequently intercepted me, as we hurried past each other going in opposite directions, with a handful of bills, saying, "This is for lunches for the Thai dancers." I stuffed the money into my pocket and kept going, wishing I had more hands and could keep records of all the persons helping.

Troupe members came to me asking whether the people hosting them could get day passes to come into the Congress and watch them perform. When I could not secure such permission, they arranged admissions themselves. At strategically placed entrances, they befriended guards who allowed them to escort their Filipino hosts and hostesses into the PICC.

On the final day of the Congress, I gave a thank-you luncheon for Mrs. Teh, who arranged housing, for all the Filipino hosts and hostesses, for the troupe, for the three stewards who helped me with general tasks, for David Padil who worked full-time caring for the troupe, and for Allan Eubank, their director. We put four tables together to accommodate our group.

Before leaving Chicago, I had purchased some gifts in anticipation of such an occasion. I presented, both to Mrs. Teh and to the troupe, a book of Chicago filled with full-page, colored photographs. The troupe gave black lacquer plates featuring a *ligay* dancer painted in gold. Speeches were made and photographs taken. We enjoyed leisure time together, a contrast to the frenetic pace of the last few days, and concluded with fancy desserts.

The Thai were especially intrigued with Ken Medema, amazed at the things he could do, such as listen to their exotic musical instruments, then reproduce the sounds on his synthesizer. We arranged a special time together for the troupe and Ken where he told them a story about a blind musician who came to Manila and "saw" beautiful people from Thailand dancing and making music at a large international congress on world evangelization. Ken is a marvelous storyteller. As he told the story about himself and them, what he could not see were the tears in their eyes as they listened.

On the final day, I settled accounts with the troupe bookkeeper, going over figures of the monies they needed to be reimbursed for Lausanne II expenses: bus, honorarium for driver, gas for the bus, pipe for the portable backdrops, and a bit of lunch money.

That evening I looked around in the plenary session, wondering who might be able to help with these expenses. David Weiss, an ardent fan of the worship team, caught my eye. As usual, he was down front where he could see and hear everything. I later wrote an explanation about this moment to Allan:

> David Weiss is sending a check for the balance Lausanne owes the troupe: $320 U.S. On the day I needed to find more money for you I went to David and asked whether he knew of anyone who might be interested in helping with the Thai's expenses. He asked how much money I needed. I figured it up, showed him, and he said he could pay all of it. He had some tithe which had accumulated and needed to be given somewhere. All this happened as we whispered during one of the plenary sessions. . . . I knew nothing about him except that he was a fan of all the music and drama and came to each session with his tape recorder and camera. He told me that he had come to Lausanne as a tentmaker. When I asked what kind of tentmaking he did I discovered he works as a writer for Walt Disney Productions.

I added a personal note for Allan regarding his wife, Joan, who did not come to the Congress because of the tight budget:

> I am so intrigued with the story of your taking Joan away from a career on Broadway, going with her to a Thai village and finally ending up with a dance and drama troupe. I know so few stories which combine the gospel and the arts in a mission context. I'm still trying to figure out how to find out more about this story, especially from Joan's perspective since my hobby for years has been biographies of women. . . . Thank you for all your work in bringing the troupe to be with us and for your work through the years which has resulted in this superb integration of faith and culture. Both the missionary in me and the artist in me applauds you.

Peruvian Musicians

When I began looking for South Americans to join the worship team in Manila, a group of five Peruvians continually popped up. Kerygma Canta came to my attention first through a missions event at Northern Baptist Theological Seminary. After hearing of my interest in indigenous music, Tito Paredes, of the Latin American Mission, offered to send me a tape of a Peruvian group. In July of 1988, after the tape arrived, I wrote to Tito:

> I've heard Peruvian musical groups performing as street musicians . . .
> in Stuttgart, Germany, and also in Vienna, Austria . . . which used many
> instruments indigenous to South America. I recognized some of those
> same instruments on the tape—the pan pipes in particular. . . . I'm look-
> ing for songs which are indigenous to the country.

At the same time I wrote to Samuel Escobar at Eastern Baptist Seminary:

Ray recommended you as a good resource person for music in Brazil and Spanish South America. I have not yet been beyond the border of Mexico and am very lacking in worship resources for that part of the world. . . . I wonder whether you have access to good worship songs in Spanish and/or Portuguese which are indigenous to the South American continent and not translations of imported songs. Secondly, would you be able to recommend a musical group which plays worship music in the indigenous styles, using South American instruments?

Samuel responded to both inquiries. He sent a copy of the Hispanic hymnbook used at Eastern, and he passed on the names of two groups: "One of them is linked to the AMEN mission (an indigenous missionary group). Their name is 'Kerygma.'"

He also sent me the name of Joel Sierra, a master of divinity student at Eastern, suggesting he would be an excellent consultant.

Joel told me about Armageddon, a musical group that performs contemporary music designed to reach students at the universities. He also told me about Kerygma Canta, a folk group that popularizes hymns from the rural areas by bringing them into city churches. He told me how to reach Marcelo Alvarado, the AMEN director for North America who lived in Pasadena and pastored the Lake Avenue Congregational Spanish Church.

I called Marcelo. He talked at length about Kerygma Canta, telling me about all five members of the group, about their songs, their instruments, their costumes, and their growing popularity as a folk group in South America. He sent me information.

I liked what I read about them in "Singing a New Song," an article from *World Christian* (March/April 198), written by Chris Christman. It explained the significance of their name and gave a short history of church music in Peru.

They formed a group and called it Kerygma Canta, after the Greek word "kerygma" meaning "proclamation" or "message," and "canta," the Spanish word for "sing." Their instruments, created from bamboo, wood and metal . . . were the instruments of the ancient Incan empire before the Spanish conquest. . . . Once the Spanish took power . . . "everything Inca was sinful. The missionaries told the churches 'Never sing popular music; it's sinful and the instruments are sinful. We cannot praise the Lord with this music.'" Hundreds of years later that attitude is deeply ingrained in the Peruvian Church. . . . "Music is the language for all people. A lot of people think American music is from heaven. They begin to spiritualize the music and the instruments."

In November, I wrote to Marcelo, inviting the group to Manila:

We are looking for groups which express the distinctive sounds of their indigenous cultures, something which seems to be increasingly difficult to find. The photos you sent, showing the group in their different costumes, are further confirmation of the diversity Kerygma has to offer. . . . Because of the limited number of slots in the program for performing groups, the Lausanne committee is planning to offer additional opportunities for ministry, such as a block of time before the evening plenary begins, informal times of playing and singing in other parts of the convention center, and ministry in a couple of churches in Manila.

In that same letter, I asked for information about Kerygma's songs:

It would be very helpful to have specific information about the songs Kerygma does such as (1) titles translated into English and a general description in English of the meaning of the words of the song; (2) time in minutes for each song; (3) similar information for instrumental music. This would enable us to put them into appropriate slots in the program or Bible study-worship times. I know this means a lot of work for you, but it would be the most meaningful and workable way for them to assist us in Manila in the official program times when they minister.

This last request was very difficult to get. In March, I wrote again:

I'll look forward to getting information about the songs. We especially need that information for a program planning meeting April 19 in Monrovia—titles of songs in both English and other language and a brief explanation of that song or piece of music.

The words for six songs arrived, the Spanish words plus the English meaning and the length of time for each.

Marcelo told me that the group enjoyed teaching their songs. That meant I had yet another musical request. Could he ask the group which of their songs they would like to teach to Lausanne II? Could he send me a tape of that music? We wanted to include all congregational songs in the hymnal.

The tape arrived with the selection indicated: "Perseveremos," a Peruvian folk tune. Tony Payne prepared a notated copy of this song for the hymnal from the tape, a difficult task because with each verse the rhythm seemed to be a bit different. He also prepared the English text and titled it "Persevere, My Brothers."

I asked for the names of the musical instruments they would bring, which I saw in the photographs Marcelo sent:

Bombo (a large drum)
Quena (a flute)
Zamponas (pan pipes)
Charango (a small guitar)

They would also bring the familiar Spanish folk guitar.

Their costumes reflected three cultures: the ancient Inca heritage and the Indian tribal identities of both north and south Peru.

The members of the group lived all over the Western Hemisphere. Jorge Robles lived in Puerto Rico, Lizardo Amaya in New York, Alberto Garces and Fernando Careca in Peru, and Wilmer Villacorta (who would substitute for Aristóteles Melgarejo) lived in California.

The ad hoc committee asked Kerygma to signal the end of coffee break each day. The morning plenary sessions went from 9:30 A.M. to noon. At 10:30, the coffee break gave people a chance to move out into the halls. The sound of Kerygma Canta at 10:50 signaled the end of the break, giving people ten minutes before activities on stage resumed. Kerygma's picturesque costumes and instruments and their highly energetic music seemed well suited for this. This would give them a slot of approximately eight minutes each day in the plenary hall.

On day three following coffee break, they were scheduled to introduce "Perseveremos" and lead the Congress in singing it both that day and day ten. In addition, they were given an evening concert time on day two. I invited them to be strolling musicians in the reception hall as they wished. At such times they could sell their tapes.

They arrived minus two members. The committee postponed their concert on day two, waiting for their delayed partners. Day after day passed. Alberto and Fernando did not arrive. Wilmer and Jorge and Lizardo continued as a trio through the end of the Congress. With all the people coming to Manila, this sort of disappointment was probably inevitable. I could be thankful that all the others in the international worship team arrived safely.

After the Congress, Wilmer, who was the most fluent in English, kept me informed about the difficulties. At my request, he sent a written explanation of what happened, enabling me to fit all the pieces together.

> July 7: Lima, Peru. Alberto Garces and Fernando Careca boarded for a flight to New York where they would connect with the other three Kerygma members and all fly together to Manila. As the plane prepared to leave, customs officials and airport police got on the plane looking for drug dealers. Alberto and Fernando were taken off to be searched and questioned. They missed the flight.
>
> July 8: Alberto and Fernando went to the airport in Lima once again. They made sure there would be no confusion with customs officials. They departed Peru for New York.
>
> July 8: JFK, New York. Wilmer Villacorta, Lizardo Amaya, and Jorge Robles left on schedule at midnight, leaving the two unused flight tickets in New York to be picked up.
>
> July 9–13: JFK, New York. Alberto Garces and Fernando Careca waited for another flight with space for them to Manila.
>
> July 13: They flew to Taipei and waited standby for a flight to Manila.
>
> July 15: Taipei. After waiting for ten hours, they gave up and returned to New York.

I rejoiced over their flexibility and inventiveness and their refusal to let this discourage them. In August, I wrote a letter to Marcelo Alvarado:

> Finally I got to meet Kerygma Canta! Three of them, at least. Wilmer and Lizardo and Jorge. Their playing and singing made a wonderful addition to the music at Lausanne II. Their colorful costumes were enjoyed by all except those sweating inside them. It was very hot in Manila. . . .
>
> I apologize that I could not help Kerygma in Manila as I ought to have. There were so many musicians and so many problems to solve. I was very grateful for the way they took charge of their own problems.

An unexpected problem, concerning the tapes they brought to the Congress, came to my attention when I received a copy of the letter written to Ed Dayton by Virgilio (Ver) Enriquez, associate director of operations for the Congress:

> Mr. Wilmer Villacorta, upon the request of Mr. Marcelo Alvarado, has hand-carried 999 missionary musical tapes to the Philippines for the Lausanne II in Manila Congress. In response to Mr. Bill Ditewig's request to help get these tapes through customs without duty, we have filed a Re-exportation Commitment with the Bureau of Customs. This means that Mr. Villacorta will have to bring the tapes out of the country after the conference.

The problem is that the tapes have now been distributed to various people in the conference and will no longer be brought out of the country by Mr. Villacorta. This means that we would have to pay the Bureau of Customs a total of P4,129.50 [$148.75] for Customs Duty and Taxes, as indicated in the enclosed Re-exportation Commitment Form.

The question, simply, is who will shoulder this expense? Mr. Bill Ditewig has asked me to refer this matter to you for decision-making. I would appreciate hearing from you as soon as possible so that we could settle things with the Bureau of Customs.

Ed wrote a response on the corner of that letter: "Ver—Charge it to program."

The magnitude of the unexpected overwhelmed many of us. Ed took it all in stride. I lamented my lack of experience. Had I known, I could have avoided this predicament by telling them to leave the tapes at home.

I wonder, if I were to be program associate for worship another time around, now experienced in anticipating problems, would there be yet other surprises?

Contemporary Youth Choir

King's Kids International (KKI) sponsored a group of children and young people to come and participate in the Congress program. Dale Kauffman selected thirty-six youth from twenty-two countries, ranging in ages from five to nineteen years old. Eight staff came, including choreographer Wynne Stearns from Glasgow, and one parent with each child under ten years of age. They arrived in Manila two weeks before the Congress began, to get acquainted and begin their training.

Nick and Mary Schreifels, Youth With A Mission (YWAM) missionaries in Manila, hosted the group, arranging for them to live at the University of Life and eat Filipino food. Each morning, the group attended classes, learning about their relationship to God, their relationship to other people, and how to share their faith with strangers. Afternoons, they learned the songs and choreography they would present to the Congress.

This intense commitment comes from believing that children and young people who want to serve God do not have to wait until they are

131

grown. They already are effective communicators to people of all ages. Every summer, many teams of King's Kids International gather in various cities of the world to train, pray, and minister as God leads.

Their presence attracts attention in high places, and they often receive invitations not normally extended to adult evangelists. While in Manila, they ministered to senators in the Philippine Senate and to generals and other high-ranking officers in the Filipino military at a special reception.

They were equally at home on the streets. They ministered in the red light district to prostitutes and in one of the garbage communities where families live in the middle of smoking refuse. They sang and shared their faith, and mixed with their audience, meeting people and praying with them. It worked. Their youthfulness, exuberance, and joy broke down barriers and won them rapport with strangers of every age and class.

On the opening night of the Congress, over two hundred young people and children, including KKI, participated in the program under Dale's direction. Four youth ran a lit torch into the huge auditorium. The torch and the youth were part of a larger project called Target 2000 Great Commission Torch Run which had begun a year earlier on Easter Sunday. At that time, Loren Cunningham, president of Youth With A Mission, and Thomas Wang, executive director of the Lausanne Committee for World Evangelization, stood on the Mount of Ascension outside Jerusalem and lit a torch. They handed it to young people who began a relay run that encircled six continents with the torch and its flame.

In a dramatic ceremony in Manila, that lit torch arrived at the Philippine International Convention Center. Four runners dressed in white shorts and T-shirts, representing the half million young people who had run with this torch, bounded down the aisle and up onto the platform. Thomas Wang, standing beside the torch he handed off months earlier, reached up and grabbed hold along with the runner. Their arms raised together, one youthful and one elderly, holding high the lit torch, symbolized the need for all generations to work together, taking the flame of the gospel to every person on earth.

King's Kids International, dressed in their national costumes, sang beautifully choreographed arrangements of "Carry the Light" and "Shine Jesus Shine." Simultaneously, with the group on stage, 225 Filipino youth moved into the darkened aisles and stairs of the auditorium, surrounding four thousand participants with music and miniature lights.

Dale handled all the details of this performance, including negotiations with the police to allow the lit torch to be carried by youth running in the street from the airport to the PICC. He arranged for live camera setups by which people inside the auditorium, watching on huge video screens, saw the runners and the torch approaching and entering the convention center.

He prepared the script for Thomas Wang to read as his part in that performance, a script which the retiring executive director for the Lausanne Committee for World Evangelization anxiously awaited as he prepared for that evening, a script which mysteriously vanished from the reception counter while Dale made a phone call, then miraculously reappeared just minutes before the dress rehearsal began. Apparently it was carried away by someone who stopped by that same counter, left a pile of things momentarily, then took everything, including the only copy of the script, off to the storage room.

All of that became part of the challenge Dale faced in working out the special program needs connected with the opening ceremony.

King's Kids International participated three times at the Congress. Sunday evening, day six, they sang and danced a medley of Jack Hayford's songs, including "Majesty." At the final closing ceremony on day ten, they joined the many others who performed for the Congress, wearing their national costumes and carrying national flags on stage.

I first met Dale when he came to meet with the ad hoc program planning committee in April, just prior to the Congress. His enthusiasm generated excitement around the table as we heard about his plan to use children and young people at the Congress. He shared his interpretation of the prophecy from Joel which describes the pouring out of God's Spirit on everyone, including sons and daughters. To Dale, the pouring out was not just on grown sons and daughters, but little ones and in-between ones as well.

My involvement with Dale focused on the choice of music for the opening processional and the closing ceremony of the Congress. Our two perspectives clashed head on. We disagreed on two matters: the use of recorded music in worship and what constitutes international music.

He and I never had a chance to discuss these issues. He sent recommendations to Ed Dayton who then sent them on to me. I responded to Ed who made the final decisions and passed word back to Dale.

Dale wanted to use a professional quality, reel-to-reel track of the hymn "Crown Him with Many Crowns" for the processional.

It will provide a majestic, uplifting opening. . . .Having used this music once before with a large group I am confident that you will be pleased with the result.

He suggested that the approximate three minutes of track could be followed by the Congress participants singing the same hymn accompanied by Ken Medema.

By the time Dale's fax arrived, a special processional had already been written for that hymn. The Filipino choir and brass group were already rehearsing it. These were the most obvious reasons why that track was not used.

The less obvious reason involved my own bias toward live performance. The influence of prerecorded accompaniment goes far beyond the brief support given to a singer or choir during a single worship service. It communicates subtle messages such as "big is better." It creates dependency on technology, diminishes motivation to learn instrumental skills, and discourages the use of indigenous instruments.

From the very beginning of my work with Ken Medema and Beverly Vander Molen, we looked for ways to avoid the popular trend of using prerecorded accompaniments. We objected to the practice of a singer coming onstage and, with the press of a button, filling the space with impressive orchestral arrangements. Part of the selection process involved finding musicians who were not dependent on that kind of support, who regularly used live accompaniment.

But elaborate choreography, rehearsed with tape, merited special consideration, a bending of the rule. The King's Kids rehearsed their stage movements with taped background. They needed that tape for their performance. Tapes needed for choreography were the only exceptions to our policy to use live music in worship at the Congress. The King's Kids performed each time with recorded accompaniment.

The second issue involved international music. In a fax sent on June 29, Dale suggested three songs for the closing ceremony of the Congress: "This Little Light of Mine," "You Are Faithful, Lord," and "Jesus Loves the Children of the World." As the congregation sang these songs, he envisioned the King's Kids, dressed in costumes from twenty-two different nations, mingling on the platform with participants also dressed in national costume.

Dale wrote, "Such a medley would strongly accentuate the multicultural expression of praise to the Lord from every continent."

The issue of what constitutes "multicultural expression of praise" was too big to get into just days before the Congress began. Ed Dayton's response focused on the commitment to using the hymnal: "We are committed to not using music that is not in the hymnal. We are also committed to not projecting words on screens."

The Kings' Kids, youth from many different cultures, represented the diverse cultures of the world in a visual way, but their choreography and music was Western and therefore monocultural.

It could be argued that their "monocultural" music has now become the music of the whole world and in that sense could be called "multicultural expression of praise." I acknowledge that American pop style can be heard everywhere, in the taxis of Cairo and the streets of Bombay, as well as in Chicago and New York. But this phenomena illustrates the multicultural audience for this music. It still remains a musical style rooted in the West and dependent upon modern technology.

At a large international gathering such as Lausanne II in Manila, people came with expectations for grand experiences they could describe in awesome detail back home. They expected Western music. They expected technology. Dale Kauffman brought the best of all possibilities together by bringing those expectations to life with children.

In August, I wrote to Dale:

> Your kids were superb. Their commitment and concentration to give their best were wonderful to observe. You are gifting them with tremendous preparation for whatever lies ahead for them.
>
> You were very gracious when the schedule for rehearsal backlogged. Everyone was. Nobody, to my knowledge, lost the spirit of cooperation needed to do what we did there at Lausanne. In the performing arts that must be some kind of a record.
>
> I never got a chance to talk with you about your effort on behalf of Lausanne. I don't know how long you had been working toward the evening of July 11. . . . Thank you for all that hard work.
>
> I had never heard about the King's Kids before working on Lausanne II. . . . They complemented the rest of the programing with their youthfulness and their energy. . . . Thanks for a job well done.

Korean Choir

The decision to locate Lausanne II in Manila gave Asians an advantage on the musical team. They were the ones who could get to Manila for the least amount of money. But out of all the Asian countries, Korea possessed yet another advantage. Its large churches had more financial resources on hand than most other churches in Asia.

An idea emerged: invite a Korean church choir to come to the Congress. Ask if the church would pay the airfares, hotel, meals, and ground transportation in Manila. A number of American musical groups had offered themselves at their own expense, but in the interests of guarding against a predominance of Western musicians, those offers were declined. The solicitation of a Korean church that would accept total financial responsibility provided an alternative to groups that could not be accepted.

Thomas Wang, chairman of Lausanne, got the idea moving by suggesting to Ed Dayton, program chairman, the excellent possibility of getting a choir from the Kwang Lim Methodist Church in Seoul. Ed wrote a letter of inquiry asking for thirty to forty choir members and explained the financial arrangement. Rev. Sundo Kim sent a prompt reply:

> We will be happy to arrange to send 40 of our men's choir to the Lausanne II Congress in Manila. However, because the men do not have a long time for vacation, they could just plan to go and stay for the first three days of the congress. We would also take care of the transportation from here and make our own hotel arrangements in Manila. If you want us to plan to do this for the three days, then let me know as soon as possible.

Thomas told me about the offer of a men's choir. My heart sank. An all-men's choir raised the gender issue. The Lausanne II planning committee had gone to great lengths to prevent Congress participants from being mostly male. It set up a quota system whereby one quarter of all participants were to be women. An all-men's choir would violate the spirit, if not the letter, of this policy. Could not women singers also come? Why did the choir have to be all men?

I protested to Thomas, "We do not want a men-only choir at Lausanne II." He agreed. He wanted to say no himself but needed to check first with Ed Dayton or me.

Kwang Lim Methodist Church continued to send inquiries to Ed Dayton asking for details of their participation.

Other things worried me. The music participation guidelines for Lausanne II requested that each group participating in the worship reflect the cultural distinctives of the home country. Those cultural distinctives included indigenous music, ethnic instruments, and national dress. The Korean church and especially its music have been strongly influenced by American church music and culture. I was fearful of this generous offer turning into a direct contradiction of Congress guidelines.

In search of advice, I picked up the phone and called Soong-In Moon, a Korean Methodist pastor in Chicago. He and I had worked together, looking for ways Koreans could affirm their cultural distinctives in worship. I consulted with him on how to negotiate Lausanne II policies with the choir from Seoul.

The next call came to me directly, from Jack Tice, missions pastor at Kwang Lim Methodist Church. I explained the need for women to be involved, not just men. I also explained how all the other musicians coming to Manila would wear national dress, sing indigenous songs in their own language, and use ethnic instruments.

Their choir, as with all other groups, would be given two different singing slots. For the first, they would be required to be culturally Korean in dress, music, and instruments. For the second, they could be as they chose. Could he help convey these policies to the church?

After several phone calls, we worked out a compromise. I would have to give up having a mixed choir of both women and men. They would agree to wear national costume, sing Korean songs in Korean, and bring two ethnic instruments: a Korean flute and the Korean drum called *chang ko*.

The committee looked for the best place in the program to schedule them and chose Sunday evening, day six in the middle of the Congress, for the choir to sing their ethnic program. On the Monday following, the choir could sing its twenty-three minute concert, with no restrictions on clothes worn, instruments used, or composers sung.

I received a fax directed to "Liaison Officer of Lausanne II" informing me of their plans to leave Seoul on Saturday, the day before they were scheduled to sing, and of their plan to stay at the Sheraton Hotel. There would be forty-five people in the choir.

In Manila, I arranged rehearsal time for them in the plenary hall and checked with security. People without official name tag bracelets were not allowed to enter the building. I talked with the guards, telling them a choir would be arriving and that I would be at the door when they arrived to escort them.

At the appointed hour, a very large touring bus pulled up at the entrance, and out stepped foty-five men all wearing identical traditional Korean costumes: white trousers and shirts belted with red and blue sashes. The performers on the ethnic instruments wore floor-length robes. The pianist, the only woman in the group, wore a traditional Korean dress.

I led them past the guards, through the main lobby, onto the covered walkway, and into the plenary hall. They followed in single file, forty-five men dressed in Korean national costume. They sang choral pieces written by Koreans, accompanied by Korean flute, Korean drum, and piano.

The next evening, dressed in Western dress shirts and ties, sport coats and trousers, they sang arrangements of American hymns in English, including "Battle Hymn of the Republic." But to my surprise, they also included some Korean music and the Korean flute. As their final song, they sang the Korean hymn in the Congress hymnal. I had requested that they sing that song in Korean, thereby introducing it to the Congress.

Upon finishing, they filed out of the plenary hall directly to the red carpeted staircase in the foyer and arranged themselves for a formal photograph, inviting me to join them. Wives who came along to share in the grand occasion took the photos. Then they left to eat their evening meal. Their short stay and lack of opportunity to experience the uniqueness of other musicians at the Congress may have prevented them from understanding my special requirements.

A conversation in Manila focused on my exacting requirements to the Korean choir. A luncheon companion questioned the appropriateness of asking for indigenous contributions from a choir that, as a rule, would not do such things in its home church. The only time Koreans wear traditional costumes to church is on Christmas, New Year's, and Korean Thanksgiving Day. Normally they wear Western clothing. Their church choirs usually sing Western music. Some of their most popular hymns are Korean words adapted to music brought by Western missionaries.

I acknowledged the possibility that my requirement perhaps made little sense to them. On the other hand, by day six of the Congress, the participants expected cultural diversity. On opening night, when even Thomas Wang wore a traditional Chinese gown, everyone recognized that multiculturalism would be an important theme at Lausanne II. If the Koreans had not appeared in national dress, with their traditional instruments, singing Korean composers, they would have been conspicuously lacking in national identity. I think people would have wondered why the Korean were not Korean. We needed Korea represented with its own unique distinctiveness.

Back home, as I prepared to write a formal letter of appreciation to the Kwang Lim Methodist Church Men's Choir, I related the story of their involvement in the Congress to Soong-In and described what they wore, which was different from anything I had ever seen him wear. He told me there is more than one Korean traditional costume. For their appearance at the Congress, they probably had all their costumes specially made by a tailor. In my letter, I thanked them for the special effort it took for them to come with national costumes. I also thanked each person in the group who had a special role.

> Please convey our deep appreciation to Song Young Woo, general manager of the choir; to conductor Baik Sun Yong; to pianist Chang Eun Joo;

to flutist Lee Chul Yee; to Kim Sung Soo, who played the *chang ko*; and to each of the men who sang for us at the Congress.

A year later, the Baptist World Alliance met in Seoul, Korea. Afterward, a report arrived at my door. It contained pictures of Korean musicians dressed in traditional Korean dress, playing traditional Korean instruments. One caption read, "Traditional Korean music and dance were presented at several sessions and programs during the Congress and women's meetings."

I wondered. If Lausanne II in Manila had not occurred the year before, would such pictures and this caption have been included in the Baptist World Alliance report? Or had the indigenous dimension of the Congress in Manila encouraged a greater use of traditional cultural expression in the Asian church?

I can only wonder.

Russian Choir

Eastern Europe was a geographical region I hoped to include on the worship team at the Congress. Viggo Søgaard, longtime Danish missionary to Asia and Lausanne senior associate for communication, sent me a letter on July 27, 1988: "You will know that Leighton Ford and I recently made a trip to the USSR and some Eastern European countries. I could envision a choir from Moscow!"

On August 31, I wrote Viggo:

Are you serious about a Slavic choir? From Moscow? Then give me something to work with in that connection. I really would like to get worship involvement from all sections of the globe and a Russian choir would be wonderful.

He sent a reply on September 20:

I do not have any specific information about the choir from Moscow, but I know that Leighton Ford heard them somewhere and that he is informed about them.

On October 6, I wrote back to Viggo:

> Leighton Ford's office says he heard of a quartet or small men's singing group. A possible contact person is Reverend Alexi M. Bichkov. . . . The Charlotte office says that letters they send to Alexi often receive no reply, so they suggest that you make the contact for me.

That same day, I called Leighton's office and received a memo in response:

> The USSR could increase its quota to Manila by making possible a musical group, but funds likely would have to be raised from outside the USSR. . . . If we can help further, please give us a call.

On November 18, I wrote to Leighton again:

> I am writing about the possibility of having a singing group come to Lausanne from the USSR. . . . Viggo Søgaard says there is the possibility of increasing the USSR participation quota through a choir. He thinks there is one in Moscow who has traveled outside the country and made recordings. A Baptist choir. I have yet to get any particulars from anyone about this group. . . . No other European group has been invited to be part of the worship.

Leighton sent a memo on December 5:

> I do not know anything about a Baptist choir. Alexi Bichkov, the Secretary of the Baptists in the USSR, did mention last June the possibility of a men's quartet.
>
> There was a large choir from the Soviet Union which sang at the Amsterdam Conference, but I think it would be totally prohibitive from the financial standpoint to bring them to Manila.

I learned that travel plans to leave the USSR often get rearranged by Soviet emigration officials. Even if we had a group ready to participate with all the necessary funding, they might encounter problems at the last minute and miss their scheduled time in the program. I gave up on a group from the USSR.

Bill O'Brien gave me a recording of a Hungarian choir and suggested I look that direction for participation from Eastern Europe. Citizen departures from Hungary were more dependable than from the USSR. But here again, I was unable to connect with anyone who could help. Eventually, all efforts to get a group of any size from Eastern Europe ceased.

When the Congress began, I learned how accurate that word of caution regarding USSR departures was. The entire delegation, from five different republics, got stuck in Moscow with visa problems. As they waited, they had time to get acquainted. By the time they arrived in Manila, on the fourth day of the Congress, they had become, in Ed Dayton's words, "a solid phalanx." Providentially, the committee scheduled Russian participation for day seven. That afternoon, as we pulled together loose ends, a spokesman for the Russian delegation suggested that they sing as part of the evening program. I listened to this suggestion with great interest, recalling my unsuccessful efforts to find a choir.

What could they sing? What did they know that would be appropriate and at the same time meaningful for the non-Russian speaking participants? A quick look through the Congress hymnal produced a hymn they all knew: "Living for Jesus, Dying for Him," presented in Russian as well as in English and written in four-part harmony, all ready for a choir to use.

That hymn, itself, is a story.

In April, after the hymnal selection committee met, I realized that we had no Russian song. The random gathering of hymns and songs failed to produce one in that language. With Russian one of the official languages of the Congress, there had to be a Russian song in the hymnal.

I called the Slavic Gospel Association in Wheaton and inquired about hymns. They told me they had several hymns which they used in their chapel services, translated into English. I arranged to pick up a copy of those hymns.

The next time Tony and I met to work on the hymnal, I gave him the Slavic hymns. Together, sitting at his kitchen table, we went through them, wishing we could choose more than one because they were so impressive.

We chose "Living For Jesus, Dying For Him." It seemed like an appropriate choice to represent the difficulties the church in Russia has experienced. We put it into our hymnal as melody only, with both the Russian words and the English translation, hoping that we were choosing a hymn well known and used by the evangelical churches in Russia.

During the course of working on the hymnal, I talked about it constantly, always open to suggestions. During such a conversation, I was told that Russians never sing melody only. They always sing in parts. I reported this practice to Tony. He added alto, tenor, and bass, which spread the hymn over two separate pages: one for Russian in four-part harmony; one for English in four-part harmony. We wanted to be faithful to Russian musical practice.

On day seven of the Congress, that hymn had not yet been used. However, it had already been scheduled for that evening. Ken planned to teach it in English. Instead, Ken accompanied seventy Russian men who sang it as a choir, thrilling people with their presence (we had all prayed for their arrival) and their fervor.

Eastern European representation in the worship at Lausanne II was God's gift. We ended up with a Russian choir without my having to do all the work of bringing a choir. They did not add to the program budget but came as participants. They sang the very hymn I would have requested that they sing, introducing it to the Congress. They sang on the very day I would have programmed them.

Their song, "Living For Jesus, Dying For Him," became one of the hymns most often sought after by people who contacted me concerning the music of Lausanne II. The memory of selecting that hymn comes back to me repeatedly. God met with Tony and me that day around the kitchen table and guided our choice.

> *Living for Jesus, dying for him,*
> *Trusting his guidance though sight is dim,*
> *May we be worthy to be his servants,*
> *Gladly forsaking all now for him.*
>
> *Living for Jesus through life's short day*
> *With death's dark shadow not far away,*
> *Not growing weary in our well-doing,*
> *Faithfully let us work while we may.*
>
> *Living for Jesus, conquering sin,*
> *Bearing our crosses, others to win,*
> *So when our journey here is completed,*
> *We may reach heaven, dwelling therein.*

Regrets

Many musicians wanted to come to Lausanne II. Some contacted me personally. Others found another person to contact me. The ad hoc committee and later the program planning committee gave me names of people to consider. I also knew people I wanted to recommend. Not all could come, but how would we choose?

From the beginning, I requested tapes from everyone recommended, feeling that there needed to be some kind of audition process. Verbal recommendations, while valuable, could not be the only factor in making decisions.

Secondly, I tried to outline the needs for the total program and avoid duplication. If we accepted all the offers of people who volunteered to pay their own expenses, we would end up with a worship team of Americans and no one else. As unreasonable as it seemed, there were times when it became important to decline offers of volunteers and instead look for people who needed financial assistance in order to come.

With these two considerations in mind, I began processing the numerous offers and recommendations that came my way as program associate for worship. In October, the ad hoc committee listened to the audition tapes I brought along. Their responses were helpful in giving me direction for the coming months of selection.

Ruth Piscopo
    The first request came as a little note attached to a publicity brochure:

    9-8-88
    Corean:
    Thomas Wang wants Ruth in the program. What do you think?
                        Gary Clark

I wrote Ruth a letter and asked her some questions:

> Would it be possible for you to send tapes and videos? I am gathering recordings of all suggested persons and groups....
>
> Could you tell us what kind of instrumentalists you sing with? As we consider soloists the accompanying needs of soloists must also be part of our planning.
>
> Could you also tell us how you use indigenous Chinese music? Do you play one of the traditional musical instruments? Do you sing any of the newly composed Chinese hymns or those using traditional Chinese tunes? What languages do you sing in?

Her husband, Rich Piscopo, wrote back:

> Mr. Thomas Wang asked Ruth to sing a year ago in Hong Kong. I am glad to be hearing from you and the Program Committee for Lausanne II. Ruth Chei Piscopo, a native of China, born in Shanghai, is a graduate of the Juilliard School in New York City. She sings in the following languages: English, Spanish, Italian, French, German and Chinese Mandarin & Cantonese. She has sung all over the world in some 30 countries on four continents. She has sung in the Peoples Rep. of China in both House Churches and Three Self Churches. . . . Ruth sings with tape background, she sings both indigenous-traditional Chinese tunes and newly composed Chinese hymns.

The ad hoc committee recommended that Ruth sing in Chinese at the Congress. I began negotiations with her to sing Chinese hymns in Chinese.

Her tape background again raised an important policy issue: Should musicians at the Congress use their own personalized tapes for accompaniment, keeping their individual identity, or should they rehearse with the small ensemble and become part of the worship team? From the beginning, I had envisioned the team approach and felt confident of the ensemble's ability to do whatever might be needed.

I wrote to Rich in November:

> Please communicate to Ruth my pleasure in having her as part of the worship team for Lausanne II in Manila. I am happy to follow through on the initial invitation of Thomas Wang and have Ruth come to sing.
>
> Her involvement should follow these four guidelines: (1) that she sing only in Chinese Mandarin and Cantonese; (2) that she sing traditional Chinese songs and hymns and newly composed Chinese hymns, not translations into Chinese of Western hymns; (3) that she forgo the use of taped accompaniments and prepare her music with the musicians at the

conference; (4) that she submit copies of her songs with English translation and approximate performance time for the program committee to use in constructing the programs.

After many phone calls and letters, Ruth was scheduled to sing on day seven of the Congress and to be part of the closing celebration on day ten. On June 3, her husband called to say that she would have to withdraw for health reasons. She was our only Chinese musician.

I wrote to Ruth and Rich in August:

> Lausanne is now over and I wished you could have been there. . . . Our Chinese representation was severely cut by the events of June in China. The 300 Chinese from the mainland did not get there. There were a few Chinese, but I never heard whether they were actually from the mainland or not. Our Chinese songs in the hymnal never got used. As music times got shortened, songs had to be left out, much to my disappointment.

Liberated Wailing Wall

The possibility of having both Jews and Arabs on the worship team intrigued me. At the same time as I was working out negotiations to have Nagieb Labeb, I pursued the possibility of inviting the Liberated Wailing Wall, a performing group connected with Jews for Jesus. I had heard them only once, at St. Albans in Oxford, England, and never forgot their spirited music with Jewish melodies, their splendid instrumentalists, their folk costuming, and their choreography and drama.

For several months during the fall of 1988, I corresponded with Jews for Jesus, a missionary organization based in San Francisco. They sent me promotional materials and background information so I could get better acquainted with the Liberated Wailing Wall. In November, I wrote them a formal letter of invitation.

In December, Jodee Steiner of Jews for Jesus wrote me expressing the concern they had over using money donated for evangelism to travel to the Philippines and minister to Christians. Ed Dayton agreed this was a serious concern. The matter needed to be resolved soon so it would not hamper their summer scheduling plans. I did not want to put them in a compromising situation. On the other hand, the worship team budget could not finance their participation.

In January, I sent a letter releasing the Liberated Wailing Wall from the invitation and thanking them for their patience as we struggled to know what to do.

Matadi Church Choir

In the summer of 1987, Ray and I traveled to Zaire to visit with American Baptist Missionaries. On a Sunday morning in Matadi, where we were guests of Martha and Leon Emmert, we observed the extraordinary skills of Lusila Katoti Nzimbu, the choir director. We asked many questions about him and learned that he had been educated in the American Baptist schools in Zaire.

Several days later, we arranged an appointment with him and inquired whether he would write some music on a commission: a cantata in French based on the Lausanne Covenant. He was very pleased. We asked that the musical manuscript be sent to us, notated in Western style notation, and that he also send a cassette recording of the cantata sung by his choir. We had some discretionary money to use for artists and from that made a down payment on the cantata. The balance would follow in two installments.

In February, the manuscript for ten choral songs arrived. The tape arrived in August. Lusila had completed the commission as we requested.

At about the same time, we got word of a choir contest in Zaire. The winning choir was to come to the United States and sing in churches across the country. In October, Ivan George, area secretary for the American Baptists' Board of International Ministries, sent word that the "sing-off" was scheduled for November 20. The Matadi choir was involved. All kinds of thoughts began whirling in my mind. What if the Matadi choir won? Could they then come on to Manila and sing the Lausanne cantata?

They lost the contest to an all-male choir from Kinshasa.

In January, I wrote to the Emmerts to ask how many singers Lusila would need to bring to have a credible choir. We wondered whether it would be possible to find the money to bring a small choir of ten plus drummer and conductor from Zaire. A major obstacle involved the matter of passports as processing took time and cost money. The Mustard Seed Foundation gave twenty-five hundred dollars for passport costs.

But all attempts to find transportation funding for the choir fell through. In May, I wrote to Lusila:

> I wish I could tell you what you have been hoping to hear. However, my news will be disappointing. No money is available to bring your choir to Manila. . . . The board of the Mustard Seed Foundation would like to receive proposals from you on ways to spend the money. It wants the money to stay there in Zaire. The board will wait for you in Matadi to

send suggestions and will then consider and make recommendations.

The choir sent proposals which the board worked through, and in October of 1989, the Mustard Seed Foundation asked that the money be released to the choir.

Faith Tabernacle Choir

I hoped to represent the United States at the Congress with an African-American church choir. In September of 1988, I asked Dale Cross of the Southern Baptist Home Mission Board what he thought of asking Calvin Bridges and the Faith Tabernacle choir in Chicago to be that choir. He agreed it was an excellent choice. I hoped his response meant some money might be available for sponsorship. In October, I took a tape to the ad hoc committee. They enthusiastically affirmed the choice.

In November, Dale cautioned me. The politics of the situation needed to be considered. The Home Mission Board could only fund projects which local people were committed to. I would have to call the Chicago Southern Baptist Association and discuss the matter. I called Everett Anthony and sent him materials on the Congress, including costs. He then asked me to consider the choir he regarded as the best in the Chicago area, the New Faith Baptist Church choir in Matteson.

The next Sunday I went to New Faith Baptist Church with my tape recorder. After that service I had two tapes of African-American choirs to compare. New Faith's choir had more polish and control. Faith Tabernacle's choir was the uninhibited folk sound of the urban black choir. That was the sound I wanted, and I tried to explain the reasons for making that kind of choice to Everett. He said he would get to work.

In April, I learned that the Home Mission Board turned down the request to help fund the choir. The dream to have an African-American church choir collapsed.

Continental Singers

In August of 1988, Ed Dayton received a memo from Ted Engstrom, vice chairman of the board for the Continental Singers.

> Ed, as you know, I am active as a Board member—Vice Chairman—of the Continental Ministries and Continental Singers.
>
> Their office called me the other day and indicated that they would be willing to have one of their Continental Singers groups share in the

Lausanne II Conference in Manila. As you may know, they performed superbly in the two conferences in Amsterdam with the BGEA [Billy Graham Evangelistic Association]. They wondered if I would endorse them to you as Program Director for Lausanne. This I do—unhesitatingly and enthusiastically!

Ed sent the memo to me. I wrote to Ted Engstrom requesting a tape. He replied, "Incidentally, these groups have sung at both of the Amsterdam Conferences of the BGEA. I do recommend them highly."

After the ad hoc committee meeting in October, which reviewed all the tapes received to that point, I wrote back to Ted Engstrom:

The worship team at the ad hoc meeting very much wanted to invite the Continentals but found themselves in the position of not enough slots to go around. With the need to represent all continents in the worship leadership and participation, we had to make some difficult choices. We decided against including the Continentals. Perhaps your office would be willing to convey our regrets and gently explain the difficulty of our situation.

I next heard from Nancy Waggoner, the Continental's director of international relations, and wrote her a similar response:

In our planning for Lausanne II, we are trying to make room for people of other countries to participate in the worship and to have each continent represented. That means the available spaces for Americans is severely limited. We regret that we cannot accept the gracious offer of the Continentals to come to Manila.

The next letter came from Ted Engstrom:

I'm fearful that there was some misunderstanding . . . since this excellent group is going to be in the Philippines at that time anyway. There would be no expense involved in bringing them from America.

On that note of frustration, our correspondence ended.

Foursquare Church of Pasadena

In March a letter came to Gary Clark from Ralph C. Torres, pastor of the Foursquare Church in Pasadena.

We would like to . . . offer some of our musicians to lead worship. We are willing to pay the airfare completely so that there would be no requirement of financial assistance in regards to the flight costs. They would come over to be in your service and to minister to the body of Christ there. Enclosed are several tapes.

Gary carried the committee's regrets to the church, saying that a small instrumental ensemble had already been chosen to lead worship at the Congress.

David Anderson

The possibility of organizing Manila concerts and church opportunities for music and drama groups coming to the Congress attracted David Anderson. He called, introduced himself, and briefly described his music ministry. He sent me a copy of the contemporary songbook he compiled to complement the official Lutheran hymnal, and tapes of himself and his wife in concert. He said he was available to do the on-site organizing in Manila for worship team ministry outside the Congress if we needed such a person.

This idea of worship team ministry alongside the Congress had been discussed for months. What about bringing in a special person to do it? I discussed it with friends whose experience I valued, then wrote a letter of regret. He responded:

> Dear Corean,
>
> Thank you for your time and consideration regarding my organizing an artistic ministry track in Manila. I'm sorry that it has been suggested that no other Westerners be brought into the planning but I definitely can understand that decision.

Thomas Eden

Tom was a personal friend whom I had hoped to include on the worship team at the Congress:

> Dear Tom,
>
> This letter is not one of my joyful ones. The ad hoc committee has decreed that I must not invite you to come to Manila. . . . There is great concern that the conference is already beginning to look too white and too Western. . . . I have been instructed to not add any more white faces. . . . The only vocalist I can look for now must be a woman—without a white face.

Bagong Kussudiardja

Bill O'Brien encouraged me to inquire whether Bagong, a choreographer known to Bill from his days as a missionary in Indonesia, would be interested in preparing a performance for the Congress. He wrote back:

> We can certainly prepare special programs both for the worship ser-
> vices as well as for performances and reflection (theological) on certain
> themes as you wish. We can easily prepare a group of 20 to 25 persons, or
> more if you so desire. We expect that you (the Organizing Committee) will
> take care of the financial needs, which will include . . .

Bill's attempts to find funding through Indonesian contacts failed.

Freddie Santos

On May 30, Mrs. Teh sent me a memo from Manila:

> GOOD NEWS: FIRST NAME headed by Freddie Santos is willing to
> present one number each day/night for free. Can you coordinate this with
> Ed Dayton to include this in the plenary program? Please let me know as
> soon as possible so I can coordinate with Freddie Santos. I believe that this
> is a blessing since these performers are first class (A-1) and they are will-
> ing to do this for free!

This came during the negotiations with Gary Granada, trying to per-
suade him to fill a very specific role on the third day of the Congress and
sing his song "Bahay." On May 25, I had sent word to Gary which removed
any possibility of having Freddie Santos: "If you are still unable to accept
the invitation, we will have one less musician. I will not replace you with
another."

Leighton Ford

The last request came on the eve of the Congress, in the departure
lounge of Narita International Airport, Japan. As I sat writing in my journal, waiting for the flight to Manila, a voice interrupted: "Excuse me, Mrs.
Bakke, but I would like to audition to sing at Lausanne II in Manila."

Leighton Ford was down on his knees in front of me. I reached for my
tape recorder, but he didn't give me a chance to audition him. He quickly
stood to his full height, out of reach of my tape player.

"If God Be for Us"

One hymn fits into this section on regrets, a hymn specially written for
Lausanne II in Manila. Ed Dayton wrote me a letter on March 30, 1988:

> There has been quite a ground swell of enthusiasm for having a
> Congress hymn or anthem. We did not do this at Lausanne '74. However,

it was done for Berlin '66. At that time there was a contest for the words, which were to be set to a traditional tune. I believe the thought probably was that it would not be possible to teach a new music score to the large group of people.

What's your thinking about this?

On April 25 I wrote:

Dear Ed,

. . . About your ideas regarding a hymn for the Congress . . . at Urbana '87 there was a special song but it wasn't successful. It was too long in my opinion, and not strong enough musically. There also seemed to be a problem in that the song leader was not interested in using the songs in the song book. . . . He did not spend much time trying to teach that special hymn. . . . A contest certainly is a possibility provided the guidelines are clear. I think many, if not most, of the best songs written today are either by a single individual or a team of persons. It may not motivate enough of a response to ask just for words. . . . The kind of music which would catch my ear in such a contest would have to be imminently singable, not long, not complex. . . . Such a simple song is the most difficult to find.

In October, a letter arrived from Robyn Claydon of Australia, program associate for women:

I have written a hymn for Manila! It is based on the major themes of Romans, the book chosen for the Bible studies . . . The hymn with accompaniment is enclosed. If you decided to use it, we would be very happy for it to be printed in the Congress program so that words and music could be taken from Manila and sung throughout the world as part of the on-going ministry of the Congress. If, on the other hand, you decided not to use it, we would not be offended!

In November, I wrote back:

Yesterday, I took it to the composition professor at Moody Bible Institute and the two of us worked for nearly an hour with the music, making some changes, simplifying the harmony and putting some boundaries around the very wide melody. . . . This coming Wednesday, I go back with the revised copy and we'll together give it another inspection. . . . Then, I will send you a revised copy.

Robyn wrote me again in February. She wanted to offer the hymn with permission to be copied. She also reported on its use:

Our school choir sang the hymn last Sunday in Chapel and it sounded great. I've heard it hummed around the school since! The girls found it easy to learn and came into the chorus each time with gusto! I'm looking forward to hearing it sung by 5,000.

When the hymnal selection committee met in April, they did not approve Robyn's hymn. It was too long and too complex. In June, I sent Robyn a fax saying that her hymn would not be in the hymnal. When we met in Manila, she thanked me for preparing her ahead of time for the disappointment.

Working with that hymn involved more than time. After one of the sessions at Moody Bible Institute, I returned to my car to find a fifty dollar parking ticket under the windshield wiper. A Street Cleaning/No Parking Sign had been attached to a fence. I am used to seeing such notices tied to parking meters or trees or street signs and never looked in the direction of the fence.

These are most, but not all, of the individuals and groups in the Regrets file. I probably spent more time with this correspondence than with letters to the people who came. I found it difficult to say no and tried to cushion disappointing news with reasons for the decision, stated as graciously as possible.

Many times, after writing a letter and setting it on the radiator in the front hall ready to be mailed, I took the dog for a walk and reflected on what I had just written. More than once, upon returning from the walk, I ripped up the finished letter and started over.

Regrets were the most unpleasant part of being program associate for worship.

AN INTERNATIONAL COMMUNION SERVICE

The program planning committee scheduled a communion service on the fourth night of the Congress. Friday night seemed a good choice. It marked the halfway point for evening plenaries. It positioned the communion into a quiet, reflective place in the schedule, several days after the exuberant opening of the Congress and several days before the celebrative closing.

Communion is always ticklish to plan when many different denominations are involved, but especially so when many different cultures, all with their own standards of appropriateness, are involved. The selection of a Presbyterian clergywoman, Roberta Hestenes, to give the communion meditation, caused problems for people coming from churches which do not approve of putting women behind pulpits. Ken Medema's contemporary musical style had the potential to create additional discomfort for those who preferred a more traditional style in worship. John Reid, the officiating Anglican bishop, was particularly apprehensive to have Ken at the keyboard that evening, perhaps not aware of Ken's versatility and ability to shape his music to fit even a traditional occasion.

As communion was served, Ken sang the short and simple Taize song, "Eat This Bread," placed in the hymnal for this time of worship. He then passed the song to each of the instrumentalists in the small ensemble. Flute and guitar and drum each improvised on that tune. When he felt that the one tune needed to be set aside temporarily, he reached back into music history for Pachelbel's Canon. As the serving of the bread and "wine" proceeded, he slipped back and forth between the two pieces of music, all the while supported and embellished by the other instrumentalists. For the postlude, following the congregational singing of "Thine Be the Glory," he improvised a fugue on that tune, using the organ sound on his synthesizer.

As a member of the ad hoc program planning committee, I worked on ideas for serving the communion and making it reflect our host country. Wearing my idealistic worship-planning hat, I proposed an active format for the service. I suggested that we move the people to the table rather than move the table (the bread and the wine) to the people.

The committee wanted the service to be efficient and quick, a considerable task when four thousand people are involved. It leaned toward the serving style which keeps people in their seats while ushers pass dishes of pre-broken crackers or pre-cut bread cubes from seat to seat, later followed by trays of miniature glasses filled with grape juice.

Moving people to the table would be neither quick nor efficient. It could be rather chaotic. There would be plenty of reflection time. The participants would watch while they waited, not beautifully synchronized ushers bringing the table to them, but people of every description taking themselves to the table, representing the Church in 170 nations. The committee discussed my plan, then put it aside and allotted twelve minutes' time during which everyone was to be served.

In retrospect, I realize we did not have access to the experience necessary to use my plan. On the other hand, we did have access to persons skilled in training ushers to serve large numbers of people quickly and efficiently.

I tried a second idea on the committee, hoping for better success. When I did some planning on location in Manila, I looked for ways to make the communion service distinctly Filipino. It seemed to me that our sacred meal together ought to reflect the place in which we were gathered.

Cristy Ticlaw, associate director of communications, told me about *pan de sal*, a soft Filipino bread. It could be made up in miniature sizes. She contacted a bakery, had a sample made up for me to take home to the United States, and asked for a price on making four thousand. The bakery quoted a price for seven thousand pan de sals, delivered: $60. This Filipino bread could be served in locally made baskets, again reflecting the local culture and supporting a local craft.

I wondered whether there was a way to use Filipino cups for the grape juice. Individual cups carved out of wood would make wonderful mementos, but even if the cost could be met, how could we serve them? Traditional trays with all the little holes for holding plastic cups would not accommodate irregular cups made by hand.

If the committee would consider dipping the bread in chalices, that would be a way to solve the problem of serving and at the same time incorporate Filipino vessels into the service. My search for locally made wooden chalices led to a young couple in the Marang Project. Teresita and Junn Sacapano had a little business producing wood carvings. They came to meet me, bringing designs for various-sized chalices.

Of all my suggestions, the only one to survive the planning discussions was the wooden chalice. The committee authorized me to order seven one-quart chalices made of acacia, unornamented. They would be placed on the long serving table as symbols of the "wine."

The next day, unexpectedly, the chalices were returned to me. The communion service had invested these simple wooden vessels with significance. They now symbolized a sacred moment in the history of world evangelization.

During the last half of the Congress, I tried to select seven recipients. Who, of all the hundreds of people who had worked to bring about this Congress, would most appreciate a chalice? I wrote and rewrote the list of seven names and looked forward to finding appropriate times when I could make the presentations.

I gave the first one to Thomas Wang, the retiring executive director of Lausanne. It had been his desire to have the Congress in Asia. For the opening-night ceremonies, he dressed in his traditional Chinese gown. Several times he mentioned to me his appreciation for the cultural diversity in the worship. I knew he appreciated the Asian pieces of that diversity.

Paul McKaughan was particularly thrilled to receive a chalice. One year before, he and his wife had sold their house and moved across the United States for him to take on the position of associate international director for the Lausanne Committee for World Evangelization. He had driven a truck with all their possessions, and Joann had followed, driving their car. He said he had no other tangible reminder of his involvement in Lausanne II.

I thought of Brad Smith for a chalice. He handled participant selection for the Congress. He worked with local nominating committees in all the countries which sent people to Lausanne II. A particular challenge involved guidelines which required that all delegations include women (25 percent). Commitment to these guidelines meant that he often ran up against the will of local nominating committees. He lost that battle in only one country.

The USSR, which had allowed only a dribble of people to attend the first Lausanne in 1974, imposed many communication and visa difficulties—so many that Brad delegated participant selection to a trusted group of international specialists on the USSR. The Soviets arrived in time to attend the communion service on day four. The Congress welcomed them with thunderous applause. Brad did not yet have their names, but they had come, seventy-one men from the USSR.

Brad spent his time at the Congress seated behind a computer and attended only one session, the last one. Afterwards, Brad told me how much he treasures that wooden chalice made by a local wood-carver. It reminds him of his role in bringing people from 170 nations to Manila to sit around the Lord's Table. While he thinks of his involvement in the Congress as a crucible, he also delights in remembering a job well done.

Bill Ditewig arranged transportation and housing for four thousand participants and hundreds of staff personnel. I took many problems to Bill during all stages of the Congress: before, during, and after. When he arrived in Manila he spent every waking moment, including many moments when the rest of us were sleeping, answering questions and resolving problems. He attended only one session at the Congress, the communion service. When I gave a chalice to Bill, he told me it would not just sit on a shelf as a souvenir. He would use it in future communion services.

Bill Thatcher supervised video productions made in advance for the Congress, produced all the plenaries, and sat in the control room wearing headphones during every session. When the Congress ended, he carried home video tapes of all the plenaries and continued working on Lausanne II. The gift of a communion chalice surprised Bill. He protested, saying that he did not deserve it. He took it on condition that anytime I needed the chalice, he would send it. It would be ours together.

Ricardo Jumawan ran the Lausanne II office at the Philippine International Convention Center (PICC) and had the herculean task of carrying out all the details of a planning committee operating on another continent. He stood in the middle when inadequate communication contributed to rising tensions between those in the United States and those in Manila. I could not find him when delivering the chalices, so I left one on his desk with a note attached.

He later told me that the use of wooden chalices, made of local acacia wood, deeply impressed him. Most churches in the Philippines use silver and gold for their communion vessels. The colonial mentality, so prevalent in his country, prefers imported materials. Wood is considered inferior. If he ever assumes leadership of a Filipino church, he would like to promote the use of wood and model the acceptability of local resources for the worship of the church.

Gary Clark set up the communion service that night at the Congress. All he had expected to do was rehearse the servers. When he arrived in the plenary hall, one hour before the service began, nothing was ready. He gathered all help in sight—the communion servers who had gathered to be coached on how to serve and the Thai dancers who were rehearsing on stage—and began setting the gigantic table. The dexterous Thai dancers filled more than four thousand tiny glasses by hand. The wooden chalice I gave Gary reminds him of their frantic, miraculous accomplishment of preparing the table in one hour's time. He had scarcely any time to give serving instructions.

Part of the delay in preparations seemed to be the reluctance of pastors in Manila to lend their silver and gold communion dishes for more than the one day. Everything had to be collected that very day, meaning that people who could have been preparing the table were stuck in Manila traffic trying to bring the dishes needed to set the table.

Had we served *pan de sal* from baskets and drunk from wooden cups, the problem of protectiveness would have been avoided. We would have eaten bread from the local bakery and purchased baskets from local artisans. We would have given the Sacapanos a larger order for wooden chalices. More than seven symbols would now remind people of that evening in Manila when they sat around the table with sisters and brothers from 170 countries.

As an American I value efficiency, but there are times when I disagree that it is the best course to pursue. Relationships are priceless and time spent around the table is precious. Efficiency often diminishes both. In my home, I set that value aside when dinner guests arrive. I revel in the enjoyment of people gathered around my table set with linens and dishes collected from various parts of the world. I would like to see churches place more emphasis on graciousness in serving communion and less on efficiency.

An extensive report on the Congress, written by a Haitian pastor in Boston, fell into my hands. It included a section on the communion service. I suspect that he spoke for many when he described his struggle. I also hope he spoke for many when he described his move toward liberation.

> On Friday the 14th in the evening, we had mixed emotions. On the one hand we were patiently waiting for the Russian brethren to arrive, but on the other hand some were wondering what it may mean in terms of our security if the people of Manila would react to their presence. We prayed silently. Soon they arrived safely and were welcomed in ovation in the midst of tears of joy from many of us. Western participants of Russian background were particularly moved.
>
> Then for some time we were disturbed by the generally unwelcome Thai dance. For me in particular, it was the first exposure to that Asian worship style, and I did feel uncomfortable. In my opinion, the whole presentation would fit well in an opera center in London, Paris, Radio City Music Hall in New York or in Hollywood where ballet dancing is usually part of the program. Little did I expect that in a worship service.
>
> On the right and on the left, people were getting upset; some sent remarks to Leighton Ford and got apologies the next day. And to make things worse, I looked at the program and saw that the next item was the Lord's Supper! I had all kinds of reflection; would taking the Lord's Supper in this context mean that I am in fellowship with those dancing Thai Christians? After all, am I really in fellowship with all these international Christians whom I know so little of?
>
> I thought of a Russian orthodox priest I had met earlier in his long black robe with a cross hanging so heavily from his neck that I felt sympathy for him. I thought of the Roman Catholic brother in the next row whom I had talked to before. I thought of the Episcopalian lady from South Africa who talked to me more about her involvement with Mother Teresa than about her relationship with Christ. And being a Baptist added to my trial when I thought of all those non-immersionists around me and of those presiding: a Presbyterian minister from the U.S. and an Episcopalian bishop

from Australia. I finally felt that I could fellowship with all of these, but not with the Thai dancers.

As the Scripture was being read, I wanted to walk out, but again the Lord encouraged me to pray; and I did. And as I prayed this thought came to my mind, "Have you ever imagined what it was like to attend a worship service at David's court? Perhaps many of those singing our beloved Psalms acted like those Thai dancers. Maybe those Thai dancers are really worshipping the Lord!"

I opened my eyes and felt I had forgiven them and was ready for Holy Communion. To my surprise, the presiding Bishop asked us to do one thing, ' "Extend your hand to your neighbor and say, 'the blood of Jesus Christ cleanses you of all sins.' " We all did and felt liberated.

The service became one of the most touching experiences in our lives, fellowshiping for the first time with the most diverse representation of the body of Christ on earth. Never to be forgotten (from "Lausanne II in Manila" by Soliny Vedrine, pp. 7–8).

CONCLUSION

A lot happened during the year I was program associate for worship. My work space, a desk in our guest bedroom, soon could not handle the enormous paperwork generated by producing a hymnal and organizing a worship team. It became an office with a bed in it, barely visible under overflow from the desk.

In April, my husband suggested making a little room in our attic into my office. So in addition to everything connected to the Congress, we welcomed a building crew and watched our attic gradually transformed into living space with an office just for me. That is why my husband was painting a ceiling that night in June when I started my foray into the State Department.

The kitchen ceiling of our hundred-year-old Victorian house was about to fall in on us. That same building crew removed the ceiling, tiled, and installed new light fixtures. All of this justified a change in the dismal wallpaper inherited from former owners nearly ten years earlier. That is why, when Steven called from Ghana, I was pulling old paper off my kitchen walls. Before leaving for Lausanne II in Manila, my husband and I had a gigantic housecleaning job to finish.

I switched hats often and quickly from the time I was appointed program associate for worship (August of 1988) until the Congress finished in July of 1989. I cannot remember ever working as hard and as intensely as during that year. There was no time for reflection.

Now, four years later, I do have the time. I can ask questions such as, Why did no one, apart from the World Council of Churches, do anything like that before? How was I able to do it? What did I learn that is important for worship in the future?

In retrospect, whenever I think about the first question, I always think about remodeling the two bathrooms in our Victorian house. When we bought it, they were the most awful bathrooms I had ever seen, but they were part of what sold me on the house. We could rip them out with no guilt and redesign the spaces to stylistically fit our vintage house. The possibility caught my attention.

Years later, when we finally had enough money to do the job, we had no models. All other Victorian houses seemed to have modern bathrooms totally out of character with the rest of the house. Nevertheless, I tenaciously stuck to the possibility. Those rooms are now finished, within stylistic hailing distance of the rest of the house. But now I know why nobody else does it. It is very hard to do.

I think I know why nobody had ever before designed international worship to reflect eight regions of the world at a Lausanne-type gathering. It is very hard to do! I did not know how hard when I started, but I was hooked on the possibility. If nothing else, I would die trying. Harold Best's Abrahamic model perfectly fit what lay ahead for me: stepping out into the unknown and following God's call, not knowing where it would lead.

There is also a second answer to why never before. Truly representative international worship may not have seemed important to groups outside the World Council of Churches. The dominant group in any gathering generally plans for its own interests and needs with little regard for the others. International gatherings are planned and funded by Westerners who are the dominant group–if not in number, in power. They plan for themselves, assuming that minority groups will fit in somehow.

The story my husband related about an encounter with a German participant at Lausanne II illustrates. The German complained that the hymnal had only two German hymns. My husband pointed out the justice of that number by comparing the number of Germans in the world population to the number of Chinese, who had only three songs in the hymnal. If anyone was under-represented, it was the Chinese.

How was I able to plan international worship as I did?

The shortest answer here is because I was a Westerner. I had access to technology: phone and fax and Xerox and computers and a city with all the foreign-language resources needed. I had access to a network of capable people around the globe. They made suggestions. People whom I had never met answered their phones to find me asking for help. They gave me their trust and their cooperation.

I also learned that a committee of one is a very efficient committee.

Whenever there is a bottleneck, it can be easily found by simply looking in the mirror. While I carried all the work of organizing the worship team, nobody got in the way of doing the job. Committees seldom work that smoothly and that quickly.

What did I learn about worship which has implications for the future?

First of all, I learned that Westerners must give a giant helping hand to non-Westerners. For instance, we must be willing to take the time to find hymns and songs from other cultures and translate them into our languages so they may be shared outside their culture. They will not come to us for this help because they are minorities seeking to find their place within a powerful and dominating majority. We must go to them.

They are coming to our churches, seeking to become part of our congregations. The task of finding their music may be as easy as arranging a conversation. The Western church is becoming increasingly multicultural, and hopefully the worship will catch up with the reality. Secondly, I found many Westerners eager to use non-Western hymns and songs. My phone rang many times with inquiries about using some of the ethnic songs in the hymnal, especially three of them: the Russian hymn, "Living for Jesus"; the Arabic song, "Bless the Lord"; and the Brazilian song with Spanish text, "Cantad al Senor." None of us on the hymnal selection committee knew those songs. We chose them because they seemed like good ones.

Thirdly, Tony and I decided to place the original language first in each song we used, and the English translation or paraphrase second. As we maneuvered unknown language symbols into place below melody notes, we discovered the beauty of non-Western scripts. Our appreciation for Asian calligraphy grew and grew.

Now, as I turn the pages of an Asian hymnal with all the languages romanized and transliterated, I reaffirm our decision. Removing Asian language script and replacing it with phonetic sounds in the Western alphabet seems to produce a language diminished in both directions. Westerners approximate sounds disconnected from meanings. Asians puzzle over transliterated texts representing their own language.

The visual distinctives of other languages, along with melodic and rhythmic distinctives, are part of the diversity of the Church at worship. I want to continue to support that diversity. Even though it makes the task of editing hymnals more difficult, the result is more satisfying and, I think, more useful.

I remember purchasing my first Chinese hymnal in Hong Kong. I stood in the shop admiring the characters, preferring the Chinese over the English because of its exquisite calligraphy, but making the practical decision to get the English-language edition. The best of both worlds, for me as a Westerner involved in the music of the Church around the globe, is to have understanding joined with beautiful non-Western script in the same worship book.

A fourth result of my work reaffirms the necessity of continuity between the contemporary Church and the Church of the past. In many churches today, discontinuity is preferred and practiced. Traditional worship is viewed as irrelevant. But contemporary churches are not an altogether new breed. They are part of the universal body of Christ which is now centuries old.

Part of the task of worship leaders is to balance between the new and the old, ever looking for ways meaningful to the congregation but at the same time retaining links with the historic Church that kept the faith and passed it on.

When comparing *Aleluya* with the first songbook for worship printed in the United States, *The Bay Psalm Book of 1640*, and the songbook prepared for Dwight L. Moody's revival meetings in Scotland in the 1870s, I was delighted to discover that all three books had one hymn in common: Psalm 100. Concern for continuity was one of the reasons why I included that hymn, with its archaic English text, in *Aleluya*.

A fifth thing I learned is that the Abrahamic model has rewards. The adventure, learning, new friends, and delightful surprises of my intensive eleven months surpass anything I might have imagined. To anyone hesitating about following God's call into the unknown, I would extend my encouragement to go. It will not be easy, but it will be fun and challenging, and unlike anything else you have ever done before.

Lastly, there still is a need to make multicultural hymnals and distribute them widely. There still is a need to teach worship leaders that just one model, just one style of worship, just one kind of song, is inappropriate for our mixed-up world where monoculturalism hardly exists anymore.

Two years after the Congress I experienced the same kind of worship which had propelled me into international worship. Unlike the first encounter, when the frustration had energized me through the most labor-intensive year of my life, this experience saddened me.

It happened at the Juniper Tree, a guest house for missionaries in southern Thailand. I was there to research a writing project. Many of the missionaries were from Norway, Denmark, and Finland. Exhausted from coping with devastating floods in Bangladesh, they were on holiday. Few were fluent in English.

I joined the group for a Sunday evening service. A worship leader from England, assisted by a guitarist, led singing using words-only books. All the songs were in English and seemed to be British. I did not know them but did recognize a few of the composers. The worship leader did not invite the Scandanavian group to sing any of their own songs.

Juniper Tree needed an international hymnal. I wish I could have recommended *Aleluya*, but there were no more copies.

The remaining loose end in my story is the doctor of ministry program I started just as plans for the Congress solidified. I took only one course, after my appointment to be program associate for worship, and from there on gave myself 100 percent to my volunteer job.

In the fall of 1989, after the Congress was over, I returned to Chicago Theological Seminary and buried myself in course work. All of us in the doctor of ministry program were required to design a ministry model involving us and describe and critique it in a professional paper. I titled mine "Music Leadership for a Global People." It was about the worship at Lausanne II.

On June 2, 1990, at the worship service which was our graduation, Bill Myers, who directed the doctor of ministry program and who had assisted me in shaping my paper, gave a charge to the graduates. I heard it as though it had been written specially for me:

> Class of 1990—your talents, your gifts, your multiple areas of study, and your diverse ministries span the world. As you go from this place, I would charge you to remember. I would charge you to remember the One who gifts you; to remember the One who has called you and who has sustained you to this time and place; to remember the One in whose image reside your considerable talents and vocations; I would charge you to remember whose you are. This will not be easy.
>
> And, remembering whose you are, tell the story. I would charge you to tell the story. There is a claim on you. You are a called people. The One who says "I am" claims you and calls you into story. Tell the story. But do not tell the story until you first listen. Listen. Sometimes we get ahead of ourselves and we gallop into the fray, messianic messengers armed with misplaced wisdom, and we forget to listen. I would charge you to listen. Listen—to those who chortle, whose God is arrogance and power. Listen—to the ones who cry out (whose brotherhood is pain); listen to the

ones who cannot find the words (whose sisterhood is sorrow)—listen . . . and remembering whose you are, leaning with hope into the future, tell the story. This will not be easy.

Nevertheless, I would charge you to embody these words—I charge you to go forth from this place singing. I charge you (listening and remembering whose you are) to be God's song wherever you find your-self . . . to be God's story with every talent; with every thought; with every gift; with every bone and sinew; with every vision; indeed, with all the sweat you can muster—be God's song. I would charge you to sing with exuberance, for I believe that wherever you find yourselves, God is already there. . . . It is because God is already present that you can join with the chorus begun before your time. You are not alone in this—you are one with an ongoing community of saints. Know your song—and sing it. Even when the notes are hard to find and you think you are off key—sing.

It was, for me, like a sending forth to collect more songs, make more international hymnals, and empower more international worship teams.

My story as program associate for worship at Lausanne II in Manila ends here, but not my involvement in multicultural worship. That contin-ues.

Notes on Hymns

These notes are like a journal, recalling the purpose for which each song was chosen. In many cases, securing and preparing a song for the hymnal became an adventure in itself. Some of those stories are also included.

1. *Alleluia*

This simple little song embodied the title of the hymnal. It was one of the praise and worship songs. Because we organized the hymnal alphabetically by title, as much as possible, it came first.

2. *Father, We Adore You*

This is another of the praise and worship songs. The hymnal selection committee tried to include three categories of worship songs: traditional Western hymns, praise and worship songs, and new indigenous songs.

3. *Amazing Grace*

The hymn had three reasons for being part of the Congress hymnal. First of all, because the hymnal would have many new hymns, it was important to have some that everyone knew. Secondly, John Stott, on the fourth morning, titled his Bible exposition "Amazing Grace." His text was Romans 3:21–5:21. The participants sang this hymn that morning. Thirdly, Tokunboh Adeyemo responded to my letter, sent to all the plenary speakers requesting hymns suited to their topic, with a request for "Amazing Grace." It was sung as a congregational hymn following his message.

4. *Amen, Praise the Father*

I found this Taiwanese song in *Hymns from the Four Winds: A Collection of Asian American Hymns*, published by Abingdon Press. We included it as an indigenous song.

5. *Heleluyan*

Ted Ward suggested a native American song, even though no native Americans would attend Lausanne II. He urged symbolic action on their behalf by including one of their songs. The committee chose this Creek song, found in the new United Methodist Hymnal.

6. *At the Name of Jesus*

As chairman of the Lausanne Committee for World Evangelization, Leighton Ford gave the final address of the Congress. He requested this hymn for his topic, "Until He Comes."

This hymn appears with two tunes. The one chosen here, a stately, modal melody, is quite different from the other one written in a major key with a lilting rhythm. We chose this tune because it identifies with the majority of the world's folk music, mostly in non-major modes, and because the more sedate setting seemed more suited to the prophetic words.

7. *All People That on Earth Do Dwell*

This hymn, based on Psalm 100, includes the whole world. It is an ancient hymn, dating back to the Reformation and the reformers who adapted the Psalms for their worship songs and collected them into Psalters. As such, it provides a link between the historical Church and the contemporary Church.

8. *Bless the Lord*

Arabic was one of the official languages of the Congress. Therefore, the Congress hymnal needed an Arabic song. This one, based on Psalm 103, came to the committee through the Egyptian soloist for the Congress, Nagieb Labeb. It arrived with notation, Arabic text, and English meaning. Bob Richardson in Ammon, Jordan, prepared a singable English text. Tony and I made a few more changes.

It holds the distinction of being the only Arabic song in any of the international hymnals I have collected thus far.

9. *Blessed Assurance*

This Gospel song was selected for use on the opening night of the Congress. The announced speaker, Billy Graham, has used this song in many of his crusades over the years. For that reason, it seemed the most appropriate choice for the occasion when he would speak. Billy Graham was replaced at the last minute by Leighton Ford, his brother-in-law.

10. *Blessed Jesus, at Thy Word*

German was one of the official languages of the Congress. Originally, this

German hymn was written to be sung as a congregational prayer just before the sermon. The committee placed it before Bible study on the second morning.

11. Called as Partners

Beverly Vander Molen found this song in *A Singing Faith*. It was programmed for the session "Mandate of the Laity." Ford Madison, one of the speakers for that session, had particular concern about the choice of a song. He listened to the words read over the phone and expressed amazement over how wonderfully they articulated his vision for the laity.

We chose the Beethoven tune, "Hymn to Joy" because of its global familiarity.

12. Spirit of the Living God

This song was part of the praise and worship category, although it was written long before such songs became popular. Unlike the newer songs, it has survived the test of time. The copyright owner wanted to make sure the words of the third line were correct, since so many textual liberties have altered the composer's work: "Break me! Melt me! Mold me! Fill me!"

13. Jesus Loves Me, This I Know

The hymnal selection committee did not recommend this song for the hymnal. As editor, I wondered about putting it in anyway but did not. At the Congress, Ken Medema appropriated it at a time when nothing else fit. It truly belongs in this revised edition of the music of Lausanne II.

Tony Payne, in formatting it, discovered the Spanish and Cherokee words in the *United Methodist Hymnal*. He included them as well.

14. Children of the Heavenly Father

This song has already become what Tony Payne and I, as editor and compiler of this little hymnal, hope will happen to all the indigenous songs in *Aleluya*. This Swedish hymn, translated into English and now much used by Americans, is a gift to the whole Church from Christians in Sweden.

15. Christ, the Everlasting Lord

Bishop Shen and his wife wrote this hymn. Shen I. Fan is the chief pastor of the Community Church in Shanghai and a prominent church leader in China. His wife is organist at the Community Church. This hymn was written for the *New Chinese Hymnal* and has become widely used.

Helen Cheung, from the Chicago Chinese Baptist Church, prepared the Chinese text, translating the simplified characters used in the first edition of *Aleluya* into the more universally understood traditional characters.

16. *Come, Everyone Who Thirsts*

The Thai Troupe planned to perform a dance to a Thai Scripture song. Joan Eubank, missionary to Thailand and strategically involved with the troupe, sent me a copy of this song along with her English translation. At the Congress, we heard and saw this song presented in Thai, accompanied by Thai traditional instruments. Ken Medema led us in the English version, preserving the distinctiveness of that Asian sound.

17. *Come, Thou Almighty King*

This hymn was chosen as one of the traditional Western hymns known around the world. Having this type of hymn in the book helped temper the many unknown songs newly translated into English.

18. *Crown Him with Many Crowns*

The opening ceremony used this hymn, first of all as a processional for the Filipino choir, then as a grand congregational hymn, drawing everyone into song. We included the Spanish translation of this hymn found in the new *United Methodist Hymnal*.

19. *Cantad al Señor*

Lorraine Florindez learned of my need for Spanish songs and sent some selections from her collection. This Brazilian tune with Spanish words caught our attention. Out of space consideration, we omitted two verses. It became a favorite song at the Congress.

Since then, I have discovered that this song was originally Portuguese. In this revised edition, all five verses are included in three languages: Portuguese, Spanish, and English.

20. *Forgive Our Sins As We Forgive*

We tried to avoid unknown Western hymns. This hymn is an exception.

We needed a corporate prayer of confession for the communion service, something people could sing or listen to or read. These words fit perfectly.

The tune, a traditional American melody, appears in hymnals both in duple and triple meter. We preferred the triple meter. It gives this hymn a distinctiveness in keeping with other songs in this collection.

21. *In My Life, Lord, Be Glorified*

This is another praise and worship song. I first heard this song at Saint Paul's and Saint George's, an Episcopal church in Edinburgh, and wrote it down in my travel journal.

22. Eat This Bread

Having never before edited a hymnal, I did not realize the implication of preparing a manuscript in Chicago, then sending it off to the Philippines for publication. International copyrights had to be secured, not always from the same publisher as the one holding publishing rights for the United States.

Not until after the manuscript left did I discover I would need to contact Taize in France for permission to use this song.

23. God So Loved the World

This song was one of the few instances when, as I looked through the *New Chinese Hymnal*, I knew what the text was. It appeared along with a biblical reference: John 3:16. The committee that put this hymnal together sent out an appeal for texts suitable for traditional Chinese melodies. Many of them, as this one, were Scripture songs.

24. God So Dearly Loved the World

French was an official language for the Congress. Tony Payne discovered a Scripture song, John 3:16, written by Pierre Lachat and used at the Billy Graham Paris Crusade in 1986. Tony made an English translation. We scheduled this song for the opening session of the Congress at which Billy Graham was scheduled to speak. The Filipino choir sang it in French. Everyone was invited to sing along in either French or English.

The English for this edition has been revised.

25. The Steadfast Love of the Lord

This is another praise and worship song. These short songs occupied an affectionate place in the worship at Lausanne II.

26. Rain on Us Your Word

Japanese was one of the official languages of the Congress. The random selection of hymns to be considered for this international hymnal failed to produce a Japanese hymn. As with some of the other official-language hymns, the search became intentional.

Remembering the Japanese hymnal on my shelf, given to me years ago by a student, I looked for something we could use, focusing on the music because I do not know the language. After selecting a few possibilities, I began looking by telephone for a Japanese-American who could assist me in choosing. With the assistance of several people, I was guided to a Presbyterian pastor. When I told him I had a Japanese hymnal, he said, "Is it the one with the brown cover?" It was. We could discuss the choices by page numbers.

After making a selection, he recommended a translator, an American fluent in Japanese. Because of the shortness of time, Gilbert Zinke read the translation to me over the phone from his computer screen. Pastor Satoh assisted in contacting the hymnal committee of the United Church of Christ of Japan for permission to use this song.

Several months later, I discovered the same hymn in the new *United Methodist Hymnal*, titled "Send Your Word," translated by Nobuaki Hanaoka. It confirmed our discovery that translation *into* one's native tongue, rather than *out of it* into the new language, is better.

With hopes for improving the English text of this hymn for the second edition of *Aleluya*, Gilbert supplied me with a literal translation of the Japanese. He also gave me several pointers on the distinctiveness of Japanese poetry which helped to clarify the difficulties of translating this hymn into English.

On a bright, cold, snowy morning, I walked to Sharon James-Ledbetter's home with all the resources I could bring together for her, including a book of poetry written in English by a Japanese poet. All day long I prayed that God would supply Sharon with the appropriate words and poetic structure to make this hymn meaningful in the English language.

She called that same evening to say it was all finished. In an astonishing way, the English translation embodied the spirit of the hymn itself. God provided the words.

27. *He's Got the Whole World in His Hands*

After tentatively selecting all the songs and hymns for the hymnal, I showed the list to James Correnti. He observed that it had no African-American spiritual. We chose this one for its global perspective.

28. *O Come, Let Us Adore Him*

This simple song was chosen to augment the praise and worship category.

29. *Jesus Is Alive Today*

Ken Medema wanted to have a Swahili song in the hymnal. Roberta King, ethnomusicologist in Africa with the Conservative Baptists, gave me this song.

30. *Jesus Shall Reign*

Leighton Ford recommended this hymn. It was another of the traditional Western hymns well known around the world and appropriate for the Congress.

31. *Jesus, Name above All Names*

This is another of the praise and worship songs.

32. I Love You, Lord
   This is another of the praise and worship songs.

33. Living for Jesus, Dying for Him
   Russian was one of the official languages of the Congress. In order to get a Russian hymn, I called the Slavic Gospel Association in Wheaton. They told me about a small collection of hymns which they had translated into English for use in their chapel services. They agreed to give me a copy.
   Tony Payne and I went through all the possibilities and chose this one. It brought a distinctive dimension to the hymnbook: the death of believers. We hoped it was an appropriate choice to be making on behalf of those who would come from the USSR.
   It turned out to be a good choice. The Soviets knew it and introduced it to the Congress. It became one of the most popular songs in the hymnal.

34. Majesty
   The hymnal selection committee omitted this song for theological reasons, asking this question: Do we worship God's majesty, or do we worship God? The program planning committee directed that it be added to the hymnal as another praise and worship song.
   Some tunes are perpetually sung incorrectly, and this is one of them. Congregations often stumble through the two ascending triadic melody patterns in the middle section and sing something else. When I negotiated for permission to use this song, I requested, and received, permission to edit the melody in those two places. I told Beverly Vander Molen about this change and asked her what Ken would do. She responded, "Ken will play what's written in the hymnal."
   I found a translation in German and added it. Unfortunately, the source and author of this translation got lost in the haste of putting together the first edition.

35. Praise God, from Whom All Blessings Flow
   This song was included as part of the praise and worship section of the hymnal.

36. In Christ There Is No East or West
   The words of this traditional Western hymn connected with the spirit of the Congress. Tony Payne, ever interested in improving musical settings, suggested this tune. It suited the text and the occasion admirably.

37. O God, We Thank You
   Howard Olson and I met at the World Mission Institute in Chicago. After learning of my need for Swahili songs, he sent me this one, part of his extensive collection of hymnody from East Africa. As music researcher at Lutheran Theological

College in Tanzania, he produced six different editions of *Tumshangilie Mungu*. The sixth edition, enlarged and translated into other languages, contains 152 songs, all of them with musical notation.

38. *O for a Thousand Tongues*

This is another of the traditional Western hymns known far and wide.

Joni Eareckson Tada, one of the plenary speakers, responded to my request for relevant hymns by requesting this one. She wanted two verses in particular. She sent a copy of the hymn, with those verses underlined, to make her request clearly understood. We found a Spanish translation of all six verses in the new *United Methodist Hymnal*.

At the Congress, this hymn was used as a congregational response after Joni finished speaking.

39. *Holy, Holy*

The committee chose this song for the praise and worship category. Theological concerns were part of the selection process. We liked this trinitarian text.

40. *The Trees of the Field*

The program planning committee chose this hymn to close both halves of the Congress: the communion service on day four and the closing ceremony on day ten. We anticipated those closures as times of celebration and joy. For totally unrelated reasons, it was used neither time.

41. *Praise to the Lord, the Almighty*

This praise hymn is widely known as a traditional Western hymn. It is originally German and so it met our need for another hymn in one of the official languages.

42. *Perseveremos Hermanos*

Kerygma Canta, the Peruvian musical group, sent a recording of this song so it could be included in the hymnal. Tony Payne transcribed the music and made a translation. When Kergyma Canta taught this song at the Congress, people opened their hymnals for extra assistance in learning it.

43. *Our Cities Cry to You, O God*

When I gave my husband, Ray Bakke, the letter requesting a hymn for his plenary on urban evangelization, he responded by sending out his own letter asking for urban hymns. This hymn marked the end result of considerable searching. Its inclusion in the second edition of the hymnal generated another kind of search.

44. Seek Ye First

This Scripture song is another of the praise and worship songs.

45. Send Me, Lord

We included this as an indigenous song from South Africa. It embodied the missionary spirit so much in evidence at the Congress.

46. Since the Lord My God Has Called Me

I asked friends in Chicago for a Korean hymn. This is the one they suggested, saying it is a very well known hymn in the Korean church. The music is stylistically Western, although written by a Korean.

47. Do You Love Him?

Roberta King, ethnomusicologist and missionary with the Conservative Baptists, gave me this Nigerian hymn. She transcribed it.

48. Spirit Lord We Pray

This song mixes two cultures together. The tune is Japanese; the text is Chinese. In addition to needing songs from both of these countries, we needed songs about the Holy Spirit. It was one of the hymns we sang in the session which focused on the Holy Spirit.

49. Bound Together

This song was not included in the first edition. It appears here because, as editor, I wanted to use the leftover space available on one of the pages.

Ken Medema used this song in the introductory session of the Congress in which he was introduced and in turn introduced the hymnal, the flutist, the guitarist, and the drummer. He announced that we were going to practice and asked everyone to stand. As four thousand people waited expectantly, he sang—and the drummer echoed—a musical explanation of who we were and what we were about to do:

> *From all around this world we've come,*
> *from places that we call our home,*
> *commanded by our God to sing,*
> *our praises now we gladly bring.*
>
> *These songs we sing are not the same,*
> *but each one praises Jesus' name.*
> *In different styles and different songs,*
> *let everybody sing along.*

This tune led into "Aleluya," sung by everyone. Later in the Congress, the tune reappeared with different words:

Bound together and
finely woven with love.

These few measures are from Ken's longer song, "Bound Together." With his unique leadership, he used this little tune to begin the worship experience of a global people at the Lausanne Congress for World Evangelization.

50. *Lord, Have Mercy*

This song comes from Bali. One member of the worship team came from Bali. It was especially meaningful to me to have his culture represented in the hymnal.

51. *The Church's One Foundation*

This is another of the traditional Western hymns known to many, the category of hymns which we consciously tried to put boundaries around in order that there be room for praise and worship songs and indigenous hymns. The committee scheduled this hymn for the second evening of the Congress, during a plenary titled Primacy of the Local Church.

52. *Come, Visit Your Church*

Portuguese was one of the official Congress languages. This hymn came through Art and Sue Brown, former missionaries to Portugal. Sue related how their church members had bonded with this minor melody from the Western church. She also warned me that the words in Portuguese differ from the words usually associated with this tune in English. From Sue's literal translation, we worked to make a singable set of English words.

53. *Thine Is the Glory*

David Penman wrote me a letter requesting this hymn in connection with the morning Bible studies he would lead. We put the hymn into the book but used it, instead, for the closing hymn of the communion service.

54. *When I Survey the Wondrous Cross*

The hymnal planning committee wanted to include a well-rounded choice of hymns for the Congress, hymns which covered all the main theological themes related to evangelization. It chose this passion hymn from the Western church to fill a significant niche in the theology of the hymnal.

55. We Are Marching in the Light of God

This is another of the indigenous South African hymns. After months of negotiation to obtain permission for reprinting, the matter was settled on the second
day of open elections in South Africa in May of 1994. The agreement came as a welcome and uniquely timed resolution to apprehensions over whether the South
African songs would be available for the revised edition.

56. What Can Wash Away My Sin?

This simple American hymn had a very tenuous place in the hymnal right up
to the end. I wanted to omit it. Not until Beverly Vander Molen did a final hymnal
content check with me, the night before going to the printer, did I put it back in for
keeps. She reminded me that unless we had that hymn, we had a serious gap: no
hymns about sin, an important subject at the Congress.

57. Speak My Heart

This song is from a collection of Khmer hymns used for worship in the
Cambodian refugee camps in Thailand. After seeing the horror portrayed in *The
Killing Fields*, a movie about Cambodia, I wanted to include one of these hymns in
its original Cambodian script. The Cambodian congregation at Uptown Baptist
Church in Chicago gave me this one written in a Khmer refugee camp by Sarin
Sam. Gioia Michelotti, fluent in Cambodian, supplied the English translation, and
John Ellison, a returned missionary, hand-lettered the ornate calligraphy used in
the first edition of *Aleluya*.

The meager supply of words—many more notes than words—and repetitious
structure of the verses in the English version seemed awkward to those of us forced
to ignore the Cambodian and sing only in English. After various attempts to add in
more words, and after a letter arrived from the composer requesting the assistance
of a poet to restore the fourth verse to its original meaning, I gathered the resources
and went to see Sharon, my poet friend. It was a Thursday evening and she had
just tucked her three children into bed for the night.

Sunday afternoon she arrived with a new translation of all four verses, explaining that she finds it impossible to do anything other than start at the beginning. She
had written while waiting in her car for red lights to change to green while sitting
in the lounge at church that morning during the second service, and while watching her children play in the park following lunch.

With her baby sitting on the floor, and her two daughters making themselves
peanut butter and jelly sandwiches at one end of my kitchen table, and my dog and
cat curious about all the commotion and new people, we sat together at the other
end of the table and sang her new words. The chaos and noise which gave birth to
this new translation is certainly only a fraction of that which surrounded Sarin Sam
as he wrote this hymn.

58. What Service Can I Do?

This Tagalog song, written in the language of our hosts in the Philippines, came to me from Melba Maggay, director of the Institute for Asian Church and Culture (ISACC) in Manila. The Filipino choir introduced this song to the Congress the first evening and repeated it the last evening. An exciting goal in revising the hymnal is to make more room for this hymn.

The paraphrase into English was prepared by poet Sharon James-Ledbetter, who had never set words to music before, and her musician friend Jackie Whowell.

59. Somos Uno en Cristo

The first time I heard this song was at Northern Baptist Theological Seminary. From that day forward, I determined to get that song. I tried writing it down, but every person who sang it for me sang it a bit differently. Finally, Lorraine Florindez sent me a notated copy from her collection of Spanish hymnody, and I gratefully discarded my attempts.

This is the only song we did not translate into English. We chose not to for three reasons. It was short, quick, and repetitive. It used words common to the historic creeds of the Church, words easy to identify. Last of all, we feared that a translation might be more cumbersome than helpful and might diminish the song's ethnic charm.

INDEX OF NAMES

Part Two
THE MUSIC OF LAUSANNE II

PREFACE

Aleluya was first prepared for an international gathering in the Philippines. It attempted to collect in one volume hymns and praise songs from traditional Western sources and from the non-Western church. The editorial committee wanted to encourage poets and composers around the globe to add their cultural distinctives to the praise and prayer of the Church worldwide.

The first printing by Overseas Missionary Fellowship in Manila provided copies for the four thousand attendees, plus an additional thousand as a special order. All five thousand were gone within a year. My carefully guarded dozen stood as a witness to the need for a second printing.

On a fall day in 1993, *Aleluya* was reborn. Tony Payne and I met with Jane Hertenstein and Pat Peterson at Cornerstone Press in Chicago to discuss the feasibility of a second edition to accompany this book. To my great delight, the consensus that day was to go ahead.

Tony wanted the second edition to reflect the greatly improved capabilities of computer programming for music production. All the pages of the second edition were prepared using Coda's *Finale* note writing software.

As editor, I wanted to remove all traces of the haste which marked our first edition and add improvements in response to comments received by those who continue to use the first edition of *Aleluya*.

Living in Chicago is a great asset in putting together an international hymnal. People of all the nineteen languages included within *Aleluya* can be found here. Friends and acquaintances gave of their time to proofread.

Everyone involved in making the first edition hoped that the music of Lausanne II would continue to enhance the worship of the Church long after the Congress in Manila ended. This second edition breathes new life into that hope.

COREAN BAKKE, editor
TONY PAYNE, compiler

1. Alleluia

Al-le-lu-ia, al-le-lu-ia, al-le-lu-ia, al-le-lu-ia, al-le-lu-ia, al-le-lu-ia, al-le-lu-ia, al-le-lu-ia.

Words & Music: Jerry Sinclair
© 1972 Manna Music, Inc.

2. Father, We Adore You

Fa - ther, we a - dore you,
Je - sus, we a - dore you, lay our lives be -
Spir - it, we a - dore you,

fore you: how we love you!

This may be sung as a three-part round
Words & Music: Tony Coelho
© 1972 Maranatha! Music (Administered by The Copyright Company).

Amazing Grace

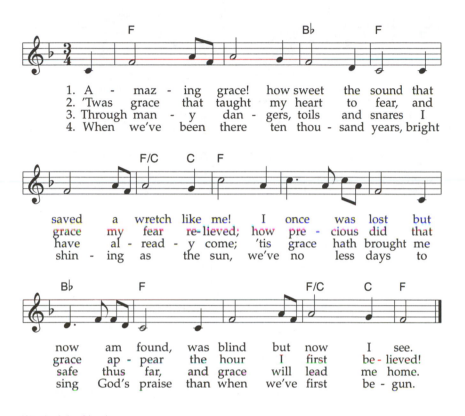

1. A - maz - ing grace! how sweet the sound that
2. 'Twas grace that taught my heart to fear, and
3. Through man - y dan - gers, toils and snares I
4. When we've been there ten thou - sand years, bright

saved a wretch like me! I once was lost but
grace my fear re-lieved; how pre - cious did that
have al - read - y come; 'tis grace hath brought me
shin - ing as the sun, we've no less days to

now am found, was blind but now I see.
grace ap - pear the hour I first be - lieved!
safe thus far, and grace will lead me home.
sing God's praise than when we've first be - gun.

Words: John Newton
Music: *North American*

4. Amen, Praise the Father

1. A - men, praise the Fa - ther; a - men, praise our Mak - er;
2. A - men, praise the Son; a - men, praise our Sav - ior;
3. A - men, praise the Spir - it; a - men, praise our Teach - er;

a - men, a - men. A - men.

Words & Music: Leng Loh
© 1983 by Leng Loh.

5. Heleluyan
Hallelujah

He - le - lu - yan, he - le - lu - yan;
Hay - lay - loo - yahn...

he - le, he - le - lu - - - yan;

he - le - lu - yan, he - le - lu - yan;

he - le, he - le - lu - - - yan.

Words & Music: *Creek, native American*
Music Transcription © 1989 by the United Methodist Publishing House.

At the Name of Jesus 6.

Dmin   Amin   Dmin   F   Dmin   Gmin   Dmin

1. At   the Name of   Je - sus,   ev - 'ry knee shall   bow,
2. Hum - bled for   a   sea - son,   to   re - ceive a   Name
3. Bore   it   up   tri - umph - ant   with   its   hu - man   light,
4. Name him, Chris - tians, name him   with love strong as   death,
5. In   your hearts en - throne him; there   let   him   sub - due
6. Chris - tians, this Lord   Je - sus   shall   re - turn   a - gain,

F   Amin   Dmin   F/C   Gmin/B♭   F/A   Gmin

ev - 'ry tongue con - fess   him King of Glo - ry   now;
from the   lips   of   sin - ners un - to whom   he   came,
through all   ranks   of   crea - tures, to   the   cen - tral height,
name with awe and   won - der   and with bat - ed breath;
all   that   is   not   ho - ly,   all   that   is   not   true;
with   his   Fa - ther's glo - ry   o'er the earth   to   reign;

C   Gmin   C   Amin   Dmin

'tis   the   Fa -   ther's   plea - - sure   it,
faith - ful - ly   he   bore - - it,
to   the   throne   of   God - - head,
he   is   God   the   Sav - - - ior,
crown   him   as   your   Cap - - - tain
for   all   wreaths   of   em - - - pire

C   C/E   G   C   Dmin/F   C/E   Amin/C

we should call   him   Lord,   who   from   the   be -
spot - less   to   the   last,   brought   it   back   vic -
to   the   Fa -   ther's   breast;   filled   it   with   the
he   is   Christ   the   Lord,   ev -   er   to   be
in   temp - ta - tion's   hour;   let   his   will   en -
meet   up - on   his   brow,   and   our   hearts con -

Amin   Gmin/B♭   F   F/A   C   Dmin

gin - ning   was   the   might - y   Word.
to - rious,   when from   death   he   passed.
glo - ry   of   that   per - fect   rest.
wor - shiped,   trust - ed,   and   a - dored.
fold   you   in   its   light   and   power.
fess   him   King   of   glo - ry   now.

Words: Caroline Marie Noel
Music: Ralph Vaughan Williams
Music © Oxford University Press

7. Vous Qui Sur la Terre Habitez

All People That on Earth Do Dwell

G / D Emin Bmin Emin / D / G

1. Vous qui sur la terre ha - bi - tez, chan -
2. Lui seul est no - tre sou - ve - rain, c'est
3. Dans sa mai - son dès au - jour - d'hui, tous
4. Pour toi, Seig - neur, que notre a - mour se

1. *All peo - ple that on earth do dwell, sing*
2. *Know that the Lord is God in - deed; with -*
3. *O en - ter then his gates with praise; ap -*
4. *For why, the Lord our God is good; his*

G / D Emin / C G / D Emin

tez à plei - ne voix, chan - tez, Ré -
lui qui nous fit de sa main: nous
pré - sen - tez - vous de - vant lui; cé -
re - nou - vel - le cha - que jour; ta

to the Lord with cheer - ful voice; him
out our aid he did us make; we
proach with joy his courts un - to; praise,
mer - cy is for - ev - er sure; his

D G / D G/B C / D/A G / D/F♯

jou - is - sez - vous au Sei - gneur, é -
le peu - ple qu'il mè - ne - ra, le
lé - brez son nom glo - ri - eux, ex -
bon - té, ta fi - dé - li - té, de -

serve with mirth, his praise forth tell; come
are his folk, he doth us feed, and
laud, and bless his Name al - ways, for
truth at all times firm - ly stood, and

G G/B Amin/C Amin / G/D D / G

gay - ez - vous à son hon - neur.
troup - eau qu'il ras - sem - ble - ra.
alt - ez - le jus - qu' aux cieux
meur - ent pour l'é - ter - ni - té.

ye be - fore him and re - joice.
for his sheep he doth us take.
it is seem - ly so to do.
shall from age to age en - dure.

Words: William Kethe
Music: *Genevan Psalter*

8.

باركي يــا نفسي الرب

Bless the Lord

Bless the Lord, O my soul; all that is in me, bless his Name.

Bless the Lord, O my soul, bless his ho - ly Name.

Bless the Lord, O my soul, bless the Lord my God.

Think up - on his ben - e - fits, all his ben - e - fits.

He will for - give your sins, all of your sins;

he for - gives all your sins. He heals your sick - ness - es,

gives you new health; O bless his ho - ly Name.

Words: Based on Psalm 103, trans. Bob Robertson, revised
Music: Boulas Bushra, harm. Habib Bahr

باركي يــا نفسي الرب

بــاركــي يــا نفسي الــرب   وكــل مــا فــي بــاطنـــــي

ليبـــــارك اســـمــه   اسمـه الـقـدوس

بـاركـي يــا نفسي الرب   بـاركـي الـرب

ولا تنسـي كـل حسنـاته

الـذي يفـر ذنوبك، جميع ذنوبك   الـذي يشفي امراضك، كل امراضك

9.   Blessed Assurance

Words: Fanny Crosby
Music: Phoebe P. Knapp

Liebster Jesu, wir Sind Hier

Blessed Jesus, at Thy Word

10.

1. Lieb - ster Je - su, wir sind hier, Dich und dein Wort
2. Un - ser Wis - sen und Ver - stand Ist mit Fin - ster -
3. O du Glanz der Herr - lich - keit, Licht vom Licht aus

1. Bless - ed Je - sus, at thy word, we are gath - ered
2. All our know - ledge, sense, and sight lie in deep - est
3. Glo - rious Lord, thy - self im - part! Light of Light, from

an - zu - hör - en; Len - ke Sin - nen und Beg - ier
nis um - hül - let. Wo nicht dein - es Geist - es Hand
Gott ge - bor - en, Mach uns al - les - amt be - reit,

all to hear thee; let our hearts and souls be stirred
dark - ness shroud - ed, till thy Spir - it breaks our night
God pro - ceed - ing, o - pen thou our ears and heart;

Auf die süs - sen Him - mels - lehr - en, Daß die Herz - en
Uns mit hel - lem Licht er - fül - let. Gut - es denk - en,
Öf - fne Herz - en, Mund und Ohr - en! Un - ser bit - ten,

now to seek and love and fear thee, by thy teach - ings
with the beams of truth un - cloud - ed. Thou a - lone to
help us by thy Spir - it's plead - ing; hear the cry thy

von der Erd - en Ganz zu dir ge - zo - gen werd - en.
Gut - es dicht - en Mußt du selbst in uns ver - richt - en.
Flehn und Sing - en Laß, Herr Je - su, wohl ge - ling - en!

sweet and ho - ly, drawn from earth to love thee sole - ly.
God canst win us; thou must work all good with - in us.
peo - ple rais - es, hear and bless our prayers and prais - es.

Words: Tobias Clausnitzer, trans. Catherine Winkworth
Music: Johann R. Ahle

11. Called as Partners

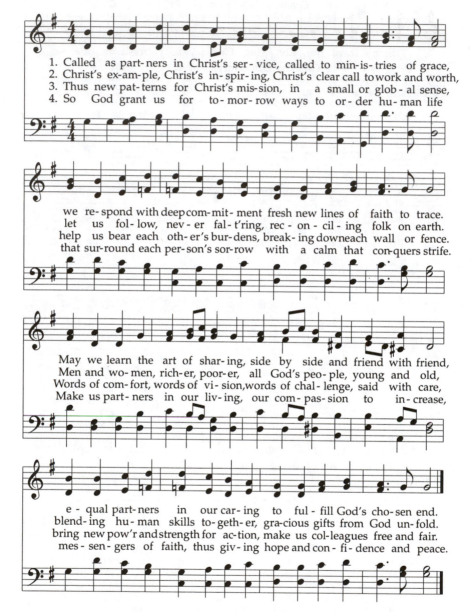

1. Called as part-ners in Christ's ser-vice, called to min-is-tries of grace,
2. Christ's ex-am-ple, Christ's in-spir-ing, Christ's clear call to work and worth,
3. Thus new pat-terns for Christ's mis-sion, in a small or glob-al sense,
4. So God grant us for to-mor-row ways to or-der hu-man life

we re-spond with deep com-mit-ment fresh new lines of faith to trace.
let us fol-low, nev-er fal-t'ring, rec-on-cil-ing folk on earth.
help us bear each oth-er's bur-dens, break-ing down each wall or fence.
that sur-round each per-son's sor-row with a calm that con-quers strife.

May we learn the art of shar-ing, side by side and friend with friend,
Men and wo-men, rich-er, poor-er, all God's peo-ple, young and old,
Words of com-fort, words of vi-sion, words of chal-lenge, said with care,
Make us part-ners in our liv-ing, our com-pas-sion to in-crease,

e-qual part-ners in our car-ing to ful-fill God's cho-sen end.
blend-ing hu-man skills to-geth-er, gra-cious gifts from God un-fold.
bring new pow'r and strength for ac-tion, make us col-leagues free and fair.
mes-sen-gers of faith, thus giv-ing hope and con-fi-dence and peace.

Words: Jane Parker Huber
Music: Ludwig von Beethoven

Spirit of the Living God 12.

Spir - it of the Liv - ing God, fall fresh on me,

Spir - it of the Liv - ing God, fall fresh on me.

Break me! Melt me! Mold me! Fill me!

Spir - it of the Liv - ing God, fall fresh on me.

Words & Music: Daniel Iverson

Jesus Loves Me, This I Know 13.

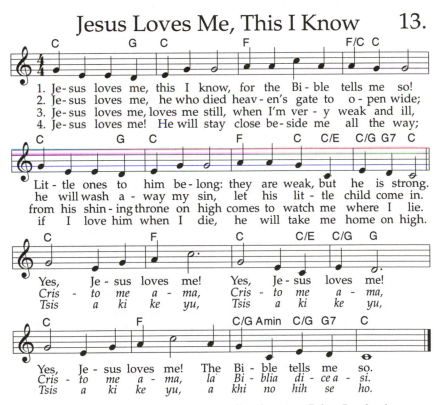

1. Je - sus loves me, this I know, for the Bi - ble tells me so!
2. Je - sus loves me, he who died heav - en's gate to o - pen wide;
3. Je - sus loves me, loves me still, when I'm ver - y weak and ill,
4. Je - sus loves me! He will stay close be - side me all the way;

Lit - tle ones to him be - long: they are weak, but he is strong.
he will wash a - way my sin, let his lit - tle child come in.
from his shin - ing throne on high comes to watch me where I lie.
if I love him when I die, he will take me home on high.

Yes, Je - sus loves me! Yes, Je - sus loves me!
Cris - to me a - ma, Cris - to me a - ma,
Tsis a ki ke yu, Tsis a ki ke yu,

Yes, Je - sus loves me! The Bi - ble tells me so.
Cris - to me a - ma, la Bi - blia di - ce a - si.
Tsis a ki ke yu, a khi no hih se ho.

Words: Anna B. Warner; Spanish trans. anon.; Cherokee trans. Robert Busyhead
Music: William B. Bradbury

14. Tryggare kan Ingen Vara

Children of the Heavenly Father

Swedish

1. Tryg - ga - re kan ing - en va - ra Än Guds
2. Her - ren si - na trog - na vår - dar U - ti
3. Gläd dig då du lil - la ska - ra! Ja - kobs
4. Vad han tar och vad han gi - ver, Sam - me

lil - la bar - na - ska - ra, Stjär - nan ej på him - la -
Si - ons hel - ga går - dar, O - ver dem han sig för -
Gud skall dig be - va - ra. För hans vil - ja mås - te
Fa - der han dock bli - ver. Och hans mål är blott det

fäs - tet, Få - geln ej i kän - da näs - tet.
bar - mar, Bär dem up - på fa - ders - ar - mar.
al - la Fi - en - der till jor - den fal - la.
e - na: Bar - nets san - na väl al - le - na.

English

1. Chil - dren of the heav'n - ly Fa - ther safe - ly
2. God his own doth tend and nour - ish; in his
3. Praise the Lord in joy - ful num - bers, your Pro -
4. Though he giv - eth or he tak - eth, God his

in his bos - om ga - ther; nest - ling bird nor star in
ho - ly courts they flour - ish. From all e - vil things he
tect - or nev - er slum - bers; at the will of your De -
chil - dren ne'er for - sak - eth; his the lov - ing pur - pose

heav - en such a re - fuge e'er was giv - en.
spares them, in his might - y arms he bears them.
fend - er ev - 'ry foe - man must sur - ren - der.
sole - ly to pre - serve them pure and ho - ly.

Words: Lina Sandell, trans. Ernst Olsen
Music: *Traditional Swedish*

基督永長久歌

Christ, the Everlasting Lord

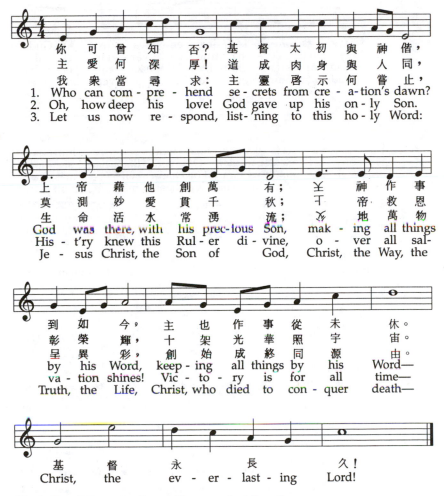

你　可　曾　知　否？　基　督　太　初　與　神　偕，
主　愛　何　深　厚！　道　成　肉　身　與　人　同，
我　衆　當　尋　求：　主　靈　啓　示　何　嘗　止，
1. Who can com - pre - hend　se - crets from cre - a - tion's dawn?
2. Oh,　how deep his　love! God gave　up his　on - ly　Son.
3. Let　us now　re - spond, list - 'ning to this　ho - ly　Word:

上　帝　藉　他　創　萬　有；　神　作　事
莫　測　妙　愛　貫　千　秋；　帝　救　恩
生　命　活　水　常　湧　流；　地　萬　物
God　was there, with　his　prec - ious Son,　mak - ing　all things
His - t'ry　knew this　Rul - er　di - vine,　o - ver　all sal -
Je - sus　Christ, the　Son　of　God,　Christ, the　Way, the

到　如　今，　主　也　作　事　從　未　休。
彰　榮　輝，　十　架　光　華　照　宇　宙。
呈　異　彩，　創　始　成　終　同　源　由。
by　his　Word, keep - ing　all things by　his　Word—
va - tion shines! Vic - to - ry　is　for　all　time—
Truth,　the　Life, Christ, who died　to　con - quer death—

基　督　永　長　久！
Christ,　the　ev - er - last - ing　Lord!

Words: Shen I. Fan, trans. Jeanne Harper, revised Tony Payne
Music: Hong Luming
Used by permission of China Christian Council.

16.

เชิญท่านทั้งหลาย
Come, Everyone Who Thirsts

Come, ev-'ry-one who thirsts, all you who

thirst, come, O come. Drink the liv-ing

wa-ter with-out price. All who thirst, who hun-ger and

thirst, come and re-ceive e-ter-nal life, e-ter-nal

life from Je-sus Christ, the Son of God.

Words: Sook Pongsenoi, based on Rev 22:17, trans. Joan Eubank
Music: *Thai*
Used by permission of Joan Eubank.

Come, Thou Almighty King 17.

1. Come, thou Almighty King, help us thy
2. Come, thou Incarnate Word, gird on thy
3. Come, Holy Comforter, thy sacred
4. To thee, great One in Three, eternal

name to sing, help us to praise:
mighty sword, our prayer attend:
witness bear in this glad hour:
praises be hence, evermore!

Father, all glorious, o'er all victorious,
come, and thy people bless, and give thy word success:
thou who almighty art, now rule in ev'ry heart,
Thy sov'reign majesty may we in glory see,

come and reign over us, Ancient of Days.
Spirit of holiness, on us descend.
and ne'er from us depart, Spirit of pow'r.
and to eternity love and adore!

Words: Anonymous
Music: Felice de Giardini

18. Crown Him with Many Crowns

A Cristo Coronad

1. Crown him with man-y crowns, the Lamb up - on his throne; Hark!
2. Crown him the Son of God be - fore the worlds be - gan, and
3. Crown him the Lord of life who tri - umphed o'er the grave, and
4. Crown him the Lord of love; be - hold his hands and side, those

how the heav'n - ly an - them drowns all mu - sic but its own! A-
ye, who tread where he hath trod, crown him the Son of man; who
rose vic - to - rious in the strife for those he came to save; his
wounds, yet vis - i - ble a - bove, in beau - ty glo - ri - fied; all

wake, my soul and sing of him who died for thee, and
ev - 'ry grief hath known that wrings the hu - man breast, and
glo - ries now we sing, who died and rose on high, who
hail, Re - deem - er, hail! for thou hast died for me; thy

hail him as thy match-less King through all e - ter - ni - ty.
takes and bears them for his own, that all in him may rest.
died e - ter - nal life to bring, and lives that death may die.
praise and glo - ry shall not fail through-out e - ter - ni - ty.

Words: Matthew Bridges & Godfrey Thring (v. 2)
Music: George J. Elvey

A Cristo Coronad

Crown Him with Many Crowns

18.

1. A Cris-to co - ro - nad, di - vi - no Sal - va - dor. Sen-
2. A Cris-to co - ro - nad, Se - ñor de nues-tro a - mor, Al
3. A Cris-to co - ro - nad, Se - ñor de vi - da y luz; Con

ta-do en al - ta ma - jes - tad es dig - no de - lo - or. Al
Rey triun-fan - te ce - le - brad, glo - rio - so ven - ce - dor; Po-
a - la - ban-zas pro - cla - mad los triun - fos de la cruz; A

rey de glo - ria y paz lo - or - es tri - bu - tad, Y
ten - te rey del paz el triun - fo con - su - mo; Y
Él so - lo a - do - rad, Se - ñor de sal - va - cíon; Lo-

ben - de - cid le al In - mor - tal por to - da e - ter - ni - dad.
por su muer - te de do - lor su gran - de a - mor mos - tró.
or e - ter - no tri - bu - tad de to - do co - ra - zón.

Words: Matthew Bridges, trans. E. A. Strange
Music: George J. Elvey

19. Cantad al Señor

Cantal ao Senhor • O, Sing to the Lord

1. Can - tad al Se - ñor un cán - ti - co nue - vo, can - tad al Se -
2. Por - que el Se - ñor ha he - cho pro - di - gios, por - que el Se -
3. Can - tad al Se - ñor, a - la - bad - le con ar - pa, can - tad al Se -
4. Es él que nos da el Es - pí - ri - tu San - to, Es él que nos
5. ¡Je - sús es Se - ñor! ¡A - men, a - le - lu - ya! ¡Je - sús es Se -

ñor un cán - ti - co nue - vo, can - tad al Se - ñor un
ñor ha he - cho pro - di - gios, por - que el Se - ñor ha
ñor, a - la - bad - le con ar - pa, can - tad al Se - ñor, a - la -
da el Es - pí - ri - tu San - to, Es él que nos da el Es -
ñor! ¡A - men, a - le - lu - ya! ¡Je - sús es Se - ñor! ¡A -

cán - ti - co nue - vo, ¡can - tad al Se - ñor, can - tad al Se - ñor!
he - cho pro - di - gios, ¡can - tad al Se - ñor, can - tad al Se - ñor!
bad - le con ar - pa, ¡can - tad al Se - ñor, can - tad al Se - ñor!
pí - ri - tu San - to, ¡can - tad al Se - ñor, can - tad al Se - ñor!
men, a - le - lu - ya! ¡can - tad al Se - ñor, can - tad al Se - ñor!

1. *Cantai ao Senhor um cântico novo, (3x)*
   cantai ao Senhor, cantai ao Senhor.
2. *Porque ele fez, ele faz maravilhas, (3x)*
   cantai ao Senhor, cantai ao Senhor.
3. *Cantai ao Sanhor, bendizei o seu nome, (3x)*
   cantai ao Senhor, cantai ao Senhor.
4. *É ele quem dá o Espíritu Santo, (3x)*
   cantai ao Senhor, cantai ao Senhor.
5. *Jesus é o Senhor! Amén, aleluia! (3x)*
   cantai ao Senhor, cantai ao Senhor.

1. O sing to the Lord, O sing God a new song, (3x)
   O, sing to the Lord, O sing to the Lord.
2. By his holy power our God has done wonders, (3x)
   O, sing to the Lord, O sing to the Lord.
3. So dance to our God and blow all the trumpets, (3x)
   O, sing to the Lord, O sing to the Lord.
4. O shout to our God, who gave us the Spirit, (3x)
   O, sing to the Lord, O sing to the Lord.
5. For Jesus is Lord! Amen! Aleluia! (3x)
   O, sing to the Lord, O sing to the Lord.

Text: Anonymous Portuguese, trans. Gerhard Cartford
Music: *Brazilian Folk Tune*

English and Spanish trans. © Gerhard Cartford.

Forgive Our Sins As We Forgive   20.

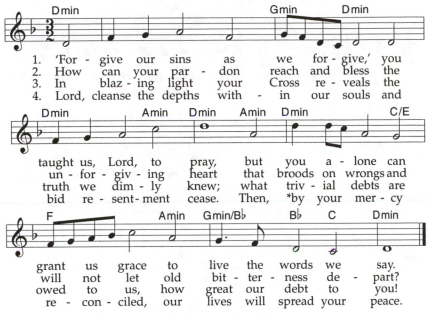

1. 'For - give our sins as we for - give,' you taught us, Lord, to pray, but you a - lone can grant us grace to live the words we say.
2. How can your par - don reach and bless the un - for - giv - ing heart that broods on wrongs and will not let old bit - ter - ness de - part?
3. In blaz - ing light your Cross re - veals the truth we dim - ly knew; what triv - ial debts are owed to us, how great our debt to you!
4. Lord, cleanse the depths with - in our souls and bid re - sent - ment cease. Then, *by your mer - cy re - con - ciled, our lives will spread your peace.

Author's original preferred version reads: "Then reconciled to God and Man."
Alteration used by permission of copyright owner.
Words: Rosamond Herklots
Music: *The Sacred Harp*
© 1969, 1983 Rosamond Herklots.
Used by permission of Oxford University Press.

In My Life, Lord, Be Glorified   21.

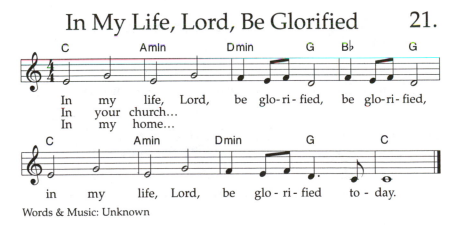

In my life, Lord, be glo - ri - fied, be glo - ri - fied,
In your church...
In my home...

in my life, Lord, be glo - ri - fied to - day.

Words & Music: Unknown

22. Eat This Bread

Eat this bread, drink this cup, come to me and nev-er be hun-gry.

Eat this bread, drink this cup, trust in me and you will not thirst.

Words & Music: Jacques Berthier
© 1984 by Les Presses Taizé (France). Used by permission of GIA Publications, Inc.

23. 神愛世人
God So Loved the World

神愛世人，甚至將他的　　獨生兒子
God so loved, loved the world that he gave his on - ly be -

賜給我們，叫一切信他的，
got - ten Son, that who-so-ev - er be-lieves, be -

不至滅亡，不至滅亡，反得永生。
lieves in him should not per - ish but have e-ter - nal life.

Words: John 3:16
Music: *Chinese*

Dieu A Tant Aimé le Monde   24.

God So Dearly Loved the World

Dieu a tant ai-mé le mon-de
God so dear-ly loved the world that he

qu'il a sa-cri-fié son Fils A-fin que qui con-que
sac-ri-ficed his on-ly Son. An-y-one who will be-

croit en lui ne pé-ris-se pas. Mais que la vie é-ter-
lieve in him will not be con-demmed but will have e-ter-nal

nel-le soit dé-sor-mais son des-tin.
life be-gin-ning now with-out de-lay.

Voi-ci la bon-ne nou-vel-le
This is the good news for ev-'ry-one.

à sai-sir à plei-nes mains! Voi-ci la bon-ne nou-
Wel-come it with o-pen lay. This is the good news for

vel-le: La vie à ple-nes mains!
ev-'ry-one: that God so loved the world!

Words: Adapted from John 3:16 by Pierre Lachat, trans. by Corean Bakke & Tony Payne
Music: Pierre Lachat

25. The Steadfast Love of the Lord

The stead-fast love of the Lord nev-er ceas-es, his
mer-cies nev-er come to an end. They are
new ev-'ry morn-ing, new ev-'ry morn-ing.
Great is thy faith-ful - ness, O Lord!
Great is thy faith-ful - ness.

Words & Music: Edith McNeil

26. み言葉をください
Rain on Us Your Word

1. Rain on us your Word, we who thirst.
2. Blow on us your Word, Spir - it Wind.
3. Bathe us with the dew of your Word.

Feed our hun - ger. Fill us with your -
Sweep with ho - ly, heav - 'nly breath through our
Cool our fire of dis - con - tent. Give us

Words: Yasushige Imakoma, trans. Sharon James-Ledbetter
Music: Shozo Koyama

self. Speak and we hear your voice.
hearts. Of - fer your cleans - ing touch.
peace. Kin - dle our thirst for you.

Com - fort our sor - row - ing hearts.
Free us from sin's vice - like hold.
En - ter our dis - cord - ant world.

Si - lence now our groan - ing fear.
Pur - i - fy, re - new our life.
Sat - is - fy us with your love.

Calm us with your lan - guage, Lord.
Let us taste sweet tri - umph, Lord.
Teach us true com - mun - ion, Lord.

Blaze our way, O Burn - ing Torch.
Storm in - to our souls with joy.
Speak the word and we are whole.

1
み言葉をください、
降りそそぐ雨のように、
恵みの主よ。
飢えと渇きに
くるしみうめき、
やみ路さまよう
いのちのために。

2
み言葉をください、
吹いてくる風のように、
救いの主よ。
からみつく罪
根こそぎはらい、
全き勝利の
きよめのために。

3
み言葉をください、
草におく露のように、
生命の主よ。
人と人との
こころかよわず、
争いなやむ
世界のために。

27. He's Got the Whole World

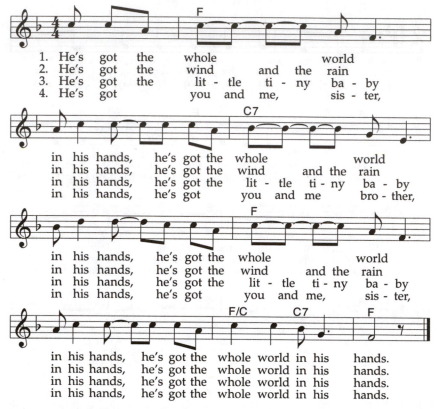

1. He's got the whole world
2. He's got the wind and the rain
3. He's got the lit - tle ti - ny ba - by
4. He's got you and me, sis - ter,

in his hands, he's got the whole world
in his hands, he's got the wind and the rain
in his hands, he's got the lit - tle ti - ny ba - by
in his hands, he's got you and me bro - ther,

in his hands, he's got the whole world
in his hands, he's got the wind and the rain
in his hands, he's got the lit - tle ti - ny ba - by
in his hands, he's got you and me, sis - ter,

in his hands, he's got the whole world in his hands.
in his hands, he's got the whole world in his hands.
in his hands, he's got the whole world in his hands.
in his hands, he's got the whole world in his hands.

Words & Music: *African-American spiritual*

28. O Come, Let Us Adore Him

O come, let us a - dore him, O come, let us a -
dore him, O come, let us a - dore him, Christ the Lord.

Words & Music: from *Cantus Diversi*

Yesu Yu Hai Leo

29.

Jesus Is Alive Today

Ye - su yu ha - i le - o, Ye - su
Je - sus is a - live to - day, Je - sus

yu ha - i le - o, Ye - su yu ha - i le - o a - si - fi -
is a - live to - day, Je - sus is a - live to - day, O praise his

we; Ye - su yu ha - i le - o, Ye - su
Name; Je - sus is a - live to - day, Je - sus

yu ha - i le - o, Ye - su yu ha - i le - o a - si - fi - we.
is a - live to - day, Je - sus is a - live to - day, O praise his Name.

A - le - lu - ya, a - le - lu - ya,
A - le - lu - ya, a - le - lu - ya,

a - le - lu - ya, a - si - fi - we.
a - le - lu - ya, O praise his Name,

a - le - lu - ya, a - si - fi - we.
a - le - lu - ya, O praise his Name.

Words & Music: *Swahili*
Transcription © Roberta R. King.

30. Jesus Shall Reign

1. Je - sus shall reign wher - e'er the sun
2. To him shall end - less pray'r be made,
3. Peo - ple and realms of ev - 'ry tongue

does its suc - ces - sive jour - neys run;
and end - less prais - es crown his head;
dwell on his love with sweet - est song;

his king - dom spread from shore to shore,
his Name like sweet per - fume shall rise
and in - fant voic - es shall pro - claim

till moons shall wax and wane no more.
with ev - 'ry morn - ing sac - ri - fice.
their ear - ly bless - ings on his Name.

Words: Isaac Watts
Music: John Hatton

Jesus, Name above All Names 31.

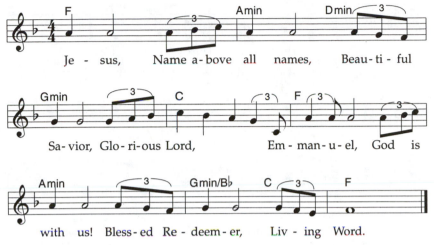

Je - sus, Name a-bove all names, Beau-ti-ful
Sa-vior, Glo-ri-ous Lord, Em-man-u-el, God is
with us! Bless-ed Re-deem-er, Liv-ing Word.

Words & Music: Naida Hearn
© 1974 Scripture in Song (Administered by Maranatha! Music, c/o The Copyright Company).

I Love You, Lord 32.

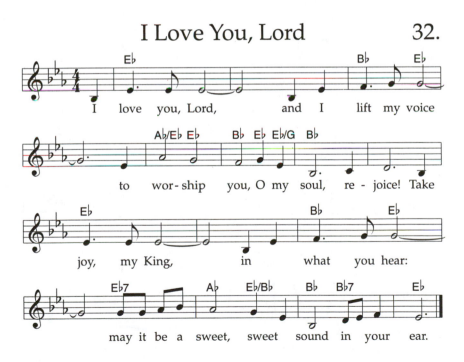

I love you, Lord, and I lift my voice
to wor-ship you, O my soul, re-joice! Take
joy, my King, in what you hear:
may it be a sweet, sweet sound in your ear.

Words & Music: Laurie Klein
© 1978 House of Mercy Music (Administered by Maranatha! Music, c/o The Copyright Company).

33. ЖИТЬ ДЛЯ ИИСНСА, С НИИ УМИРАТЬ

Living for Jesus, Dying for Him

1. Жить для Ии-су- са, сНим у- ми-рать,
2. Жить для Ии-су- са, кра- ток хоть день
3. Жить для Ии-су- са, грех по- бе- дить;

Луч- щу- ю до- лю мож- ноль же-лать?
И не- да-ле- ко смерт- на- я тень,
Крест по- но-щень- я бод- ро сно-сить.

Сто- ит смирять- ся, сто- ит бо-роть- ся,
Не у- ны-ва- я не у- ста-ва- я,
Кон- чив путь жиз- ни, что- бы вот-чи- зне

Сто- ит за з- то мир весь от- дать.
Вер- но тру-дить- ся пусть нам не лень.
Сла- вои бес-смер- тья вен- чан-ным быть.

Words: I. I. Vecherok
Music: *Russian Folksong,* arr. A.F.E.

Living for Jesus, Dying for Him   33.

ЖИТЬ ДЛЯ ИИСНСА, С НИИ УМИРАТЬ

1. Liv - ing for Je - sus,   dy - ing   for him,
2. Liv - ing for Je - sus through life's short day
3. Liv - ing for Je - sus, con - quer - ing sin,

trust - ing   his guid - ance   though sight is dim,
with death's dark shad - ow   not   far   a - way,
bear - ing   our cross - es,   oth - ers   to win,

may   we   be wor - thy   to   be   his ser - vants,
not grow - ing wear - y   in   our   well - do - ing,
so when our jour - ney   here   is com - plet - ed,

glad - ly for - sak - ing   all now for him.
faith - ful - ly let us   work while we may.
we   may reach heav - en, dwell - ing there - in.

Words: I. I. Vecherok
Music: *Russian Folksong,* arr. A.F.E.

34. Majesty

Words & Music: Jack Hayford

Praise God, from Whom All Blessings Flow 35.

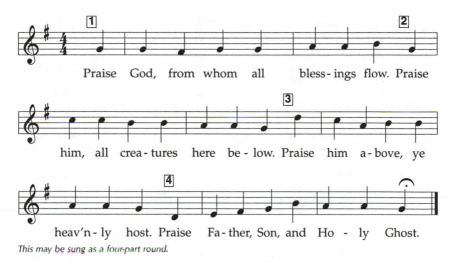

1 Praise God, from whom all bless-ings flow. Praise **2**
him, all crea-tures here be-low. Praise him a-bove, ye **3**
4 heav'n-ly host. Praise Fa-ther, Son, and Ho-ly Ghost.

This may be sung as a four-part round.

Words: Thomas Ken
Music: Thomas Tallis

In Christ There Is No East or West 36.

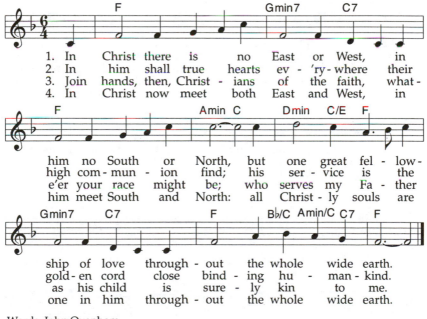

1. In Christ there is no East or West, in
2. In him shall true hearts ev - 'ry-where their
3. Join hands, then, Christ - ians of the faith, what -
4. In Christ now meet both East and West, in

him no South or North, but one great fel - low-
high com - mun - ion find; his ser - vice is the
e'er your race might be; who serves my Fa - ther
him meet South and North: all Christ - ly souls are

ship of love through - out the whole wide earth.
gold - en cord close bind - ing hu - man-kind.
as his child is sure - ly kin to me.
one in him through - out the whole wide earth.

Words: John Oxenham
Music: *American*

37. Hazina Yangu
O God, We Thank You

1. Ha - zi - na ya - ngu na - i - we - ka Mi - ko - no - ni mwa-
2. Po - ke - a, Bwa - na, fu - ngu la - ngu, Le - o na - li - to-
3. I - ma - ni tu - pu bi - la te - ndo Hu - ta - i - ku - ba-
4. Ha - la - fu mwi - sho ni - je kwa - ko Kwe - nye u - tu - ku-

ko. Ro - ho ya - ngu ya - to - she - ka I - ki - du - mu kwa
a. Li - we ma - li ya - ko, Mu - ngu, Li - we la ku - fa-
li. Sa - sa, Bwa - na, ni - pe mwe - ndo Pi - a, u - ni - ja-
fu. U - ku - ba - li ni - we wa - ko, E - e, Mta - ka - ti-

ko. Na - o - mba mwi - li ku - u - we - ka
a. Ni - a - che cho - yo ki - la fu - ngu,
li. Ki - do - go cha - ngu cha ma - ten - do
fu. Ha - zi - na ya - ngu i - we kwa - ko,

Pe - nye u - sa - la - ma. Pe - nye nji - a ya ku - nyo - ka
Ni - we na - li - to - a. Du - ni - a - ni si - o pa - ngu,
U - si - ki - ke - je - li; Ni - ki - to - a bi - la fun - do,
Ha - ta ni - we m - fu. Ni - je pa - ko m - cha wa - ko

U - li - po - si - ma - ma. U - pe - ndo Wa - ko u - me - fi-
Kwa - ko na - ji - to - a. Ni - we wa a - di - li.
Ni - we wa a - di - li.
Kwa u - ta - ka - ti - fu.

ka. Na kwa - ngu U - me - fa - ha - mi - ka. A - sa - nte

Sa - na, Bwa - na Mu - ngu. U Bwa - na Mwe - nye u - tu - ku - fu.

Words: Enock A. Kalembo
Music: *Tanzanian*, transcribed by Howard Olson
Used by permission of Lutheran Theological College, Tanzania.

O God, We Thank You

Hazina Yangu

37.

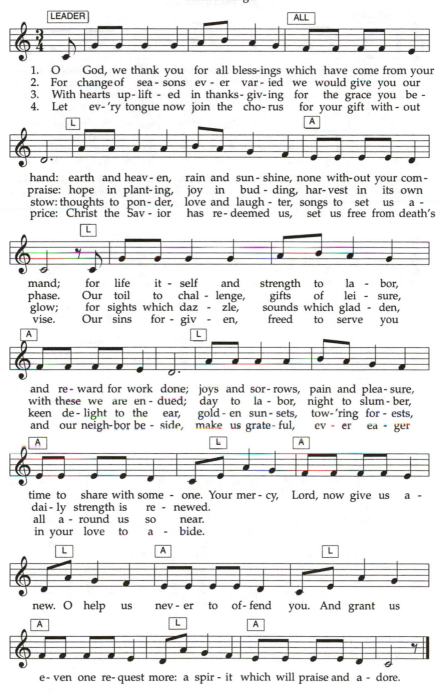

LEADER

1. O God, we thank you for all bless-ings which have come from your
2. For change of sea-sons ev - er var - ied we would give you our
3. With hearts up-lift - ed in thanks-giv-ing for the grace you be -
4. Let ev-'ry tongue now join the cho-rus for your gift with-out

hand: earth and heav-en, rain and sun-shine, none with-out your com-
praise: hope in plant-ing, joy in bud - ding, har-vest in its own
stow: thoughts to pon-der, love and laugh - ter, songs to set us a-
price: Christ the Sav-ior has re-deemed us, set us free from death's

mand; for life it - self and strength to la - bor,
phase. Our toil to chal - lenge, gifts of lei - sure,
glow; for sights which daz - zle, sounds which glad - den,
vise. Our sins for - giv - en, freed to serve you

and re - ward for work done; joys and sor - rows, pain and plea - sure,
with these we are en - dued; day to la - bor, night to slum - ber,
keen de - light to the ear, gold - en sun - sets, tow-'ring for - ests,
and our neigh-bor be - side, make us grate - ful, ev - er ea - ger

time to share with some - one. Your mer - cy, Lord, now give us a-
dai - ly strength is re - newed.
all a - round us so near.
in your love to a - bide.

new. O help us nev - er to of - fend you. And grant us

e - ven one re - quest more: a spir - it which will praise and a - dore.

Words: Howard S. Olson
Music: *Tanzanian*, transcribed by Howard Olson
Words & Music © Howard Olson (Mudimi Ntandu).

38. O for a Thousand Tongues

Mil Voces Para Celebrar

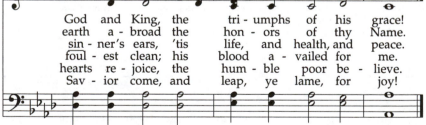

1. O for a thou-sand tongues to sing my
2. My gra-cious Mas-ter and my God, as-
3. Je-sus! the Name that charms our fears, that
4. He breaks the pow'r of can-celed sin, he
5. He speaks, and lis-t'ning to his voice, new
6. Hear him, ye deaf; his praise, ye dumb; your

great Re-deem-er's praise, the glo-ries of my
sist me to pro-claim, to spread through all the
bids our sor-rows cease; 'tis mu-sic in the
sets the pris-'ner free; his blood can make the
life the dead re-ceive; the mourn-ful, bro-ken
loos-ened tongues em-ploy; ye blind, be-hold your

God and King, the tri-umphs of his grace!
earth a-broad the hon-ors of thy Name.
sin-ner's ears, 'tis life, and health, and peace.
foul-est clean; his blood a-vailed for me.
hearts re-joice, the hum-ble poor be-lieve.
Sav-ior come, and leap, ye lame, for joy!

Words: Charles Wesley
Music: Carl G. Glaser

Mil Voces Para Celebrar 38.

O for a Thousand Tongues

1. Mil vo - ces pa - ra cel - e - brar a
2. Mi buen Se - ñor, Mæs - tro y Dios; que
3. El dul - ce nom - bre de Je - sús nos
4. Des - tru - ye el po - der del mal y
5. Él ha - bla y el o - ir su voz el
6. Es - cu - chen, sor - dos, al Se - ñor; a -

mi Li - ber - ta - dor, las glo - rias de su
pue - da di - vul - gar tu gra - to nom - bre
li - bra del te - mor, en las tris - te - zas
brin - da li - ber - tad; al más im - pu - ro
muer - to vi - vi - rá; se a - le - gra el tris - te
la - be el mun - do a Dios, los co - jos sal - ten,

ma - jes - tad, los triun - fos de su a - mor.
y su ho - nor, en cie - lo, tie - rra y mar.
tra - e luz, per - dón al pe - ca - dor.
pue - de dar pu - re - za y san - ti - dad.
co - ra - zón, los po - bres ha - llan paz.
ve - an hoy los cie - gos al Se - ñor.

Words: Charles Wesley, trans. Frederico J. Pagura
Music: Carl G. Glaser

Spanish translation © 1989 The United Methodist Publishing House.

39. Holy, Holy

1. Ho - ly, ho - ly, ho - ly, ho - ly, ho - ly,
2. Gra - cious Fa - ther, Gra - cious Fa - ther, we're so
3. Pre - cious Je - sus, Pre - cious Je - sus, we're so
4. Ho - ly Spir - it, Ho - ly Spir - it, come and
5. Hal - le - lu - jah, hal - le - lu - jah, hal - le -

ho - ly, Lord God Al - might - y; and we
blest to be your chil - dren, Gra - cious Fa - ther; and we
glad that you've re - deemed us, Pre - cious Je - sus; and we
fill our hearts a - new, Ho - ly Spir - it; and we
lu - jah, hal - le - lu - jah; and we

lift our hearts be - fore you as a to - ken of our love, ho - ly,
lift our heads be - fore you as a to - ken of our love, Gra - cious
lift our hands be - fore you as a to - ken of our love, Pre - cious
lift our voice be - fore you as a to - ken of our love, Ho - ly
lift our hearts be - fore you as a to - ken of our love, hal - le -

ho - ly, ho - ly, ho - ly.
Fa - ther, Gra - cious Fa - ther.
Je - sus, Pre - cious Je - sus.
Spir - it, Ho - ly Spir - it.
lu - jah, hal - le - lu - jah.

Words & Music: Jimmy Owens

The Trees of the Field 40.

You shall go out with joy and be led forth with peace.
(clap) etc.

The moun-tains and the hills will break forth be-

fore you. There'll be shouts of joy and all the trees of the

field will clap, will clap their hands.

And all the trees of the field will clap their hands.

The trees of the field will clap their hands.

The trees of the field will clap their hands

while you go out with joy.

Words: Isaiah 55:12, adapted by Steffi Geiser Rubin
Music: Stuart Dauerman
© 1976 Lillenas Publishing Company/SESAC (Administered by Integrity Copyright Group, Inc.).

41.
Lobe den Herren
Praise to the Lord, the Almighty

1. Lob-e den Her-ren, den mäch-ti-gen Kön-ig der Ehr-
2. Lob-e den Her-ren, der al-les so herr-lich re-gier-
3. Lob-e den Her-ren, der dein-en Stand sicht-bar ges-eg-
4. Lob-e den Her-ren, was in mir ist lob-e den Na-

en! Mein-e ge-lieb-e-te See-le, das ist mein Be-
et, Der dich auf Ad-e-lers Fit-ti-chen sich-er ge-
net, Der aus dem Him-mel mit Strö-men der Lieb-e ge-
men! Al-les, was O-dem hat, lob-e mit A-bra-hams

geh- ren. Kom-met zu-hauf! Psal- ter und
führ- et, Der dich er- hält, Wie es dir
reg - net! Den-ke da-ran, Was der All-
Sa- men! Er ist dein Licht, See- le, ver-

Har-fe, wacht auf! Las- set die Mu-sik an-hör- en!
sel-ber ge-fällt. Hast du nicht die-ses ver-spür- et?
mäch-ti-ge kann, Der dir mit Lieb-e be-geg- net!
giss es ja nicht! Lob- en-de, schlies-se mit A- men!

Words: Joachim Neander
Music: *Stralsund Gesangbuch*

Praise to the Lord, the Almighty 41.

Lobe den Herren

1. Praise to the Lord, the Al-might-y, the King of cre-a-tion! O my soul, praise him, for he is thy health and sal-va-tion! All ye who hear, now to his tem-ple draw near; join me in glad ad-o-ra-tion!

2. Praise to the Lord, who o'er all things so won-drous-ly reign-eth, shel-ters thee un-der his wings, yea, so gent-ly sus-stain-eth! Has thou not seen how thy de-sires e'er have been grant-ed in what he or-dain-eth?

3. Praise to the Lord, who doth pros-per thy work and de-fend thee; sure-ly his good-ness and mer-cy here dai-ly at-tend thee. Pon-der a-new what the Al-might-y can do, if with his love he be-friend thee.

4. Praise to the Lord! O let all that is in me a-dore him! All that hath life and breath, come now with prais-es be-fore him! Let the a-men sound from his peo-ple a-gain: glad-ly for-ev-er a-dore him.

Words: Joachim Neander, trans. Catherine Winkworth
Music: *Stralsund Gesangbuch*

42. Perseveremos Hermanos
Persevere My Brothers

Emin

Per - se - ve - re - mos her - ma - nos por la Fe, por
D.C. Per - se - ver-e - mos her - ma - nos can - tan - do o -
We per - se - vere, my bro-thers in faith, in
D.C. *We per - se - vere my bro-thers in sing-ing and*

G   **Emin**

la Fe, La ve - ni - da del Se - ñor cer-ca es - tá, cer-ca
ran - do, La ve - ni - da del Se - ñor cer-ca es - tá, cer-ca
faith, the com-ing of the Lord is near, is
pray-ing, the com-ing óf the Lord is near, is

1.   **2.**   *Fine* **C**   **3**   **G**

es - tá. Per - es - tá   En la san - ta Bi - blia tu me
        es - tá.   *In the ho - ly Bi - ble you*
near.   We near.
        near.

Emin   **C**   **3**   **G**

di - ces que me a - mas. En la san - ta Bi - blia tu me
tell me that you love me. In the ho - ly Bi - ble you

Emin   **3**   **G**

di - ces que me a - mas. Y has da - do a tu Hi - jo por
tell me that you love me. You have giv - en us your Son to

Emin   **3**

lim - piar nues - tros pe - ca - dos. Y has da - do a tu
clean a - way our sins. You have giv - en us

G   **Emin**   *D.C. al Fine*

Hi - jo por lim - piar nues - tros pe - ca - dos.
your Son to clean a - way our sins.

Words: Anonymous, trans. Tony Payne
Music: *Peruvian Folk Tune*, transcribed by Tony Payne
Used by permission of Kerygma Canta.

Our Cities Cry to You, O God   43.

1. Our cit-ies cry to you, O God, from out their pain and
2. Yet still you walk our streets, O Christ! We know your pres-ence
3. Your peo-ple are your hands and feet to serve your world to-
4. O heal-ing Sav-ior, Prince of Peace, sal-va-tion's Source and

strife; you made us for your-self a-lone, but we choose a-lien
here where hum-ble Chris-tians love and serve in god-ly grace and
day, our lives the book our cit-ies read to help them find your
Sum, for you our bro-ken cit-ies cry— O come, Lord Je-sus,

life. Our goals are pleas-ure, gold and power; in-jus-tice stalks our
fear. O Word made flesh be seen in us! May all we say and
way. O pour your sov-'reign Spir-it out on heart and will and
come! With truth your roy-al di-a-dem, with right-eous-ness your

earth; in vain we seek for rest, for joy, for sense of hu-man worth.
do af-firm you God In-car-nate still, and turn men's hearts to you.
brain; in-spire your Church with love and pow'r to ease our cit-ies' pain!
rod, O come, Lord Je-sus, bring to earth the Cit-y of our God!

Words: Margaret Clarkson
Music: Henry S. Cutler
Words © 1987 Hope Music Publishing Company.

44. Seek Ye First

1. Seek ye first the king - dom of God
2. Ask and it shall be giv - en un - to you,
3. Man shall not live by bread a - lone,

and his right-eous - ness, and all these things shall be
seek and ye shall find, knock and it shall be
but by ev - 'ry word that pro - ceeds from the

lu - ia, al - le - lu - ia!
add - ed un - to you; Al - le - lu, al - le - lu - ia.
o - pened un - to you;
mouth of the Lord;

Words & Music: Karen Lafferty
© 1972 Maranatha! Music (Administered by the Copyright Company).

Thuma Mina

Send Me, Lord

45.

Thu - ma mi - na.

Thu-ma mi - na, thu - ma
Je - sus, send me
Je - sus, lead me
Je - sus, fill me

mi - na, thu-ma mi - na So - man -
Je - sus, send me Je - sus, send me,
Je - sus, lead me Je - sus, lead me,
Je - sus, fill me Je - sus, fill me,

1.—2.—3.

4.

Send me, Lord.
Lead me, Lord.
Fill me, Lord.

dla.
Lord.
Lord.

Send me
Lead me
Fill me Lord.

46. 부름받아 나선 이 몸

Since the Lord My God Has Called Me

1. 부름 받아 나선이 몸 어디든 지가오리 다 괴로 우나 즐 거 우나 주만 따 라 가오리니 어 느 누 가 막 으리 까 죽음 인 들 막 으리 까 어 느
2. 아 골 골짝 빈들에 도복음 들 고 가오리 다 소돔 같 은 거 리에도 사 랑 안 고 찾아가 서 종의 몸 에 지 닌 것 도 아 낌 없 이 드 리 리 다 종 의

1. Since the Lord, my God has called, I will go where-ev-er he leads; I will fol-low on-ly Je-sus, I will fol-low on-ly him! Who can hin-der while he leads me? Je-sus guides me all the way. Who can
2. I will bring good news to the world, to the place of great-est need. To the streets of ev-ery cit-y I will bring the love of God! All my trea-sures for Christ's king-dom, I will free-ly give my all. Since the

Words: Lee Ho Woon, trans. John T. Underwood
Music: Lee Yoo Sun

누 가 막으리 까 죽 음 인 들 막으리 까
몸 에 지닌것 도 아 낌 없 이 드리리 다

hin- der while he leads? Je- sus guides me all the way.
Lord, my God has called, where he leads me I will go.

Do You Love Him?   47.

LEADER   A

1. Do you love him? O, yes! I love my Lord.
2. Do you trust him? O, yes! I trust my Lord.
3. Will you serve him? O, yes! I'll serve my Lord.

L   A

Do you love him?
Do you trust him?
Will you serve him?

(clap) A - le - lu - ya, when we

go to see the Lord. A - le - lu - ya, when he

1.—2.   3.

comes to take us home. take us home.

Words & Music: *Nigerian*, adapted by Roberta King
© Roberta R. King.

48.

聖靈洗心歌
Spirit Lord We Pray

1. 敬　求　主　聖　靈，慰　我　繁　心　使　安　寧；
2. 敬　求　主　聖　靈，施　恩　照　我　心　救　洗　光；
3. 我　心　有　迷　靈，求　主　照　出　海　拯　死　亡？
4. 誰　能　救　我　靈，脫　離　苦　光　出　死　亡？
5. 若　蒙　主　聖　靈，賞　賜　光　輝　照　我　心，

敬　求　主　聖　靈，洗　我　凡　心　罪
使　我　離　污　淘，使　我　離　煙　賜
救　拯　光　照　處，迷　疑　主　新　賜
主　是　生　命　源；靠　主　認　識
心　清　不　染　塵，方　能　認　識

使　潔　清；導　我　煩　心　離　愁　城。
成　清　潔；潔　我　花　英　白　如　雪。
盡　消　亡，胸　襟　明　頓　輝　煌？
生　命　光，死　亡　攻　擊　又　何　妨？
愛　之　神，免　遭　魔　障　致　沉　淪。

Words: Ernest Y. L. Yang
Music: *Japanese*
Words used by permission of Chinese Christian Literature Council, Ltd.

49.

Bound Together

Bound to-geth-er and fine-ly wov-en, we're
A-le-lu-ya, a-le-lu-ya,

bound to-geth-er and fine-ly wov-en with love.
a-le-lu-ya, a-le-lu-ya, a-men.

Words & Music: Ken Medema
© 1989 Briar Patch Music.

Spirit Lord We Pray
聖靈洗心歌

1. Spir-it Lord we pray, com-fort give and peace al-way.
2. Spir-it Lord we pray, cleans-ing grace be-stow to-day.
3. Prone our hearts to stray, shine, O Lord, sal-va-tion's ray.
4. Who our souls can save, save from death and grief's dark wave?
5. Ho-ly Spir-it, come, shine with-in our hearts, your home,

Spir-it Lord we pray: wash us clean from
Wash our guilt a-way: free from sin, more
Shine a-long our way: mists of doubt will
Christ to us God gave. To his own new
'till all shame is gone. Then the God of

sin's al-loy, lead and change our grief to joy.
pure we grow, as the lil-y, white as snow.
dis-ap-pear, and the mean-ing will shine clear.
life he'll bring. Now, O death, where is thy sting?
love we'll know. He will save us from the foe.

Words: Ernest Y. L. Yang, trans. Ivy Balchin
Music: *Japanese*
Used by permission of Chinese Christian Literature Council, Ltd.

O duh Aji
Lord, Have Mercy

O duh A-ji Sang Hyang Wi-dhi,
O Lord, my God, my Fa-ther,

A-ji dong swe ca-nin-ke ti-tiang.
have mer-cy, have mer-cy on me.

Words & Music: Wayan Mastra
© 1988 Asian Institute for Liturgy and Music.

51. The Church's One Foundation

1. The church-'s one foun-da-tion is Je-sus Christ, her
2. E - lect from ev-'ry na-tion, yet one o'er all the
3. Though with a scorn-ful won-der this world sees her op-
4. Through toil and trib-u-la-tion and tu-mult of her

Lord. She is his new cre-a-tion by wa-ter and the
earth, her char-ter of sal-va-tion: One Lord, one faith, one
pressed. By schi-sms rent a-sund-er, by her-e-sies dis-
war. She waits the con-sum-ma-tion of peace for-ev-er-

Word. From heav'n he came and sought her to be his ho-ly
birth. One ho-ly Name she bless-es, par-takes one ho-ly
tressed. Yet saints their watch are keep-ing. Their cry goes up, "How
more. Till with the vis-ion glo-rious her long-ing eyes are

bride. With his own blood he bought her, and for her life he died.
food, and to one hope she press-es with ev-'ry grace en-dued.
long?" And soon the night of weep-ing shall be the morn of song.
blest, and the great church vic-to-rious shall be the church at rest.

Words: Samuel J. Stone
Music: Samuel S. Wesley

Vem Visita
Come, Visit Your Church

52.

1. Vem, vi - - si - ta a tu - a i - gre - ja,
2. Sem tu - a gra - ca e - la mur - cha
1. *Come, vis - it your church, O blest Re - deem - er,*
2. *With - out your grace she weak - ens and with - ers*

ó ben - di - to Sal - va - dor!
fi - ca - rá, e sem vi - gor.
Come and re - new her fal - ter - ing hope.
as a dry plant with no pow - er or strength.

Vi - vi - fi - ca, vi - vi - fi - ca
Come and re - vive us, come and re - vive us,

nos - sas al - mas, o Se - nhor!
hear our prayer: re - vive us, O Lord!

Vi - vi - fi - ca, Vi - vi - fi - ca
Come and re - vive us, come and re - vive us,

nos - sas al - mas ó Se - nhor!
hear our prayer, re - vive us, O Lord!

Words: Wright
Music: Thomas J. Williams
Music © Dilys Evans

53.

A Toi la Gloire

Dein ist Macht und Ehre • Thine is The Glory

1. A toi la gloi - re, O Res - sus - ci - té!
2. Crain - drais - je en - core? Il vit à ja - mais,
1. *Dein ist Macht und Eh - re, e - wig Dein der Sieg,*
2. *Was kann und schei - den von der Lie - be Sein?*
1. Thine is the glo - ry, ris - en, con - q'ring Son;
2. No more we doubt thee, glo - rious Prince of Life!

A toi la vic - toi - re Pour l'é - ter - ni - té!
Ce - lui que j'a - dor - e, Le Prince de la paix:
Held, der dem Gra - be sei - ge - krönt ent - stieg.
Trüb - sal od - er Lei - den, ir - gend ei - ne Pein?
end - less is the vic - t'ry thou o'er death hast won.
Life is naught with - out thee; aid us in our strife.

Bril - lant de lu - miè - re, L'ange est des - cen - du,
Il est ma vic - toi - re, Mon puis - sant sou - tien,
Wir auch sol - len le - ben mit dem Herrn zu - gleich.
Wo - vor soll mir grau - en? Als ein Kind des Lichts
An - gels in bright rai - ment rolled the stone a - way,
Make us more than con - q'rors through thy death - less love;

Il rou - le la pier - re Du tom - beau vain - cu.
Ma vie et ma gloi - re: Non, je ne crains rien!
Er will uns er - he - ben in Sein himm - lisch Reich.
darf ich Ihm ver - trau - en: Nein ich fürch - te nichts.
kept the fold - ed grave - clothes where thy bod - y lay.
bring us safe through Jor - dan to thy home a - bove.

Words: Edmond L. Budry, trans. B. Hoyle
Music: G. F. Handel

Refrain

A toi la gloi - re, O Res - sus - ci - té!
Dein ist Macht und Eh - re, e - wig Dein der Sieg.
Thine is the glo - ry, ris - en, con - q'ring Son;

A toi la vic - toi - re Pour l'é - ter - ni - té!
Held, der dem Gra - be sei - ge - krönt ent - stieg.
end - less is the vic - t'ry thou o'er death hast won.

When I Survey 54.

1. When I sur - vey the won - drous cross,
2. For - bid it, Lord, that I should boast,
3. See, from his head, his hands, his feet,
4. Were the whole realm of na - ture mine,

on which the Prince of Glo - ry died,
save in the death of Christ, my God;
sor - row and love flow min - gled down.
that were a pres - ent far too small;

my rich - est gain I count but loss,
all the vain things that charm me most,
Did e'er such love and sor - row meet,
love so a - maz - ing, so di - vine,

and pour con - tempt on all my pride.
I sac - ri - fice them to his blood.
or thorns com - pose so rich a crown?
de - mands my soul, my life, my all.

Words: Isaac Watts
Music: Lowell Mason

55. We Are Marching in the Light

Words & Music: *South African*
© 1984 Utryck. Used by permission of Walton Music Corporation.

light of God, we are march-ing, march-ing, march-ing, we are

march-ing, march-ing, Oo— we are march-ing in the light of God.

What Can Wash Away My Sin? 56.

1. What can wash a-way my sin? Noth-ing but the blood of Je-sus.
2. For my par-don this I see: noth-ing but the blood of Je-sus.
3. Noth-ing can for sin a-tone: noth-ing but the blood of Je-sus.
4. This is all my hope and peace: noth-ing but the blood of Je-sus.

What can make me whole a - gain? Noth-ing but the blood of Je-sus.
For my cleans-ing, this my plea: noth-ing but the blood of Je-sus.
Naught of good that I have done: noth-ing but the blood of Je-sus.
This is all my right-eous - ness: noth-ing but the blood of Je-sus.

O pre-cious is the flow that makes me white as snow;

no oth-er fount I know, noth-ing but the blood of Je-sus.

Words & Music: Robert Lowry

57. ពិ ប្រ ប្ញុំ ផ្ដែច ពី ស្អរ ឡេិត
Speak My Heart

Words & Music: Sarin Sam
Used by permission.

Speak My Heart

57.

1. Speak my heart with thou - sand tongues a - bout
2. See the stars in blaz - ing gal - ax - ies
3. God is ho - ly, pow - er - ful a - bove
4. On - ly God can love us, save us from

God to tell of his love and life he gave for
burn, cre - a - ted by God, the bril - liant light of
all. His right - 'ous - ness pu - ri - fies my mind and
sin though we are not free, by dust and death still

me. He is my Lord, un - e - qualed and ex -
life. Let all the earth pro - claim his might - y
heart. I con - tem - plate his ev - er - faith - ful,
bound. God choos - es us as his be - lov - ed

alt - ed, Lord of heav'n and earth, Great King of the un - i - verse.
pow'r. His mir - a - cles a - bound, his hand - i - work sings his Name.
nev - er chang - ing love for me, his grace re - deem - ing me.
chil - dren, with his Spir - it helps us know the mind of Christ.

Words & Music: Sarin Sam, trans. Sharon James-Ledbetter
Words © 1994 Sharon James-Ledbetter.

58. Paglilingkod

What Service Can I Do?

1. A - nong u - ring pag - li - ling - kod, a - nong pag - a - a -
2. Ga - a - nong ha - bang pa - na - hon ang gu - gu - gu - lin
3. Ang ba - wat a - lay o han - dog kung su - su ka - tin
4. A - nong u - ring pag - li - ling - kod, a - nong u - ring a -

lay Ang na - ra - ra - pat i - han - dog sa Dios A - mang ba -
ko; Ga - a - nong la - lim ng pan - sin ang i - u - u - kol
ko Na - wa - wa - lan ng ha - la - ga, ka tu - lad ay a
lay Ang na - ra - ra - pat i - han - dog sa Iyo, Ha - ring ba -

nal; Na Siyang la - ging nag - bi - bi - gay, la ging ma - pag - pa
ko Pa ra sa Kan - yang na - ma - tay, sa a - ki'y tu - mu -
bo; I - bi - ni - gay Niya ang la - hat do - on sa Kal - bar -
nal? Bu - hay ko at ka - lu - lu - wa, ya - man at la - hat

la; A - nong u - ring pag - li - ling - kod ang da - pat sa Kan - ya?
bos; Da - ki - la ang pag - i - big Niya at di ma - ta - ta los!
yo; At di Ni - ya i - ti - na - nong a - no ang ba - yad ko.
na; Kai - lan ma'y di ma - tum - ba - san, Dios, ang Iyong pag - sin - ta!

Words & Music: Samuel V. Guerrero, harm. Imelda Ongsiako
© 1988 *Institute for Studies in Asian Church and Culture (ISACC).*

What Service Can I Do?

Paglilingkod

58.

1. What ser-vice can I do for you? What off-'ring shall I
2. I ask, O God, to mul-ti-ply my hours and my
3. For death, O Christ, you took my flesh and jour-neyed in-to
4. Now foun-tains gush from gran-ite self, you sat-is-fy my

bring? What wor-thy praise is due to you, my Fa-ther and my
days. Give sub-stance to my falt-'ring thoughts and words with which to
shame, so cru'l a tor-ture for a King to bear for me my
thirst. You flush the blind-ness from my eyes and give me sec-ond

King? What can I give, what ho-ly gifts are wor-thy of your
praise. Grant cour-age now to touch the world and speak the mys-ter-
blame. How can I com-pre-hend your pain, your sad and lone-ly
birth. The pow-er of your love for me in-vades my soul and

Name? For by your will all things were made, by Word cre-a-tion came.
y of your re-deem-ing love and grace. A-noint my fra-il-ty.
way? Carve out the stone from my cold heart and teach me how to pray.
mind. I give you now all that I am. My heart leaps to re-spond.

Words & Music: Samuel V. Guerrero, Harm. Imelda Ongsiako,
trans. Sharon James-Ledbetter & Jackie Whowell
© 1988 Institute for Studies in Asian Church and Culture (ISACC).
Translation © 1989 Sharon James-Ledbetter.

59. Somos Uno en Cristo
We Are One in Christ

Somos uno en Cristo, somos uno, somos
uno, uno solo. Somos uno en Cristo, somos
uno, somos uno, uno solo. Un solo
Dios, un solo Señor, una sola fe, un solo a-
mor; un solo Bautismo, un solo Espíritu; y es es el Consolador. (Hey!)

Words & Music: *Spanish* (Anonymous)

HYMN ACKNOWLEDGEMENTS

All People That on Earth Do Dwell: public domain.
Alleluia: by Jerry Sinclair. © Copyright 1972 by Manna Music, Inc., PO Box 218, Pacific City, CA 97135. International copyright secured. All rights reserved. Used by permission.
Amazing Grace: public domain.
Amen, Praise the Father: words and music © 1983 by Leng Loh. Used by permission of I-to Loh, Asian Institute for Liturgy and Music.
At the Name of Jesus: music by Ralph Vaughan Williams (1872-1958), from *Enlarged Songs of Praise 1931*; reprinted by permission of Oxford University Press.
Bless the Lord: words based on Psalm 103, translated by Bob Robertson, revised. Permission to use not required in country of origin.
Blessed Assurance: public domain.
Blessed Jesus, at Thy Word: public domain.
Bound Together: words and music by Ken Medema. © 1989 by Ken Medema Music. All rights reserved. Briar Patch Music, 3825 Meadowood SW, Grandville, MI 49418, 616-534-6571
Called as Partners in Christ's Service: reprinted from *A SINGING FAITH*, © 1981 Jane Parker Huber. Used by permission of Westminster/John Knox Press.
Cantad al Señor (O Sing to the Lord): English and Spanish translations © Gerhard Cartford. Used by permission.
Children of the Heavenly Father: text translation copyright © Board of Publication, Lutheran Church in America. Reprinted by permission of Augsburg Fortress.
Christ, the Everlasting Lord: reprinted from the *New Chinese Hynmnal*. Used by permission of China Christian Council.
Come, Everyone Who Thirsts: music, public domain; words used by permission of Joan Eubank.
Come, Thou Almighty King: public domain.
Come Visit Your Church: music used by permission of Dilys Evans.
Crown Him with Many Crowns: public domain.
Do You Love Him?: words and music © Roberta R. King. Used by permission.
Eat this Bread: © 1984 by Les Presses de Taize (France). Used by permission of GIA Publications, Inc., exclusive agent. All rights reserved.
Father, We Adore You: words and music by Tony Coelho. © 1972 Maranatha! Music (Administered by The Copyright Company, Nashville, TN). All rights reserved. International copyright secured.Used by permission.
Forgive Our Sins as We Forgive: words reprinted by permission of Oxford University Press.
God So Dearly Loved the World: © by Pierre Lachat. Used by permission.

God So Loved the World: reprinted from the *New Chinese Hymnal* by permission of China Christian Council.

Heleluyan: music transcription © 1989 The United Methodist Publishing House. Reprinted from *The United Methodist Hymnal* with permission.

He's Got the Whole World: public domain.

Holy, Holy: © 1972 Bud John Songs, Inc. (ASCAP).

I Love You, Lord: © 1978 House of Mercy Music (Administered by Maranatha! Music c/o The Copyright Company Nashville, TN). All rights reserved. International copyright secured. Used by permission.

In Christ There Is No East or West: public domain.

In My Life, Lord, Be Glorified: public domain.

Jesus Is Alive Today: words and music © by Roberta R. King. Used by permission.

Jesus Loves Me: Cherokee phonetic transcription © 1989 The United Methodist Publishing House.

Jesus, Name above All Names: © 1974 Scripture in Song (Administered by Maranatha! Music c/o The Copyright Company Nashville, TN). All rights reserved. International copyright secured. Used by permission.

Jesus Shall Reign: public domain.

Living for Jesus, Dying for Him: public domain.

Lord, Have Mercy: © 1988 Asian Institute for Liturgy and Music. Used by permission of Wayan Mastra.

Majesty: © 1981 Rocksmith Music c/o Trust Music Management, Inc. PO Box 9256, Calabasas, CA 91372. Used by permission. All rights reserved.

O Come, Let Us Adore Him: public domain.

O for a Thousand Tongues: Spanish translation © 1989 The United Methodist Publishing House. Reprinted from *The United Methodist Hymnal* with permission.

O God, We Thank You: © by the Lutheran Theological College. Used by permission. English text and tune reprinted from *Lead Us, Lord* © Howard S. Olson.

Our Cities Cry to You, O God: words © 1987 Hope Publishing Company, Carol Stream, IL. All rights reserved. Used by permission.

Persevere My Brothers: used by permission of Kerygma Canta & Marcelo Alvarado, A.M.E.N. International Director.

Praise God From Whom All Blessings Flow: public domain.

Praise to the Lord, the Almighty: public domain.

Rain On Us Your Word: words © by Yasushige Imakoma. Music © by Shozo Koyama, administered by Japanese Society for Rights of Authors, Composers & Publihers (JASRAC). Used by permission. Translation © 1994 by Sharon James-Ledbetter.

Seek Ye First: © 1972 Maranatha! Music (Administered by The Copyright Company Nashville, TN). All rights reserved. International copyright secured. Used by permission.

Send Me Lord: copyright © 1984 Utryck. Used by permission of Walton Music Corporation.

Since the Lord My God Has Called Me: public domain.

Somos Uno en Christo: public domain.

Speak My Heart: used by permission Sarin Sam. Words © 1994 by Sharon James Ledbetter.

Spirit Lord We Pray: used by permission of the Chinese Christian Literature Council Ltd.

Spirit of the Living God: © 1935, 1963 Birdwing Music (A Division of Sparrow Corp.). All rights controlled by the Sparrow Corporation, PO Box 5010, Brentwood, TN 37024-5010. All rights reserved. Used by permission.

The Church's One Foundation: public domain.

The Steadfast Love: © 1974, 1975 Celebration, PO Box 309, Aliquippa, PA 15001, USA. All rights reserved. Used by permission.

The Trees of the Field: © 1975 Lillenas Publishing Company/SESAC. All rights reserved. Administered by Integrated Copyright Group, Inc.

Thine Is the Glory: public domain.

We Are Marching In the Light of God: © 1984 Utryck. Used by permission of Walton Music Corporation.

What Can Wash Away My Sin: public domain.

What Service Shall I Give: © Institute for Studies in Asian Church and Culture (ISACC). Translation © 1994 by Sharon James-Ledbetter.

When I Survey the Wondrous Cross: public domain.

COPYRIGHT DIRECTORY

It has been our experience that securing copyright information can be a tedious task. Our hope is that this directory will assist you in your own permissions searches.

Asian Institute for Liturgy and Music
P.O. Box 3167
Manila 1099, Philippnes.
Phone: 632-70-75-91 to 94
Fax: 632-722-1490

Augsburg Fortress
426 South 5th Street
Box 1209
Minneapolis, MN 55440.
Phone: 612-330-3300
Fax: 612-330-3455

Briar Patch Music
3825 Meadowood SW
Grandville, MI 49418.
Phone: 616-534-6571
Fax: 616-534-1113

Bud John Songs, Inc. (ASCAP)
2505 21st Avenue South
Nashville, TN 37212.
Phone: 615-269-7000
Fax: 615-269-9525

Cartford, Gerhard
2279 Commonwealth Avenue
St. Paul, MN 55108

Celebration
PO Box 309
Aliquippa, PA 15001.
Phone: 412-375-1510
Fax: 412-375-1138

China Christian Council
169 Yuan Ming Yuan Road, 3/F
Shanghai, China 200002.
Phone: 86-21-321-0806
Fax: 86-21-323-2605

Chinese Christian Literature
Council Ltd.
138 Nathan Road, 4/F, Flat A
Kowloon, Hong Kong.
Phone: 852-367-8031
Fax: 852-739-6030

(The) Copyright Company
40 Music Square East
Nashville, TN 37203.
Phone: 615-244-5588
Fax: 615-244-5591

Eubank, Joan
Christian Communications
Institute
Payap University; PO Box 48
Chiang Mai 50000, Thailand.
Phone/Fax: 66-53-248-191

Evans, Dilys
Tan-y-coed, Uxbridge Square
Caernaruon
Gwynedd, N. Wales, LL552.

GIA Publications, Inc.
7404 South Mason Avenue
Chicago, IL 60638.
Phone: 708-496-3800
Fax: 708-496-2130

Hope Publishing Company
380 South Main Place
Carol Stream, IL 60188
Phone: 708-665-3200 Fax:
708-665-2552

Imakoma, Yasushige
3-3-2-401 Hikarigaoka
Nerima-ku
Tokyo 179, Japan.
Phone: 81-3-5998-2815

Institute for Studies in Asian
Church and Culture (ISACC)
PO Box 10078
Q.C. Main
Quezon City, Philippines.
Phone: 632-922-9621
Fax: 632-922-9893

Integrated Copyright Group, Inc.
P.O. Box 24149
Nashville, TN 37202
Phone: 615-329-3999
Fax: 615-329-4070

Japanese Society for Rights of
Authors, Composers and
Publishers (JASRAC)
1-7-13 Nishishinbashi
Minato-ku
Tokyo 105, Japan.
Phone: 81-3-3502-6551
Fax: 81-3-3508-8183

James-Ledbetter, Sharon
1614 West Cullom
Chicago, IL 60613.

Kerygma Canta:
Marcelo Alvarado, A.M.E.N.
International Director
PO Box 41292
Pasadena, CA 91104.
Phone: 818-791-4076

King, Roberta R.
Daystar University College
PO Box 44400
Nairobi, Kenya.
Fax: 254-2-7283-38

Lachat, Pierre
Association Chantre
40, rue de Goussainville
F-95400 Villiers-le-Bel
France.
Phone: 33-1-39-85-70-42
Fax: 33-1-39-85-13-23

Lillenas Publishing Company
(SESAC)
PO Box 24149
Nashville, TN 37202.
Phone: 615-329-3999
Fax: 615-329-4070

Lutheran Theological College
Makumira
PO Box 55
Usa River, Tanzania.

Manna Music
PO Box 218
Pacific City, OR 97135.
Phone: 503-965-6112
Fax: 503-965-6880

Mastra, Wayan
Gereja Kristen Protestan di Bali
PO Box 72
Denpasar, Bali
Indonesia.
Fax: 62-361-751-463

Oxford University Press
3 Park Road
London
NWI 6XN,
England.
Phone: 44-71-724-7484
Fax: 44-71-723-5033

Sam, Sarin
37 Kirkham Road
Dandenong, Vic 3175
Australia.

(The) Sparrow Corporation
PO Box 5010
101 Winners Circle
Brentwood, TN 37024-5010.
Phone: 615-371-6800
Fax: 615-371-6997

Trust Music Management Inc.
PO Box 9256
Calabasas, CA 91372.
Phone/Fax: 818-591-2473

United Methodist Publishing
House
201 8th Avenue, South
Nashville, TN 37202.
Phone: 615-749-6422
Fax: 615-749-6512

Walton Music Corporation
170 Northeast 33rd Street
Ft. Lauderdale, FL 33334.
Phone: 305-563-1844
Fax: 305-563-9006

Westminster/John Knox Press
100 Witherspoon Street
Louisville, KY 40202-1396.
Phone: 502-569-5043
Fax: 502-569-5018

Index to Hymnal